LEARNING. services

01209 722146

Duchy College Rosewarne
Learning Centre

This resource is to be returned on or before the last date
stamped below. To renew items please contact the Centre

Three Week Loan

Also by Pauline Kidner:

Life with Bluebell

My Secret World

Glade's Journey

Videos:

Raining Otters

Photographic book:

Exploring the Secret World of Wildlife Rescue

All the above are available from:

PK Publishing
Secret World Wildlife Rescue
New Road
East Huntspill, Nr Highbridge
Somerset TA9 3PZ
Tel. 01278 783250
Email: info@secretworld.org

To order online, see our website:
www.secretworld.org

A Place of Safety

The highs and lows of working with wildlife

Pauline Kidner

Best Wishes from Pauli 15

Cartoons by Jason Venus

PK Publishing
SOMERSET

PK Publishing
Secret World Wildlife Rescue
New Road, East Huntspill, Nr Highbridge
Somerset TA9 3PZ
Tel. 01278 783250
Email: info@secretworld.org
Website: www.secretworld.org

First published in the UK by PK Publishing 2014

A copy of the British Library Cataloguing in
Publication Data for this title
is available from the British Library.

ISBN 978-0-9536628-2-1

To my son, Simon

Without you, Secret World would never have
survived. Although it's my name that is connected
to this charity, you have always been my rock
behind the scenes who has made it all happen.
Thank you.

In memory of Jeff Clark

Jeff supported me and my charity for many
years. He was a person who I knew would help
out in any way that he could. That was the kind of
person he was. Because he was quiet and
unassuming, maybe he wasn't valued as much as
he should have been. He cared passionately for
badgers but loved all animals.
Thank you, Jeff, for your friendship –
we all miss you.

Contents

Foreword

I have spent a lot of time around the Mendips and Somerset Levels with my family over the years, but I had never heard of the great work being done by Secret World Wildlife Rescue.

They came to my attention suddenly in early 2011 during a most unfortunate incident when I saw Pauline Kidner on our local television news, conveying the unthinkable that someone had been taking potshots at the swans, ultimately killing thirty-one of them. Thirty-one! I was incandescent with rage. These beautiful creatures are protected, but alas not protected all the time and for someone to kill them simply for fun was unthinkable. I felt sick and had to do *something*. I called Pauline immediately and offered to bolster their reward because these people simply had to be caught. Alas, although the same names came up time and again during the police investigation, nothing could be proved and so no charges were ever brought. However, my relationship with Secret World was cemented and it wasn't long before I was bottle-feeding baby badgers in Pauline's kitchen.

And to be able to say that takes dedication, but to say that she is dedicated, kind and with a heart of solid gold is a ridiculous understatement. Pauline connects with wildlife in ways I have never seen before. Nothing fazes her – *nothing* – she just rolls up her sleeves and gets on with it and always makes things better. Over the years she has taken in, cared for and reared just about every creature native to these shores and a considerable number of visitors, too. The wild can be a terrible place, but Pauline's dedication and expertise make it just a little more bearable in so many wonderful ways for its inhabitants, especially those who cannot help themselves, because they really do need all the help they can get.

I raise a glass to you, Pauline, because you are quite unique and so from those who you teach and from those with no voice, I say thank the gods for you.

Terry Pratchett
Salisbury, June 2014

1

It's a family affair

'Oh! Thank goodness you're here.' I enthused at the man waiting for me in the reception of our Visitor Centre. 'You can have as many cups of tea as you want!'

No trace of a smile appeared on the face of the washing-machine repairman and I made a mental note that he obviously had no sense of humour. He probably wasn't going to be too impressed when I explained what was wrong with the machine, but I guided him through the farm and into the farmhouse, where the ground floor is now our tearoom.

Making my way upstairs to the flat where myself and my husband, Derek, live, I chatted. 'We do a lot of wildlife work and all their washing is usually done in the launderette downstairs, but those machines have broken down so we were using mine until those are mended. Unfortunately, something has blocked the filter and so my machine has stopped too.'

A nod of his head showed that he had followed my explanation so far, but I somehow thought he was going to flinch at the next information bulletin.

Taking him to the washing machine, which was in the bathroom, I took a deep breath and explained the possibilities. 'You might find that something like a dead chick may have got picked up inside the washing or meal worms may not have been shaken off before putting the washing in the machine. But you never know,' I breezed, 'it may only be something like a sock. Erm ... would you like a cup of coffee?'

His face had paled somewhat.

'Coffee with milk and I think I'd better have two sugars,' said the man, scratching his head and looking distastefully at the washing machine.

I left him and went into the kitchen to put the kettle on. Mr Woo, a baby wallaby, was sitting in his rucksack hanging from the cupboard door. Now covered in soft white fur, this albino was just old enough to get himself 'out' and 'into' his bag whenever he wanted. The strange voice meant that there was something new to explore and before I could stop him he had hopped into the bathroom to find out what was happening. Wooey had an unfortunate habit of gripping limbs and trying to mate, which is all too common in all juveniles of the mammal species!

Quickly following Mr Woo into the bathroom, I 'unclipped' him from the man's leg. 'I'm sorry, he's so inquisitive – but he obviously likes you!'

The man was not impressed, but we had woken a vestige of interest as he asked, 'What is that?'

'It's a wallaby, a baby wallaby that we are rearing. I didn't think he would get out of his bag, but he is just too nosey.' I apologised. 'Kettle's boiling, so coffee is coming up.' I smiled brightly.

Perhaps this incident could have been accepted as a usual occurrence, but whilst I finished making the coffee, Robbie the runt, a young piglet who had been asleep in the dog basket, trotted into the bathroom to see what he was missing. Taking the coffee through to the washing-machine man, I realised that Robbie thought it was all a game as he ran back out with a screwdriver in his mouth that he had managed to acquire from the open tool box on the floor.

'What ... what was that? A pig? He's got my bloomin' screwdriver,' the startled man gasped.

'Yes, I'm so sorry,' I explained as I retrieved the screwdriver from Robbie. 'It's a young piglet that we are hand rearing – he will go outside once he's weaned,' I remarked as if it made things any better. 'We do hand rearing of animals and so get used to having them around while they're small.' I smiled and wiped the saliva off the screwdriver before returning it to its rightful position.

'I'll shut the kitchen door to stop them from coming out and bothering you again, as I have to go downstairs to do a talk in the courtyard to the visitors.' I nodded towards the washing machine. 'Good luck!'

Making my way to the courtyard, I made sure that other members of staff had animals to show the visitors who had all congregated in the courtyard. It was a lovely summer's day, not too many visitors as it was term time so it was mainly young families or older people.

* * *

We originally opened our farm to visitors in 1984, to show the public where their food came from. This was something we were almost forced to do as we were hit by milk quotas in the 1980s, which made our farm non-viable. Opening to the public was our way of keeping the farm that had belonged to Derek's father. Sadly, our Friesian herd was sold and money invested in the tearoom and other necessary facilities. We had kept a few cows so that we could demonstrate milking to visitors.

However, over the years I had become very interested in wildlife and we'd had many casualties brought into us. We therefore had some wild animals that could not go back to the wild, such as foxes, badgers, owls and bats that other people had tamed whilst caring for them. They then realised what a commitment this was as these animals require lots of space and once imprinted, they needed to have human contact for the rest of their lives. It meant that we were able to show visitors not only farm animals but also wildlife – the 'Secrets of the Countryside', which is why our Centre eventually became known as Secret World instead of New Road Farm.

Each of us took it in turn to speak over the microphone with different animals and tell our visitors all about them. I had our two resident noctule bats, Himmy and Bertha. Neither of these bats could fly and they had belonged to a bat worker for some time, but she felt that she really wasn't using them enough and very kindly gave them to us.

They lived in a large bat box in my office. Being one of the largest species of bats found in Britain, they were good examples to show people how bats not only use their arms to fly but that their webbing includes their hands too. It is the elongated fingers with all the joints that allow them to change the shape of their wings so quickly, which is why bats seem to change direction at a 90 degree angle so fast that they can fly up walls.

In my talk I am able to explain how they can live up to 25 years and having placed them so that they were hanging from the front of my T-shirt, visitors could see them preening themselves with their tiny back feet and then Himmy and Bertha would settle to being hand fed some mealworms. Talk over, they remained on my T-shirt as I quickly went up to see how the washing-machine man was doing.

'All sorted,' he said, turning towards me as I came into the room. 'It was the pump that was jammed with a sock, a fifty pence piece [my husband never empties his pockets before putting his clothes in the laundry basket], and you were right – there was a dead chick and some insect things and ... What on earth is that on your jumper?!'

'Oh, these,' I said, 'they're bats.'

Quickly picking up his tool box, he hastily made his way out of the room. 'No, don't worry, I'll find my way out and we'll send the bill. I've never been in a house like this,' and he was gone.

Obviously not another fan, I thought.

I checked the kitchen before I went back downstairs. Woo was back in his bag sucking his preening claw on the end of his long leg (like a baby sucks its thumb) and Robbie was back asleep in the dog basket. All was quiet, so it was safe to go and put the bats away and check that everything was okay in the tearoom now that it was lunchtime.

Indeed it was busy as a coach party had arrived and Liz, who ran the tearoom for us, was quickly making up the orders with Jenny and Sue, both people from our village. Liz was a larger-than-life character who could be sharp, but also be a fantastic mother hen. With a selection of homemade foods, especially cakes, the tearoom was very popular.

We used the whole of the ground floor of the farmhouse for the tearoom. The kitchen was the original farmhouse kitchen and was the first room I saw when I arrived 22 years ago as housekeeper to Derek and his three small children. The house had then been almost derelict with not very many rooms in use. Hard to believe that the lovely eight foot pine dresser with copper kettle and saucepans shining in the tearoom kitchen was once painted green and yellow and was outside with all the tractor tools in it. The old Rayburn in the kitchen was the only form of heating for the whole of the house and once that had been allowed to go out, you knew that summer had arrived.

With the thick walls in this seventeenth-century listed building, the house was always lovely and cool in the summer and warm in the winter – once the Rayburn was alight! We used the three reception rooms as the tearoom and could seat fifty. Visitors enjoyed the beams, open fires and inglenook, which gave the tearoom such character. With a lovely front garden and a play area, all with outside seating, we could cater for nearly 100, but it was quite a pace!

Derek, my husband, was helping out by doing the washing-up. Not that he enjoyed it, but he loved the thought that every time he washed up a cup he had made 50p! (Farmers are all the same.) My son, Simon, who arrived with me so many years ago, also worked at the Centre – as did his very attractive girlfriend, Nikki – so it was a real family affair. Simon had met Nikki five years ago when they were at Leeds University.

Derek looked after the advertising, ran the tearoom and stocked the shop. Simon was the Administrator of our charity, then known as the Bluebell Sett, and Nikki was the Centre Manager. My role was looking after the animals, particularly the wildlife, and I did talks to promote our work. Having said that, all four of us were just as likely to be washing-up, serving in the shop, going out on a wildlife rescue or cleaning the toilets – variety was the spice of life!

With everything under control, I was going to go over to reception, across the courtyard, when I met an excited Nikki coming the other way. 'Guess what!' she enthused, and I knew from her manner that it was something special. 'Someone is bringing in a fawn! It should be here in half an hour.'

'We'd better get the cubby hole ready,' I said. 'The washing machine is mended but I'll tell you about that later on.'

We both made our way to the kitchen of my flat where the bottom of the airing cupboard door had been cut off and this area of the cupboard had been tiled to create a warm space next to the hot water tank. A wooden board across the front, it makes a secluded area where animals could feel safe but we could keep an eye on them and they could see us without feeling at risk. With an infrared lamp in there, it could be made really warm for animals that may come in very chilled.

The cubby hole had only just been vacated as our badger cubs that had been living there were now weaned and had moved to an outside pen. Because Nikki and I had done the bottle feeding, the cubs were now cared for by other members of staff as it was important for the cubs to revert to being wild prior to eventually being released back into the wild in the autumn.

We always know that once the badger cubs have gone out, it will only be a matter of weeks or even days before the fawns arrive. In the past, up to five fawns have been our usual number and it's always good to have Nikki to help as when the babies are tiny, they will need feeds every four hours and that's during the night as well. Although Simon and Nikki had another part of the house as 'their' flat they only had a kitchenette, bedroom and no bathroom, so we did live very much together.

As soon as we came into the kitchen both Woo and Robbie decided it was time for their feeds. It was easier to settle Robbie first, so Nikki mixed the feed and fed him while I had to put up with Mr Woo jumping around me as I tried to disinfect the cubby hole and then lay the newspapers. I can understand the amazement of the washing-machine man as I look across at Nikki who by now has Robbie over her shoulder waiting for him to burp as he has just cleared a complete bottle of milk. Normally animals would feed small amounts from their mothers ad lib so this is not a problem, but the very fact of taking large feeds means winding can be quite important. Even though Robbie has finished his feed, he just loves to suck and we even have a photo of him with a dummy in his mouth!

Leaving Robbie to run around, the next bottle of feed was for Mr Woo. He was impatiently jumping up at Nikki, making his silly hiccup noise. 'I'll go and get some browse,' I said, 'and I need to put these bats away.'

By now they had disappeared down the top of my T-shirt and were hanging quite contently on my bra. There's a story to that, but I'll tell you later!

Within the hour, Kate, a response driver, had arrived with the fawn curled up in one of our cardboard carriers. It was one of those stories where the stupidity of people sometimes makes me so cross. A young couple were out walking and had found the fawn lying quietly in long grass on its own, which is perfectly natural as the mother will come back to their young when they are ready to feed. They had decided to take the fawn back home to show their children when they came home from school. It was only when the lady who contacted us went to the house to help with a barbeque that she had heard about the fawn that they had left out in their back garden. She was very quick in telling them they should never have moved it and seeing as this had happened the day before, there was little chance of finding its mother again.

Nikki gently lifted the tiny roe kid out of the box and placed it in the cubby hole. She was only a few days old and so small. The long legs looked so fragile. Her golden brown colour was sprinkled with white spots on her back – all so useful in the camouflage of the countryside. The small wet velvet nose nuzzled the browse of dog rose, willow and hawthorn which almost hid the nervous face, but folding her thin long legs, the tiny fawn laid down.

Unless they are in bad condition and they need to be assessed immediately, we find the best thing is to leave the fawns to get used to their surroundings. Eventually, driven by hunger, they start to 'peep' and then it is possible to dribble milk into their mouths without moving the board away. It's so hard to get them to feed as they normally just nuzzle for milk under the doe. They are not held in anyway and this is hard to mimic.

The Centre had closed for the day and we had just finished dinner before the fawn stood and stretched. Her velvet nose sniffed tentatively above the board and she started to peep. We have a camera in the cubby hole and there is a monitor on the side in the kitchen, so we can see all that goes on in the cubby hole without being near to it.

Mixing some lamb's milk and filling a syringe with a teat on the end, Nikki sat legs crossed murmuring to the fawn. Slowly offering the syringe over the board she managed to slide the teat into the fawn's mouth. Nikki gently syringed a small amount of milk onto her tongue. Doh, as Nikki had named her, wrinkled her nose as the milk didn't taste the same as usual. This is the time when patience and bonding is necessary to build up trust with such an exquisite animal. Doh snorted with disgust and settled again on the fleece. Nikki stayed for a while just talking to her before leaving the fawn to rest for a while.

By 10 p.m. the peeping started again and this time the call was more urgent. Nikki, who had been curled up in the armchair in the kitchen with Robbie the runt, quickly made some fresh milk

7

and this time the teat was sucked and the syringe of milk quickly emptied. Doh took another syringe before deciding that was enough. She snuffled in the saucer of earth and ate some, which always surprises me but in the wild, this would be the way for her to get minerals. Doh stretched – always a good sign of a contented animal – and settled down again.

I had just come in from giving the last feeds to the birds in the hospital room where the incubators hummed with an assortment of babies being kept warm. Switching the lights off in the Hospital room, there was just a red glow of the infrared lamps that kept many tubs warm that were housing all manner of animals, from hedgehogs to owls and herring gulls.

In the kitchen the smell of milk had brought a wallaby out of its bag and a grunting piglet was rubbing his nose up my trouser leg as if to enquire if milk was about to arrive for him too.

'Ow!' I said. 'That piglet's snout is really hard! Shall I feed him?' I offered.

'Don't worry,' said Nikki, 'I'll do them because I shall try Doh with another feed before I go to bed!'

I laughed, knowing full well what was coming. 'Perhaps you would like to do the early morning feed?'

'What a good idea!' I mocked. I got ready for bed and crossed my fingers that there wouldn't be a call-out during the night. Derek was already in bed – and asleep. It was another end to a busy day. Little had I known when people started to bring orphaned and injured wildlife into me that it was going to take over my life.

* * *

I woke up to find Derek putting a cup of coffee by the bedside table. Already the sun was up. 'Someone's hungry,' was my husband's first words, 'and noisy too.'

Wildlife in the house has never brought much joy to Derek, but to be fair, he only snaps occasionally, despite having to share the kitchen with badger cubs, fawns – wallaby and piglet obviously – and the odd swan in the bath or bats being test flown in our hall. A life, I often tell him, many people would give their eye teeth for, but this does not impress him.

Luckily in the summer his spare time is spent either playing or watching cricket, followed by skittles in the winter (a Somerset pastime conveniently held in pubs). Even the cricket in the summer has to have at least one or two hours after the match spent in the pub to be able to discuss the match and either commiserate or celebrate – although if it is to celebrate, the two hours often gets extended!

The 'and noisy' was my cue to do something about it and it was just as well that I got up straight away as Derek was not amused at the amorous advances of Mr Woo, a piglet charging around and Murray my dog, an Alsation-cross, trying to save me the bother of clearing up the messes that all these activities had produced after being asleep all night. God, dogs are so disgusting!

Sweeping up Woo's 'currants' with a brush and dustpan, giving Mr Woo a custard cream to chew, checking that Robbie was content looking to see if there was a shred of food at the bottom of the cereal packet that Derek had put by the bin, I was able to turn my attention to Doh, who by now was running out of patience and thinking of jumping the board.

Having made the milk, I risked using a wet tissue to toilet the fawn just by wiping under her tail. This is what the mother would do, while the fawn feeds, but also to 'toilet' them very often triggers the response to feed. Doh was now so excited she was nudging me for her milk and drank 100 ml, which was really good. I risked taking the front of the board down and while she was sniffing the new area, I was able to clean out the cubby hole and put fresh bedding in. She seemed quite calm, so I went on to get the milk ready for Mr Woo who by now had eaten his biscuit. Robbie was still excavating the cereal box and was almost wearing the remains of the packet as a hat, so I knew time was of the essence!

Woo luckily never takes long to finish his bottle and a quick run up and down the hall usually follows the feed. He was duly joined by Robbie who by now had discarded the packet completely and was showing Woo how to jump sideways. The return to the kitchen meant that both the wallaby and the piglet dived under the table (where Derek was still eating his breakfast), completed the circuit and both ran back up the hall.

'That ruddy piglet's got my slipper,' Derek shouted. Doh dived into the cubby hole for safety. 'It's alright,' I replied, 'he's bringing it back!' By this time the slipper had covered the piglet's head and he ran straight into the fridge. Deftly retrieving the slipper, I handed it back. 'I'm going outside to get on,' said Derek and disappeared. Maybe not a good start to the day.

'That ruddy piglet's got my slipper'

Doh had settled again under the browse, Woo had jumped back in his clean rucksack, busy sucking his preening claw on his back leg like a dummy, and I was in the armchair with Robbie just falling asleep as I winded him on my shoulder after him finishing his bottle. Luckily the staff would be in soon as there would be plenty of trilling going on in the hospital room with all the birds wanting their first feeds.

Simon put his head around the door just as Robbie started to snore. 'All's quiet then,' he said.

'Well, it wasn't a few moments ago and your father's not had the best start to the day, but he's already downstairs.'

'You haven't forgotten that Tish is here today with the film crew, they'll be pleased to see the fawn,' said Simon. And with that little reminder he was gone.

We'd had rather a lot of film crews with us during this year. A series called *Pet Rescue* often picked up storylines and were occasional visitors. We were very lucky because all the television coverage did help us attract supporters – the downside being all the extra wildlife casualties that found their way to us too. It was really only Derek, myself, Nikki and Simon that were doing all the rescues and after full days, it was sometimes hard to keep the hours needed to go on call-outs – especially during the night. The police soon realised that we would be quick to respond when called at night and we would find ourselves travelling quite long distances to pick up a road traffic accident animal casualty. This would often require a visit to the vets, sometimes not returning until 3 a.m. or later. Work still had to be done the next day and it could sometimes be so draining – but stubborn me wasn't going to give up helping wildlife.

Tish was filming for a series due to go out the following year in 2000. It was going to be called *Secret World* and it was all about our work and the Centre. We were hoping it was going to be the answer to all our dreams.

They usually came for a full day to make the most of the time with the camera and sound men. Today was obviously going to be spent looking at all the orphans that we had in and they were bound to be excited at the arrival of Doh. As it happened, even before they had arrived and Nikki had risen from her bed, another fawn had been brought in. This little male had sadly been found near the remains of its mother. Sometimes the stories behind these animals are sickening. Deer are poached with little thought for the dependant fawn that may be around. This little roe buck had not had a feed for quite some time, his little body was pinched and he was calling for food. Checking him over quickly, I tried him with some liquid lectade – the Lucozade of the animal world. If you feed milk to youngsters that are really hungry then they will some-times just gorge themselves and end up with diarrhoea. He cer-tainly was hungry and actually took from a proper baby's bottle as he was so keen to drink. We usually feed with a syringe in the first place to get the fawns used to the taste of the milk, we then change them to a baby's bottle on the first feed in the morning when they are really keen for their food. This little guy was happy to drink from anything!

A tousle-haired Nikki drifted in for her first cup of coffee. 'Please meet Rae,' I said, waving my hand with a flourish to the little male who was snorting and gave a quick skip. 'Oh,' said Nikki excitedly, 'is that another one? I thought it was Doh!' A peep from the cubby hole made it clear that there were now two. Placing Rae gently in with Doh, she immediately stood up and sniffed her new friend. Fawns always do so much better if there is more than one. Well, to be honest the same applies to any species. Apart from feeding and cleaning, with company there isn't any need for us to interact with them, which means they revert to being wild much quicker and establish a bond to help them through the rehabilitation process. They both settled under the browse, preening each others' necks.

'I must get going,' said Nikki. 'Tish will soon be here,' and with that she was gone. The second feeds were going to be due soon but that could take place once the film crew had arrived. We work a lot with film crews but have always made sure that they fit in with the animal's timetable. That way it's not intrusive and the animal acts normally.

I made a quick check around downstairs to make sure everyone had turned in for work and that everything was going smoothly. Derek was off delivering leaflets as it was Whitsun soon, one of our busiest weekends. The more leaflets we could get around the better. Derek had a very good rapport with many other tourist attractions and did actually deliver some leaflets for other centres around Somerset. He was always a popular visitor as he often had complimentary tickets for different places, which he gave to the owners or their employees. (I think this was also a very good ploy to get a cup of tea and a piece of cake!)

Simon was caught up getting a skip that had arrived manoeuvred as near as possible to the cellar at the end of the farmhouse. This is not a cellar in the usual way of being under the house. Here on the Somerset Levels where it frequently floods, it would not be a good thing. This was the room that way back in the seventeenth century was used to salt the meat to make it last through the winter. In fact, in our kitchen upstairs there are shelves around the chimney breast where the grain was stored and large hooks in the beams where the salted meat would have been hung. The aim of the skip was to reduce the amount of rubbish that was in this room.

Pete Rudd was our maintenance man and was one of those incredible people who could do anything – electrics, building, tiling, vehicles – you name it, he could do it. Pete was also into antiques. He was quite a small man but always drove a big Volvo Estate because he could get so much into it – but he could hardly see over the large steering wheel! It was a very much-loved vehicle. The only trouble with Pete was that he saved everything that was likely to be of use as a replacement. We had now got to the position where it was cheaper to go and buy what you needed rather than to spend the time trying to find it – his Aladdin's cave was a nightmare. He still maintained that he knew where everything was but Simon was out to 'organise' it so that we could *all* find things. I silently wished him luck as I saw Pete joining in the directing of the vehicle.

Tish had arrived with Mike the cameraman and Rory, his son, who was the sound man. They were really pleased to hear about the fawns and within minutes we were joined by Nikki. Rory started to sort out our microphones. When filming for a day, you usually keep the radio mikes on, discreetly hidden beneath your top, and just switch off the battery pack tucked in your back pocket when it's not needed. It was imperative to remember this was in your pocket when you go the toilet otherwise 'accidents' can happen. I was already used to the fact that every so often it was necessary for the sound man to pull your top forward and glance down to ensure that the microphones were still in place. Nikki, a blonde bombshell, is very much better endowed than me, so I'm sure no matter who the crew was, she had her microphone checked a lot more than mine was!

We usually make sure that the rest of the staff know when we are filming to make sure we don't get any interruptions, which would necessitate a second take. Filming had started in the kitchen and both the fawns had walked calmly out of the cubby hole to Nikki who was ready to feed them. I was just in the background 'doing things'. The kitchen door flew open as an irate Simon entered, immediately apologising for disturbing us. Speaking as calmly as he could through clenched teeth he said, 'Can you come and sort Pete out before I do something I might regret. There's me and Norman clearing out the cellar and Pete's bringing everything back again – we're not getting anywhere!'

I duly excused myself and went to soothe ruffled feathers. Pete eventually decided it was too painful to watch and the clearance went ahead. It did mean, though, that for the next year there was going to be the well repeated sentence – 'Of course, I had one of them but it all got thrown away when Simon cleared out the cellar ...'

The rest of the day went well with a lot of filming done so Tish was more than happy. The next time they were due to come in was on a day that we had the vet visiting to do the weekly check-up. They had got some really super footage of the fawns and were so pleased that there was two of them. We certainly didn't know that only three weeks later we were to have Doh, Rae, Me, Fah, Soh,

Lah, Te, Doh (2) and had had to resort to Minor and Major as extra names. One mad day of filming consisted of eight fawns in the kitchen with Woo jumping out of his bag getting really excited but not sure whether he was a fawn or a wallaby. This was far more fawns than we had ever had – both Nikki and I had bags under our eyes showing how the number of late night feeds had taken their toll. But the sight of the fawns, when they were eventually weaned, down in the enclosure at the back of our Rehab block, was fantastic.

* * *

The care of all the animals takes a lot of patience, time and money but the biggest problem is finding release sites for the orphans. Adults are easy because, if they recover to full health, then they are returned to where they came from. They know these areas, know where to find food and water, where to hide and I'm sure there are members of their families that are glad to see them back. Colin Seddon was the manager at the RSPCA Wildlife Unit near Taunton and he helped us in many ways with release sites. Most of the orphans would go to their release sites in the autumn as we copy the time that they would disperse from their parents.

We worked with Colin in particular with badger cubs. For many years we have had a reputation for looking after badger cubs. We did the hand rearing of the young cubs and then once weaned, they were passed down to the RSPCA unit as they had the grassed enclosures necessary for them to be mixed into groups as families. This was a period of time that was hands-off care to enable them to revert to being wild prior to eventually going for release. He invited me to go with him to one of the releases and it was a question of being up at 4.30 to be collected at 5 a.m. with the van and all the badgers already caged up in the back. He always liked to travel early at the coolest time of the day and with little chance of being held up by traffic.

There was no point in offering to drive – Colin does not like women drivers! It was still dark as we made our way to the release site but within the next hour dawn started to erupt with fantastic hues of blue and red in the distance over the fields. The mist was rising as the day was warming up, a typical September day telling us that autumn was just around the corner.

As I look at our beautiful countryside it's hard to believe that out there in parts of the country people are digging up badgers for their sport. I find it amazing that men will go to such extremes of digging deep down into setts, sometimes as deep as 1–2 metres, to dig badgers out so that they can set dogs on them, either stabbing or shooting them eventually to end their terror. Having gone to a conference where they talk about badger baiting and show clips of film, the excited barks of the dogs and the terrible whining and snarling of the badger being attacked all too easily come to mind. Other sick people cage the badgers up when they get them and take them to towns where they either create a metal-lined pit or do it in the back of a van to force the badger to fight against selected dogs as it has no way out. The amounts of money that are bet on these kinds of contests are incredible. The badger is disadvantaged by having its jaw or leg broken. They wager which dog will win the fight, completely oblivious of the injuries that these dogs themselves often suffer in the fights. This is why the badger and its sett were protected by law to put a stop to this horrendous sport which is sadly now on the increase, as well as dog and cock fighting. Sometimes I despair of the human race. What chance have we got if we cannot respect animals?

The conversation naturally falls to the Randomised Badger Culling Trial (RBCT) which had started two years ago. It amazes me that a large experiment – the largest ever held in the world on Bovine TB – should hardly be given any media coverage although it still continues. When it first started in 1997 there was a huge outcry because of the badgers that were to be killed and many of the traps used to catch them were destroyed and moved by activists, but eventually it carried on with little disturbance. This was meant to be the final experiment to see if culling of badgers played a part in the control of Bovine TB in cattle. Since the 1970s, when the first badger was found with Bovine TB, there has been many different methods of culling badgers but none of them were completely successful.

Ten triplet areas of 150 km square were chosen in counties where there was a high incidence of TB in cattle. Each area in the triplet had to be of similar geographical aspects. In one area no badgers are to be killed – this is the control area to show what happens if you do nothing. In the second area badgers are killed where there are outbreaks in cattle – called reactive culling. And the third area is where they kill as many badgers as possible to see if this reduces the incidence of Bovine TB in cattle. This is called the pro-active cull area. It is a seven-year experiment to finally find out whether culling badgers works. I suppose the fact that the Labour government stopped all badger culling in any other areas whilst this experiment is going on is something and we are told that every badger will be given a post mortem. No wonder this experiment was going to cost in excess of £53 million. The whole experiment is being controlled by the Independent Scientific Group (ISG) who we hope will be totally independent but we will have to wait and see.

Badgers were being blamed for the increase of this terrible disease and were often still persecuted despite the protection afforded to them by the legislation. We had a TB outbreak in our herd a few years ago and had to have three cows dispatched. Two beautiful Highland cattle and a Guernsey – it was tragic to see them being loaded on a lorry to be killed. This was followed up by the then MAFF representative (Ministry of Fisheries and Food) who was quite adamant that this was caused by the badgers that we had on site – as was the usual remark made by MAFF. People don't understand how attached you become to your animals on a farm. You can't care for them, milk them twice a day, having often watched them grow from calves, without building a bond. Being given compensation doesn't take away the loss experienced. Especially in our case as we were to be told that on slaughter, all three cows were clear of Bovine TB and had been false positives.

Our only hope, we agreed, was that finally the experiment would give us the answer – good or bad – that killing badgers was or wasn't the way forward. Glancing back at the beautiful healthy badgers sleeping in the cages behind me in the back of Colin's van, I hoped that they would have a life in the wild well away from those trials and prayed that they would never experience the cruelty that man can cause.

We were at the release site by 11 a.m. and met the landowner who then showed us the way through the fields to the artificial sett that had been created for them. As we arrived in a deciduous woodland, the golden leaves had already started to fall. Old tree stumps had fallen and been left so there was plenty of bark for the badger cubs to scratch through in search of beetles and bugs. Bramble patches gave natural cover as well as a supply of blackberries that badgers love. It was perfect. A large area was marked out with electric wire where all the undergrowth has been cleared away so that the fence won't cut out. Here a deserted sett was in the middle of the enclosure. This area had all been surveyed by

Colin the winter before to make sure there were no other badgers resident in this area. Winter is the time to do surveys as with all the undergrowth dying back, it is much easier to find tracks and signs. Badgers are very territorial and will fight and even kill badgers that don't belong to their clan.

Colin checked the fence and made sure that everything was as he had left it a few weeks ago when he had come to install the fence, bringing bedding with him and plenty of food for the badgers. The landowner will feed the badger juveniles through to the spring when food would become naturally available to them. Lifting the cages over the fence, each cage was put with the end to the sett entrance and the gate lifted to allow access. Each badger quickly shot into the sett and eventually all seven were in their new home.

Softly blocking the sett entrance with hay, we pulled away so that the badgers could sleep off their journey. It would be evening before they would tentatively emerge from their new home. The electric fence was a way of keeping them within the area while they got used to their new surroundings. After three weeks Colin would return to take the fence down and they would then have the chance to move out further, but they would still be assist-fed for the next few months.

The journey home was quieter with both Colin and myself contemplating the chances of survival of these young cubs. They had relied so much on us to care for them and to get them through to adulthood. They didn't have a matriarch with them to help them find food or to show them new territorial paths, but everything possible had been done to give them a second chance. Little did I know that in subsequent years, we would be able to prove that many of them had indeed survived for many years.

People always ask me how you can bear to let them go, but release is the ultimate goal and they will show you each step of the way that they want freedom. We rear the cubs in the kitchen but as soon as they are weaned they are causing trouble opening cupboards and pulling up carpets. It's time for them to go to our larger casualty pens where they can have more natural materials like logs and sack bags full of hay to play fight with and large pipes as tunnels to run through and play. Then eventually they are digging at the metal gates that lead out to the grassed enclosures as they want more space to dig and forage naturally. It is with lots of huffing and puffing that they excitedly run around the grass enclosure for the first time with all their hair standing on end looking like huge puff balls. They revert to being nocturnal and soon even the grassed paddock isn't enough and they are digging at night by the fences because they want out. If you love them, you let them go and give them a chance of life in the wild, their true destination.

* * *

We were excited that we had managed to get an invitation to appear at the pet section of Harrods in London. It was to promote my last book, *Glade's Journey*, so we hoped this would increase sales and be a good way of meeting people who might be interested in helping us as a charity. It was another early start but one that still didn't mean we missed the huge traffic jam as you get into London. It took two hours to reach London and then two hours to reach Harrods which is actually on our side of London! I was there with Simon and Nikki and we had brought some animals to show to customers and explain about our work. Animals, books, display boards were all taken up to the right floor by a lift. We had taken a hedgehog, Sage our barn owl who has been going to talks for years, a couple of African land snails and Woo, who was still happy to be in his rucksack for most of the time.

As you can imagine there was a huge amount of interest in the animals and the time went so quickly as we were constantly talking to people, showing them our animals and explaining the work that we do. The number of people that came up asking how much Woo was and could they buy him, without even asking what he was and what sort of accommodation and feeding he would require, was amazing. We were very quick to explain he was not for sale. Nikki was quite upset and I suppose that's always the problem with having animals in an instant buy situation without people really thinking about the responsibility of keeping pets – or the expense. Not that many people in Harrods would have much of a problem in that department! This was no different than any other event that we attend inasmuch as people very often ask the same questions over and over again.

'Oh, isn't he lovely.'

'What's his name?'

'What is it?'

'How old is he?'

The African snails are great because the children love the slime and whilst we don't find them in our gardens, we can talk about the importance of slugs and snails to attract wildlife into gardens.

It was getting late in the day and I was beginning to flag. One lady came up to me and said, 'Oh, African snails, I like them.'

'Well done!' I replied. 'Not many people know what they are.'

'Oh,' she said. 'I think they make super pets because they're so quiet.'

Boredom was overcoming me so just to liven things up, I said to her, 'Well they do hum.'

'Do they?' she said. 'What – as in smell?'

'Oh, no,' I replied. 'Hum as in humming, *mmmmmmmm*.' I demonstrated.

'Well,' the lady said, 'I never knew they made any noise at all!'

Sadly at this point I became distracted and by the time I turned around to explain that I had only been joking, the lady had disappeared. So if you ever hear about humming African snails – I started the rumour! Sadly we didn't meet anyone that was going to help us run the charity.

The wildlife was costing us more each year and the Centre as it grew had to deal with all sorts of rules and regulations, all of which cost money. Health and safety meant proper surfaces for the play areas, more hand washing facilities for the school groups, an extra phase of electricity was needed to service all the heat lamps and incubators. We ourselves were finding the rescues and rehabilitation were taking up almost all of our lives and yet we desperately wanted to be there for wildlife casualties and to reduce suffering.

December brought the annual meeting with the bank manager. We weren't getting as many school visits as we used to with the new seat belt rules meaning that more coaches had to be booked to bring them in to us. The periods of making money, that is the summer holidays and bank holidays, were being cancelled out by the periods of time that we were quieter, such as the winter. Early summer would bring young families with little to spend and there were more and more farm attractions opening. We had created our Centre on an educational basis and were no contest to tourist attractions with rides and indoor ball play areas – there was little doubt that the wildlife work cost money and required a lot of man hours.

It was not surprising when we went to the bank to hear that they weren't happy to see so little reduction in our overdraft and that they were considering withdrawing their support. The new television series was due to go out in spring the following year on HTV and possible book sales swung the decision in our favour, but it was clear that this was the last winter we would be allowed to continue to trade. 2000 had to be a much better year.

2

Millennium bogs

The Millennium rolled in with much expectation of better things and I tried to feel the same excitement but had enough sense to realise that unless things really improved, the end of this year could be very sad indeed.

It was New Year, Simon and Nikki arrived home from Edinburgh just as we received a message that an otter cub was on its way. We had never had one at our Centre so mild hysteria would not be too strong a word! The reference books were out and Nikki was ringing Colin at the RSPCA to get information. We had also been given the rearing sheets from the people in Scotland who did the rearing of otters, the Greens, so we had very good advice.

The cubby hole was prepared. January is not a time for orphans as most arrive in the spring, but otter cubs are born all year round and surprisingly, cubs are just as likely to survive having been born in the winter as they would if they were born in the summer. Little Oscar arrived in the early evening but it was already dark. A fluff ball of chocolate brown was curled up in the towel inside the box as we opened it. He was very thin and had been found near a swollen river, freezing cold and crying. Sometimes it is possible to get them back with their mother as their plaintive whistle carries a long way. Unfortunately when the weather is starting to freeze you don't have the same time to wait and see.

When there is heavy rain and rivers rise, the holt can sometimes be flooded. When very young, cubs have long fluffy fur that traps air and, too young to swim, makes them buoyant. Carried by the strong current the cubs can be a long way away from the holt by the time they struggle out of the water, often they just drown.

Nikki sat with Oscar on her lap soothing him while I got some milk ready for him. His fur was so dense. Otters need this to protect them with natural insulation as they are in and out of the water even in the winter. Oscar had very tiny ears but huge whiskers that were going to be so important when he was old enough to swim under water to find fish, as much by sense of touch as sense of smell. The feet were webbed and the huge muscular tail was almost as long as his body, the tail being used as a rudder when swimming. Although Oscar was only about six weeks old he was already the size of a ferret. So often people say to me, 'I think I saw an otter the other day – or it may have been a mink.' The size difference is huge and a fully grown dog otter could be as much as a metre and a half in length including its tail. It was quite obvious that an otter cub is probably one of the prettiest babies in the British wildlife (although I still prefer badgers!).

First, Nikki toileted him with a wet tissue. If you watch mammals, this is usually the first thing the mother will do when disturbing them from sleep. Once they have cleaned them, the mother will settle down to feed. Sometimes, they will hardly pass any urine or faeces, especially if they have been without food for a while, as the body will have absorbed all that they had eaten previously. Even so, the toileting process makes the orphan realise food is on the way and it is all part of the bonding process. Oscar was keen to take the bottle straight away, both his front paws splayed out and gripped the bottle, showing the webbing on his feet and the big thick tail was flicked around in pleasure.

'What's that about?' Nikki gestured with her free hand and raised eyebrows.

'That's what lambs do. Haven't you seen them down on their front legs with their tails madly wagging?' I said, and we both laughed. Oscar certainly wasn't bothered that the milk tasted different from his mother's and the bottle was soon empty. You could see Nikki was smitten and I concluded to myself that she may even be prepared to do the feeds during the night!

As I thought, Nikki was happy to do most of the feeds so it gave me a chance to catch up on some paperwork. I was surprised when I was in the kitchen how like the badger cubs this new little one was. Once Oscar was a little bit stronger and able to lift himself up on his legs, he started to discover the rest of the kitchen while Nikki was cleaning out the cubby hole. He liked to go behind the armchair, which is a favourite place of the badgers, and loved playing with the cones that I keep in the fireplace.

Once we saw him starting to play with the water in the dog's water bowl, we knew that it was time to try him with some small fish. Oscar was dipping his head in the water although hadn't learnt how to close his nostrils so it was all accompanied by a lot of spluttering and snorting, but once he could smell the tiny fish we had put in the bowl, he was desperate to catch it. Eventually he had success and held the fish up high to show that he had caught it. Then, moving it around in his mouth to get it head first, it was quickly swallowed and soon Oscar had his head back in the dog's water bowl to see if there was another one.

We had bought some small troutlings from a local trout farm. They were only about 8cms long and had soft bones. They were 50p each which doesn't sound a lot of money until he was eating about 10–12 a day. Just as the mother would now take them down to the water to teach them how to swim it was time for Oscar's first lesson. We were able to use our lovely clawfoot bath, which is so big that when the children were small, I could get all four in together! All manner of things had been in our bath – swans, ducks, terrapins – and Derek no longer used it as most animals go to the toilet as soon as you put them in and the otter cub was no different. To start with we only put in a small amount of water so Oscar could walk about. It was obvious that he didn't like it. He was walking around like a baby with a wet nappy on showing that the whole process, as far as he was concerned, was very distasteful.

'Oh, he doesn't like it,' wailed Nikki.

'Just give him a chance,' I replied. Again the snorting and spluttering continued as he nosed under the water, but eventually he was snorkelling very well. After five minutes, Nikki had him wrapped in a nice warm towel, just as would happen in the wild, I'm sure! After a quick rub, he was placed on the floor and found the rug himself so that he could squirm himself dry. A bottle was very quickly polished off and Nikki placed him back in the cubby hole. Tired out after his first swimming lesson, Oscar was soon fast asleep on his back with his legs flopped in a way that made him look like an empty hot water bottle cover. He must have been feeling very safe to lay in such a vulnerable position and once he started dreaming, his legs twitched. A very contented otter cub was sound asleep.

Slowly we were able to increase the depth of the water in the bath and eventually Oscar was swimming perfectly, ducking and diving and amazing us by the amount of time he spent underwater. He was now totally weaned. Otters are big strong animals and need to have a healthy fear of humans, so time away from the person who bottle fed them is best. They have incredibly sharp teeth to be able to hold on to fish and eels. I once went to pick up Oscar without him realising I was there and was given quite a strong nip, which is good as it shows the natural reaction of a wild animal when frightened.

We keep orphans until the time that they would normally disperse from their mothers. For otter cubs that is a long rehabilitation time as they remain with their mothers until they are 15–18 months old. It is really necessary for them to have another otter cub for this long period of time. Someone to play with and someone to compete with for food. It was time for him to find a friend.

The Otter and Owl sanctuary in Southampton rears a lot of otter cubs and when we contacted them, they had a similar aged otter cub that Oscar could go with. Nikki, although she had an overpowering love of animals, knew that the time was right for the break to be made. The sad whistle that could be heard during the night was a sign that he wanted someone to play with.

Company was paramount during that long period of growing in order to have a balanced socialised animal. Colin Seddon often took on the release of the otter cubs when they were ready to be released, so we were happy that Oscar would have the best chance of returning back to the wild. Nikki took Oscar down to Southampton, wanting to be sure that he would be looked after. However, she came home happy that he was in the best place, although I suspect a few tears were shed on the journey back.

Thank goodness that Robbie was now outside with the rest of

his family and Woo was now weaned but still having the complete run of the house. Nikki was quite sure Woo wasn't ready to be outside. For Simon, with a hay-strewn carpet in their lounge and a few currants here and there, that couldn't come soon enough (although I have to say he was equally as fond of Woo as Nikki).

* * *

It was a time for decorating and general maintenance as well as gardening and redesigning of leaflets etc. ready for the new season. Being open every day, there was still talks to do and the tearoom was always busy, even on the coldest of days and especially on Sundays with Liz's famous roast dinners. Local clotted cream made cream teas a must, or some of the crumbles or desserts that were also offered with cream or custard. Not a good place to be if you were on a diet!

Simon had recently purchased a very old Land Rover, which was his prized possession despite its antiquity. Someone had kindly offered us some really good pens and chicken houses that were in good order. Simon had been to look at them and had come back saying we would need a few pairs of hands to get it all moved. It was arranged that Simon would have a trailer hitched to his Land Rover, Derek was taking his van, I was in our car and Pete was following in his car.

We all followed the wonderful Land Rover to our eventual destination. Simon had already been there so he knew the way. We all followed when he indicated to go up a hill, following a lane which as time went on got narrower and narrower. We arrived near the top by a house, wondering how we were going to turn around to go back down but, still with complete faith in Simon, we all parked in our line and made our way to the top. Here Simon had to admit he had taken the wrong turning and there was no way that he could turn around with the trailer attached so we decided to unhitch the trailer. Simon turned the Land Rover around and we manoeuvred the trailer by hand and then placed it back on the hitch. To our horror, Simon hadn't put on the hand brake and the Land Rover started to roll downhill and picked up momentum as both Land Rover and trailer started to slide towards each of the vehicles – all in a line, each going to be shunted into the next. We all stood and watched with mouths open, not making a move.

To his credit, Simon moved at great speed that could almost be compared with a James Bond film, throwing himself into the cab

To our horror, the Land Rover started to roll downhill!

and wrenching on the hand brake with inches to spare before it would have hit the first of our lined-up vehicles and shunted them all into each other.

'That was close,' Simon cheerfully stated with a smile on his face. Pete, with the sign of the cross, gave thanks that his beloved car was safe and Derek was speechless. No wonder I'm going grey.

We all eventually managed to turn around with no further dangers and found our way to the farm in question where cups of tea were very welcome. The runs and chicken houses did make it all worthwhile.

* * *

March arrived and the daffodils around the farm were signs that we would soon be very busy with baby birds. Mr Woo was actually spending whole days out in his pen and the decision was made that we needed a mate for him as he was lonely. Luckily we knew Colin Fountain, who was the manager at the Cotswolds Wildlife Park where they had plenty of wallabies, and he was happy to let us have one. (Derek had said when we were first offered Woo as an ugly, naked pink baby that if we were successful in rearing him, we had to promise that we would let him go to somewhere that had other wallabies for company. Luckily we were able to overcome this problem of loneliness by getting another one for him!)

Nikki and I travelled up with a large deer box to house the female friend. Luckily, experienced zookeepers had the new Mrs
Woo already contained and we just needed to transfer her from
one box to another. We were warned of the fact that they had very
fragile skulls, could kick with a vengeance and the best way to
catch them was by their tail with their backs to our legs. It all
sounded very easy! Travelling back there was excited talk of
'Wouldn't it be great if they had a baby' but I warned Nikki that it
wasn't guaranteed that Mr Woo would even like his new friend. It
was nearly evening by the time we got back so Simon helped us
move Mrs Woo into the wallaby shed and Mr Woo came in as
usual.

The next day was full of anticipation. We hoped that the fencing around the pen would be enough to keep Mrs Woo in and, of
course, there was the expectation that they would like each other.
Mr Woo was taken down to his pen as usual and Nikki stood by
the door of the Woo shed to let Mrs Woo out. As soon as the door
opened, Mrs Woo came out like a bullet and was at the end of the
enclosure with four or five huge bounds. Luckily she made no attempt to jump the fence but stayed in the corner refusing to even
look at us. Mr Woo was not impressed with the intruder and spent
his time as far away as possible. At the end of the day, the relationship was no different and Mr Woo was more than ready to come
out and go back into the house. The door to the Woo house was
left open so that Mrs Woo could go inside if she so wished, but
even a sneaky look late that night proved that she was still sulking
in the corner of the enclosure. We all went to bed with heavy
hearts. Maybe we just hadn't done the right thing.

Mr Woo was put into his enclosure the next morning, completely indifferent to Mrs Woo who had moved but was now
watching him with suspicion from another part of the enclosure.
She had a mark on her forehead so we wondered if she had tried
to get out but she seemed very steady despite everything being
different. Two hours later there were screams of 'Pauline, Pauline
come quickly', from Nikki who was shouting up the stairs. Certain
there was bound to have been a disaster, I quickly followed her
disappearing image towards the Woo pen. Mr and Mrs Woo were
sitting back to back like bookends.

'Look, look,' enthused Nikki. 'They're next to each other!'

'Well,' I replied, 'it's not exactly love at first sight is it?'

'No, but they're NEXT to each other, they're bound to fall in love,' Nikki exclaimed with her large blue eyes shining brightly – she always wanted everything to have a happy ending. And indeed this story did have a happy ending. Mr Woo was soon besotted with Mrs Woo and they were always together. Mrs Woo never tamed and you could only get near to her, never allowed to touch. But at least the Woo family was a success.

* * *

Never one to miss a trick, Nikki was the first to claim a very pretty kitten that was found in a plastic carrier bag down on the Moors. Luckily, someone took the time to look inside the bag. I'm so incensed when we get involved with this kind of situation. There really is no excuse to dump animals with so many rescue places about. Even if someone *is* going to dump an animal, at least they could put it somewhere that it is likely to be found. But then I suppose these people have no feelings for animals whatsoever, I doubt that they have any respect for human life either.

The beautiful kitten was long-haired and with gorgeous blue eyes. How long it had been since it was discarded in the bag we couldn't tell but it wasn't starving.

'I could look after it,' she wailed. 'We haven't got anything in at the moment that is taking up our time.' Completely forgetting that Mr Woo tended to turn up indoors on occasions.

'No,' I said sensibly, 'it's going to be so easy to find a home for this one because it's so pretty. Wait until we have something that really needs a home.' A pouting Nikki had to put up with three days of joy before she had to surrender the kitten to its new owner.

Actually she didn't have long to wait because a kitten was brought in, just a few weeks later. It was very small and had been hanging around this gentleman's garden. He already had a cat and didn't want another one. The black kitten glared out of the container that the man had left behind, wishing us luck with getting the kitten out, brandishing a hand with two plasters. The kitten was feral and was prepared to prove it by swiping at any bit of flesh that was handy. We could see it had been very wet as its fur was all in clumps and the tail was broken as it hung over the body the wrong way. (I have to admit it looked like the bumper cars at the fair.) Nikki thought I was cruel to think it looked funny and the kitten was taken upstairs away from such uncaring people.

The carrier was placed on the floor whilst Nikki and Simon

watched television. With the door open it was over an hour before the black kitten decided to bolt from the carrier to under the television table and remained there for the rest of the evening. Just before going to bed Nikki tried to cajole him out from underneath by sliding her hand towards the kitten. With a painful swipe, the kitten showed he was going nowhere. Nikki, sucking the blood from the scratch on her hand, decided he could stay where he was as far as she was concerned and kitten was named Gremlin.

With the patience of a saint, Nikki eventually won Gremlin over and he became besotted with her. He is a very talkative cat and, not a good thing from our point of view, a very good catcher. With cats now exceeding dogs as the favourite pet because they are less needy, so many people sit with a cat on their laps complaining about birds of prey, magpies, crows and how horrible they are because they kill small birds and mice. They only kill to survive – as all predators do – foxes, stoats and weasels to name but a few. Research has found, on average, one cat will kill 3,000 wild creatures in its lifetime – all for fun.

Two of our volunteers, Pete and Norma, come from Glamorgan to help on open weekends throughout the summer and they stay in the car park in their camper van. Gremlin adores cheese and as soon as they arrive Gremlin will be sat at their doorstep waiting for some. He had to have his tail amputated but has grown into a sleek black panther who, I'm afraid to say, does tend to boss all the other cats around.

* * *

We knew as we moved into March that we would soon be seeing orphaned badger cubs and fox cubs too. I had done a talk at one of the local schools, sorted out some orders with Derek for the shop and was off out again in the evening for a talk with Good Companions in Bristol. I needed to leave with all the equipment by 6 p.m. to get there on time. Tea was going to have to be missed so a chocolate bar and packet of crisps were grabbed before I left. Not the best diet to have. It was quite a long drive but I was there in good time to set up the projector with the slide carousel. They were a really nice group and enjoyed the talk so I felt it had all been worthwhile as I was leaving. I had all the equipment stacked up in my arms on the way out when an elderly gentleman walking with sticks called me back. Legs astride he pointed with his stick to a slide underneath him that I had dropped on the way out.

'Gosh, thank you,' I said, 'I would never have realised I had lost it until I got home.' Putting everything down, I bent down and picked the slide up and placed it back in the carousel.

'That's alright,' the gentleman said. 'It's a long time since I had a young lady between my legs!' and he winked. That kept me smiling all the way home.

Arriving back, I decided to do the late feeds in the hospital room before I went up to the flat. I thought Derek was probably asleep in front of the television. Having done the late feeds and changed a few beds for the hedgehogs (they're so dirty), I arrived back up in the flat where I was met by a rather annoyed Derek. It was just gone 11 p.m. and there had been a phone call about an RTA (road traffic accident) badger outside a lady's house near to Exeter, about an hour away. 'I'll go,' I volunteered.

'No,' answered Derek, pulling on his coat, 'I'll go because I've got all the details and I know where it is. But this is getting silly, all the call-outs that we seem to be getting.' He slammed the door and was gone. I didn't answer. He had a point but maybe, just maybe, the television series when it goes on HTV might bring in more money to help us with our wildlife work. But Derek had heard it all before, so there was no point in saying it out loud.

The trouble with these call-outs late at night to uncontained animals is that although injured, they often aren't still there when you finally arrive. Badgers particularly, once they regain consciousness, will desperately try to get back to their setts as a place of safety. We have had badgers that on x-ray have had a broken pelvis or broken legs but have obviously laid up somewhere until they have healed. They have the amazing ability of surviving for a long time without food.

One sow we rescued with an infected womb was near three tiny week-old cubs so we collected the cubs as well. The sow, called Carey, needed to have a course of injections so we installed them in a quiet pen at the bottom of the farm. She had a heat lamp to keep warm and was cleaning up after her suckling cubs. But despite clean water and food being put in her pen every night, she didn't drink for two weeks and only started to eat the food after four weeks yet was still perfectly healthy. I'm sure sows with small dependent cubs wouldn't normally leave them at least for a couple of weeks.

Saddened by all the problems we were having, I sat in the kitchen with a cup of coffee. I love my kitchen – with or without animals in the cubby hole. So much had changed over the years and I knew deep down that the wildlife work was costing us more than we could afford. Murray, my Alsatian cross, came over to lick my hand, I was close to tears. He was a lovely old dog and always knew when I was down.

I had started a charity called the Bluebell Sett, named after one of my first three sibling badger cubs that arrived in 1989. Bluebell stayed with me for several years even though she was free to go. Even so, the charity never really brought in the cost of caring for the wildlife. The wonderful members of the committee that ran the charity with me worked so hard, but we never really brought in enough funds. If everything failed, where would our resident animals go? What was going to happen to all the wildlife casualties that came in to us? The thoughts were too painful to think about and I went to get a casualty pen ready for the badger. I put a fresh blanket in for him and made sure the heat lamp was the right height, leaving it on so that the pen would start to warm up.

I decided to go to bed with my phone by my side. Derek could then ring me once he was on his way back and let me know if he needed to go to the vets first. At least I could catch a bit of sleep before I needed to get up again. It wasn't worth getting undressed. I closed my eyes and it seemed like seconds before the phone rang.

'I'm on my way back,' said Derek, sounding in better form than when he left. 'I've got the badger and it doesn't seem too bad so I think he can wait and go to the vets tomorrow. I should be about another hour.'

'OK, thanks,' I said. 'The pen is ready but I'll go down and get some food and water to go in for him. Thank you for going.'

'It's OK,' he said. Derek knew how much it all meant to me.

Getting up and filling the kettle, as I knew Derek would want a cup of coffee when he got back, I then went out and checked the other casualties in their pens to make sure they were alright. My heart lifted with the contentment of the inmates. A swan injured with fishing hooks stuck deep in his throat, now recovering from the operation, a hedgehog on patrol in the pen – we would soon be sending the hedgehogs home once spring arrived – and a tawny owl recovering from being found in a water trough so close to death. As far as I was concerned, every effort to stop the suffering of wildlife had to be worth it. I would do as much as I could for as long as I could.

Badger meal prepared and water bowl ready to go in the pen, I arrived in the courtyard from the prep room just as Derek drove in. It was now nearly 3 a.m. I helped Derek carry the cage to the casualty pen.

'It must be in good condition,' I said, 'or he's more down my end than yours!'

'No,' Derek said, 'he's a fair-sized badger in good condition and I think he must have been just clipped by the car. He was thinking of moving just as I got there.'

We placed the cage inside the pen and opened the door. The badger tentatively walked out of the cage. Leaving him to settle in the pen, we switched all the lights out so all that could be seen was the red glow of the infrared lamp that was placed above the badger. Derek was more than ready for his coffee by the time we had got back into the kitchen. 'It was a very nice lady that called us out,' said Derek. 'She said she is a friend of Valerie Singleton.'

'There you go,' I said, 'you just don't know who you might come in contact with!' I think we were both asleep as soon as our heads touched the pillow.

* * *

The badger was doing well the next morning. I was almost sure it was a boar because of his broad head and he was in really good condition. He had made the most of his supplied meal and was enjoying the hotel comforts of the heat lamp by lying belly up without a care in the world. With little sign of injury, I thought he could wait until Liz came out the following day for our weekly check-up of wildlife casualties. Today was going to be a badgery day as within the next two hours, David Stevens from the Somerset Badger Group had brought in a badger that had been reported to us in someone's garage. We have a list of people that we can call out to badger problems. These are people that are experienced in catching badgers and have the necessary graspers and cages to contain them. Badgers are very strong animals and can get out of the normal kind of animal carriers quite easily. It's never a good idea to put an unconscious badger loose in a car, as several people can verify.

Spring is the time of year when the sows are underground with the cubs that are usually born between February and May. The sows keep the males away from the cubs for the first weeks of their lives and the males spend their time patrolling their territories. They make sure that subservient male badgers within their group, or even those that are thinking of moving into the territories, will know who is the boss. In their fights the badgers get wounded on the rump and sometimes around the ears. This is when badgers will find somewhere out of the way to lick their wounds and recover before returning home when things have quietened down.

The badger that David had brought to us had rump wounds, but other than that he seemed to be fine – another casualty that was going to make the most of a rest and good food for a few days. Liz would now have two badgers to look at tomorrow.

By the afternoon our first badger cub had arrived. He had been discovered in a field by a farmer. I met the farmer in reception and thanked him for bringing the cub to us – not every farmer would have brought him in although many do care as much for their wildlife as they do for their own animals. I left the receptionist to take the details of where he was found and carried the small cub, wrapped up in a warm towel, upstairs to the flat. I sat in the arm-chair in the kitchen and held him against me to slowly warm him up, stroking him. He must have been so terrified out in the field all alone.

We always have a theme for naming the badger cubs and this year there was so much talk about the Millennium bugs that were going to destroy our computers. Looking through a wildlife book I realised that there were several plants which started Bog such as Bog Bean, Bog Sedge, Bog Cotton, Bog Violet so we decided it was going to be the year of the Bogs! Bog Bean was duly named, rather an unattractive name for such a bundle of grey fur with a black and white face that was only six weeks old. This poor little boy was freezing. He'd either been taken out of a sett by a dog or be-ing moved by the sow was dropped, but there were no injuries. He certainly wouldn't have survived for much longer if he hadn't been found by the farmer out checking his sheep. The farmer had put the cub in his pocket and came straight out to us.

Warmth was what this little mite wanted before he would want any milk. The incubator had been switched on in the kitchen and the sound of the motor whirring meant it was slowly reaching the right heat. I was happy sitting in the armchair with the little form held against my body gaining the warmth from me. Derek came in and saw me in the chair. 'You're in your element, aren't you?' he said smiling. 'Coffee?'

'Yes, please. Sorry – the "badgers in my kitchen" bit is about to start all over again,' I apologised.

'And you wouldn't have it any other way,' he said, placing the mug on the side by my chair and kissing the top of my head. 'I'm off to close up because everyone has gone. If Nikki is cooking tea, it means pasta again!' he smiled, and grimaced jokingly.

Whatever happens, I thought to myself, I know we shall be OK.

I heard footsteps clattering up the stairs that was bound to be Nikki having heard that the cub had arrived. She burst into the room. 'Is it alright? Can I see? Oh, isn't he lovely,' she enthused. I offered to hand him over to her but she said, 'No, he looks lovely and comfy where he is,' and laughed as Bog Bean scratched his side with his back leg, a sign that he was feeling better. His eyes still looked milky as they had only just opened. I'm always amazed how different badger cubs are from fox cubs that open their eyes after ten days. Badger cubs don't come above ground until they are at least eight weeks old. Underground there is no need to be able to see and hear, so both their ears and eyes are sealed until they are five weeks old. The one sense that they do use is their sense of smell.

I fondled his paws that were so soft and yet already had the shiny claws. 'First badger cub of the Millennium,' said Nikki. 'I'll cook tea tonight if you want, how do you fancy pasta?'

'That would be lovely,' I said, and smiled.

Before Nikki started to cook tea, she mixed me up a small amount of milk and put it on a chair by my side with a bowl of warm water and a 1ml syringe with a small teat on it. As the little man had started to move around, I thought I would try him with some milk. Wiping under his tail and sliding underneath to his penis with a wet tissue, he immediately started to suckle and pushed out his anal gland. A strong smell of musk was evident, this was his way of laying his scent on his mother just as his siblings and mother would do so that they all had the same smell which, when mixed with the others of the group, would be individual to that social group. Badgers can recognise each other as much by smell as recognition, having a sense of smell as strong as a dog, about 800 times stronger than our sense of smell, so we're told. It's not an unpleasant smell and musk is actually the base of a lot of perfumes.

I filled up the syringe and slowly released the milk into the cub's mouth. He wrinkled his nose in distaste – this was not like mother's milk. Slowly letting him have a second and third syringe, the reaction was the same. It's never right to try to get them to feed too quickly, it takes time and really the feeding regime is part of the bonding, telling the orphan that they are safe and you are there to help them. Feeding them too quickly means that sometimes the lungs will get flooded and this in turn develops into pneumonia. Then you really do have a problem as it's very difficult to help them to survive. Bog Bean thought he'd had enough of that terrible white stuff, he stretched and yawned and settled down to sleep. Placing him into the incubator, it was time for dinner. Derek and Simon were upstairs having closed everything down. 'Our first badger cub of the year then, huh?' said Simon, looking into the incubator. 'He looks quite content.'

'Yes,' mimicked Derek. 'Isn't it lovely – the orphan season has started.' And he pulled a face.

Nikki laughed. 'Best time ever,' she enthused and dinner was served.

Bog Bean was the size that when he started to feed properly, he would only need to be fed every four hours and certainly wouldn't need a feed during the night. So last thing, when everything else was fed and watered, I settled with him on my lap in the armchair. This time the wiping under his tail was followed by a rush of warm urine. Thankfully, I had several kitchen tissues to hand and managed not to end up with a wet lap. I filled the syringe and placed it in his mouth. Perhaps he knew this was the last chance before the morning and his tongue curled around the teat and he started to suck. One syringe after the other was quickly consumed until he had drunk 30 mls. Just like human babies, he fell asleep on the last syringe and stayed with his mouth slightly open so you could see his tongue still curled while he comfort sucked.

Placing him carefully into the incubator, I turned the kitchen lights out. Everyone else was already in bed. Both Bog Bean and I fell asleep much happier.

* * *

It was a Sunday evening, just a few days away from Easter. Simon and Nikki were out and Derek and I were about to sit and enjoy a Sunday dinner just on our own. It was all ready to be served but we hesitated as the weather forecast for the coming week came on the television. Warnings of bitterly cold winds coming our way with a flippant remark that there could be snow, did little to raise our hopes of a successful Easter. The first public holiday after the winter has always been one of our best weekends for visitors and shop sales. We needed this to be exceptional this year.

The joint was carved and plated and I was about to serve up the vegetables. The telephone rang. 'Who on earth is that?' Derek said vehemently. 'I bet it will be someone wanting to know how their animal is. Fancy ringing at this time on a Sunday. Who would think of ringing on a Sunday night, for goodness' sake?!'

We do tell people they can ring and find out how their casualty is after 48 hours and they sometimes tend to ring when they think about it, without realising sometimes how early or late it can be. I tried to get to the phone with pan in hand but unfortunately Derek got there first. I cringed.

'Good evening, Secret World,' he started.

Well, that wasn't too bad was it?

'Oh, hello, yes, I know all about it. He's doing fine,' Derek chatted. 'No, it was no trouble at all. That's what we are here for. We always go out, night or day. The aim is to reduce suffering as much as we can.' He listened. 'Yes, that's fine. Of course you can come and visit him.'

I was totally bemused. Not only was he talking to the person 'on a Sunday night' but even agreeing to visiting times for casualties!

'No trouble at all,' he repeated 'Thank you for calling.'

'What was that all about?' I asked, with upturned hands.

'That,' said Derek smiling, 'was Valerie Singleton!'

* * *

It was Good Friday morning and we awoke to hailstones hammering on the window. I had that terrible sense of dread that it was all going wrong. The badger cubs were all scrabbling against the board in front of the cubby hole. Little did they care about the weather, it was all nice and warm in the kitchen.

Bog Bean by now had been joined by twin cubs that had been found in Weston-super-Mare by people out walking. They were above a badger sett whimpering. A sow badger had been killed on the road three days before and we think it was probably their mother. Bog Violet (female) and Bog Sedge (male) were duly named. They were a little bit older than Bog Bean but badgers mix as cubs very easily and they were all at the stage of starting to play with each other. Moved from the incubator, they had more space in the cubby hole and were old enough to explore the kitchen at feed times. This is the time that Derek hates as badgers love feet and will attack (only in play) but the fuss Derek makes about it, you'd think that they drew blood. Bare feet first thing in the morning were particularly popular.

Easter is always advertised as the one and only time that we take the badger cubs, still on milk, down onto the front lawn, briefly for visitors to see. It's all cordoned off so that nobody can actually touch them. Each of our carers takes a cub down wrapped in their own towels and if or when they become upset, we bring them straight back upstairs. People are fascinated as you so rarely see badger cubs so small. After Easter the cubs soon wean and then it's time for the cubs to go into pens away from the kitchen with hardly any contact with Nikki or me as we want them to revert to being wild.

If it continued to rain and hail, there was no way that we would be able to take them out in the open to show people. Derek and Simon were already outside getting ready for the day, unlocking the offices and making sure that the cleaners were in. The animal carers were already starting their daily chores. Time to let out the poultry, feed the pigs and pet lambs to name but few. Everyone was walking around with hoods up just trying to get it all done, despite the horrendous weather. Volunteers were already in looking after the many orphan birds that were now trilling in the hospital room – probably the best place to be today.

Nikki came through to the kitchen.

'Do you want to feed?' I said, 'and I'll try and get the cubby hole cleaned out.'

She looked thoroughly drained and I probably did as well. We had been so late last night trying to get all the new stock out in the shop. The men had given up and gone to bed. Even with the gas fire on it had got very cold towards midnight in the barn with its high ceiling and elm beams. We were really cold and tired by the time we were back in the kitchen to do the last feeds for the badger cubs. It had all been done in silence because, without voicing our thoughts, we both knew this weekend was going to be an important one for trying to pay off our loan.

'OK,' said Nikki flatly, and she got the milk ready while I started to clear the newspaper that had been shredded through the night.

The cubby hole all had to be disinfected and then clean fleeces and toys placed in the clean pen. The cubs were oblivious to our moods and excitedly chased each other around the legs of the chairs. Having made their fur stand on end, which they do when they are frightened or excited to make themselves look bigger, they looked like black and white balls of fluff.

I was having difficulty hanging on to the bucket with inquisitive cubs trying to look and see what was inside. All that water tipped over was the last thing I wanted so I cleaned with one hand and was holding on to the bucket with the other. As soon as Nikki was in the armchair my troubles were over because that meant the milk was ready and Nikki was trying to bottle feed one cub with the other two doing their best to climb up on to her lap – there was no such thing as queuing.

'They did say that it might brighten up today,' said Nikki, showing that we still had the same thoughts on our minds. 'The television programme starts on Tuesday and that's sure to make a difference,' she said.

I pulled a face. 'I'll leave you to it,' I said, 'the cubby hole's ready.' Nikki's eyes were beginning to brim. Any more time together and we'd both be in tears.

What's it they say in life, you either have a glass half empty or half full? I believe in it being half full, count your blessings. I breezed into the tearoom with a smile.

Liz in the kitchen looked serious. 'This isn't what we wanted, is it?' she said, pointing to the rain running down the window pane.

'Oh, it'll be fine,' I said, 'and if it stays cold, the tearoom will be the favourite place, so you'll be the busy one.' We both laughed.

Sadly the whole four-day period remained cold and wet and the only place that did indeed take more money than usual was the tearoom. With log fires burning in both the rooms and the Rayburn in the kitchen, it certainly was the best place to be. We had to try and do all our talks in the buildings around the farm but it wasn't the same as doing it all to a large audience. Ferret racing was rained off and we took half of what we would normally take in admissions and shop takings.

The Tuesday after the Easter weekend, our first programme of *Secret World* went out on HTV. It was a six-part series with Mr Woo every inch a star. Nikki was very much the presenter and Derek and Simon involved more with the rescues. It was very popular and at the launch party, which was held in Bristol, the television company were more than pleased with the viewing figures.

We did see our visitor numbers rise but the wildlife casualties rocketed. We had never been so busy. Things like making beds were a thing of the past, we just pulled the covers back over when we managed to get there. I suspect Nikki already did this! Most of her clothes remained on the floor until next required and yet she could walk out looking like a million dollars. I have never seen anyone staple holes in their clothes rather than sewing! Within a week the kitchen crew had risen by another six badger cubs and the arrival of baby birds seemed endless. We did have a lot of volunteers that helped us in collections and care of the wildlife but it seemed never-ending.

* * *

As if Easter wasn't bad enough, we were expecting great things with our visitor numbers over the Whitsun weekend, another busy time for us. On the Friday before the bank holiday the M5, which we can see from our house, was busy with people travelling for the weekend. I was outside shutting the chickens in just as it was getting dark and there was a huge bang. There was a sound of screeching brakes, of metal making impact and I knew there had been a bad accident on the motorway. Simon came out from the house and went up to the motorway bridge, which is just outside our farm. Almost immediately there were sirens and police, ambulances and fire engines were soon in attendance. Simon came back as there was little he could do to help, it all appeared to be under control.

It makes you realise how lucky you are. A large articulated lorry had tried to avoid a car that had already crashed with another and had driven straight into the pillars of our motorway bridge. There are some people who won't be spending this weekend as they had planned, I thought. I remember when Simon was visiting Nikki in Leeds after he had finished his own university course. Nikki had a gap year in France as she was studying media and languages, so had an extra year to do. Simon had studied business studies and law. He had taken our car up, it was one of the nicest cars we had ever had. Derek had got it from the auction near us. I'm pretty useless with makes of car so let's just say it was automatic, was blue and had four wheels but was pretty fast.

Strangely we had been watching *Crime Watch* the week before and they had flagged up on the programme that Leeds had a high incidence of stolen cars. 'Ooh!' I commented to Simon, who was watching with me. 'Perhaps you didn't ought to take our car up,' I said jokingly.

'Don't worry, Mother – I have a safe place where I can park it,' remarked Simon. I just nodded.

Well, his second night up there, he heard the car being started up (safely parked outside on the side of a road in university land!). He threw his clothes on and ran downstairs but the car was just disappearing into the distance. Simon reported it to the police, hoping that a quick report would mean they would find it and indeed, the police rang the next morning to say it had been found dumped outside a grocery shop. Relief sank in as the officer explained that it was now in the police compound. Simon's mind was working overtime. He could go and collect it, get any repairs done and then ring and tell us what had happened. The officer said he could collect it anytime during the day.

When Simon arrived at the compound, he innocently asked for his car back. The officer in charge looked over his shoulder and said, 'Where's your pick-up truck?' Simon started to get nervous.

'No-one said anything about it being very damaged,' he said.

'You're going nowhere in that car, mate. The car thieves had a good joyride mounting kerbs and along alleys and then dumped it outside a grocery shop, where we are then given to believe that some other kids tried to ram raid the shop front.'

The car didn't look anything like it used to. In fact it was somewhat shorter and smaller than it had been.

A hesitant Simon rang to explain the situation. I was more thankful that he hadn't got there as the first thieves were driving off, stood in front of them to stop them and then got run over for his troubles. 'We can always get another car,' I said, 'but thank goodness you haven't been hurt.'

Mind you, a couple of years later, when Simon wrote off another car (not his fault I have to say) the telephone conversation started with, 'You know you said last time when our car got wrote off – we can always get another car, it's much better that you haven't been hurt, well ...'

What we didn't realise that evening was that the lorry had damaged the supports of the motorway bridge. When we started to get ready the next morning we found that our road was closed and people could only access us from country roads instead of a tourist signposted road directly off the A38. It was another weekend where our normal takings were halved, not showing the huge increase we were hoping for after the TV series.

I didn't have too much time to dwell on it as on the night of the bank holiday, I had a phone call from my mother to say that Dad had been taken into hospital with a heart attack. I went over immediately and we both went through to the Weston-super-Mare hospital. They lived in a flat overlooking the sea. They had moved several years ago to be near to me and to be honest had been towers of strength in helping us get the tourist attraction off the ground. Dad would cover reception and Mum would help in the tearoom but now in their eighties, their health was not so good. Dad in particular had slowed down, which in turn had made things harder for Mum having to do things that she hadn't normally done.

We made our way to the ward that Dad had been transferred to by the time we got there. Mum, ever the organiser, had fresh bed clothes, wash bag, money to buy a paper. Dad looked very grey but was better than I expected. He was lucky, it had been more of a warning but he was really going to have to slow down and stop doing a lot of what, in the past, he had enjoyed doing.

He remained in hospital for a few days and then was sent home. I helped as much as I could with the shopping until they got themselves into a pattern of how they could cope – and I was only a phone call away. I hadn't said anything to either of them about the problems we were having, but they had an idea that things were not good. I consoled myself that no matter what our problems were, we were all healthy and if need be, we could all go and get other jobs.

Our road was opened to light traffic and it remained like that for two years before it was finally repaired.

During the summer, Valerie Singleton did visit us. Her badger had already gone home but she enjoyed seeing what we did and very kindly offered to join Simon King as one of our patrons. Valerie loves clotted cream and we were sat out in the sun on the front lawn with warm fruit scones, you could smell the vanilla in them, and a dish laden with clotted cream. I asked her if she would attend an auction and ball that we were hoping to hold in November as one of our largest fund-raising events for the charity. She agreed and we were thrilled.

It wasn't the best of summers and as autumn approached, there were strikes by drivers on the tankers and there was a petrol shortage. People were not going out unless they really had to. Scenes of huge queues and the arguments on forecourts of petrol stations had to be seen to be believed. You wouldn't have thought so many things could go wrong in one year. Simon received a phone call from Tish about the television series. It had been very popular and she was hoping to get another series commissioned. However, huge cuts were being made at ITV. HTV was being sold and the commissioning director was no longer the same person. There would be no second series. Simon came to tell me the news.

'Well, that's that then,' I replied. 'Our next committee meeting of the charity is not going to be an easy one.'

'We couldn't have done more, I'm sorry.' Simon knew that was the final nail in the coffin.

'And just to throw salt in the wound,' he said, 'the glis glis have escaped from the nocturnal house.'

'How did that happen?' I asked.

'They've gnawed a hole at the back and nobody noticed,' came the reply.

'Oh dear, how am I going to explain that one to Doug?' I sighed.

Simon grimaced and went to tell the others the bad news. Doug Woods was someone I had met years ago. He was a retired butcher but there was little that he didn't know about wildlife. He was my guru. He taught me how to do talks, took me on walks and really opened my eyes to the natural world. He took me to my first Badger Conference and I have so much to thank him for. He had a particular interest in the common dormouse, one of our three hibernating mammals in this country.

Doug did a tremendous amount of work in the Cheddar Woods where there is a lot of hazel, the main diet of these beautiful animals that were believed to be very rare. They are arboreal so it was his idea to put small wooden boxes attached about two metres up a tree and indeed the dormice used them. I, like many others, was treated to an enchanting walk checking the boxes and finding the dormice curled up inside. Doug would point out where the deer had broken off the branches as they grazed, the paths where badgers walked every night and took me on magical badger watches shared by other very lucky people. He was an amazing man.

He got me involved in the breeding programme for dormice and I had sheds where the juvenile dormice were looked after, having been picked up under licence when discovered in the boxes as late litters that wouldn't gain the weight to survive the winter. They would then return to the wild the following spring. Amazing little creatures they eat pollen when they first emerge, then take seeds and fruit, finally eating the hazel nuts in a distinctive way while they are still green and on the trees before, having tripled their weight, they hibernate through the winter. They create a tight ball of moss and leaves and hibernate between the roots of the hedge on the ground.

We had been given the glis glis (fat dormice) from a research programme in Tring. The idea was to record their breeding patterns and growth period. These animals are not indigenous but were first brought in by the Romans. This is where they get their name – fat dormice – as they are nearly the size of squirrels but look very much like bush babies. They were kept in clay pots that they couldn't climb out of and fattened on walnuts, then they were eaten. The species died out but were later re-introduced by Lord Rothschild on his estate in the Tring area at the beginning of the twentieth century. Just as our common dormouse has to have hazel, glis glis survive where there are beech forests as they eat the mast seeds.

My problem was two-fold. One to tell Doug what had happened and two, how were they going to survive as their diet did not suit them in this area, which is why they have remained contained in the Tring area. My cup that floweth half full made me think that at least if we closed, that was one lot of animals we didn't have to find homes for. But I worried how they would survive. They'd be fine at the moment as they love apples and our orchard was full of laden trees.

My stomach lurched and I felt sick. We really were facing the fact that Secret World was about to close. Pulling myself together, I remembered that I had an appointment with Mr and Mrs Havercroft. The name seemed familiar to me but I couldn't think why. Going downstairs, I made my way to reception just as they arrived. They were a young couple that looked very serious. Taking them up to the kitchen, I made us all a drink.

In no way was I prepared for what they were to tell me. Philip, the father of Millie, was driving a tractor with their four children on the wheel arches and Millie had fallen off. Before he was able to do anything, the tractor had gone over Millie and killed her. Philip reached for his wife Nicki's hand, as he explained. I remembered reading about the awful accident in the local paper. Secret

World was Millie's favourite place and they wanted donations for her funeral to come to us towards our work with wildlife. The words stung me. Just how do you cope with such an experience so terrible, especially knowing how many 'what ifs' there must have been going over and over in their minds? I knew that I couldn't offer them a tree or anything in remembrance, knowing that we probably wouldn't be there for much longer, but my heart went out to them. They were such a lovely couple and thanking them for coming and trying to find the right words for their generosity, arrangements were made for donation envelopes in memory of Millie, who had only been ten years old.

After they had gone, I sat quietly in my kitchen. No radio or television on, just the ticking of the clock. Me and my foolish ideas. I had to accept if we weren't doing the wildlife work, we wouldn't need so many staff. Our vet bills would be smaller. Even the filming took a lot of time and they very rarely pay a facility fee, believing that anything shown on TV is kind of advertising. It had all drained our finances. This wasn't totally the reason though, other larger, similar tourist attractions had opened in the same county in the past couple of years and were competition, but at least our visitor numbers were remaining static.

But I had been so convinced that our own television series would make the difference. It certainly had. Nikki had added up our casualties for the year and we had gone from 1,000 wildlife casualties annually to nearly 3,000 just in the current year.

Where were we going to be in six months' time? What will happen to all our animals – especially my resident badgers, Glade, Nippy and Foxglove? Didn't what had happened to the Havercrofts put everything into perspective. In life there are some things that money can't buy.

It was time to face what was coming. Maybe it wasn't going to be easy but we had our health and we had each other. Murray, my shadow, yet again found my lap and I stroked his head.

3

The new Secret World

If ever there were people who saved Secret World, it was the committee of the Bluebell Sett Trust. With the help of professional people giving their advice freely to us, the committee members decided to try and carry the charity on even once the tourist attraction closed. They would have to rent the property. Simon had already been employed by them as the Charity Administrator for the past two years and the hope was that two of the animal carers would be able to be employed to help with the wildlife casualties. The rest of the work would need to be done by myself and other volunteers. Maybe I could manage on the money I gained from talks about the charity, we'd have to see.

The charity would only be able to finance the care of wildlife so all the commercial animals that we had such as cows, sheep, donkeys, chickens, pigs and farm stock would all have to be sold.

We were still hoping to have our Celebrity Auction in November as a large fundraiser and that just might bring in enough money for the charity to continue into 2001 for a couple of months. It was just a few weeks away now. We couldn't afford for it to fail. There would be no job for me, Derek or Nikki and everyone else on the payroll of the tourist attraction would be laid off, but at least there was a chance that the Bluebell Sett Trust would survive. It was a huge gamble.

I couldn't imagine how Derek was feeling. This was his father's farm, handed down to him and now that was all going to go. He would even have to find a job. The shop, tearoom, advertising and promotional work, all his side of the business, were all going to go, it was going to be a huge change. When we started a tourist attraction there was to be so many ups and downs. We created a tearoom in the bottom of the farmhouse only to find that we didn't have enough electricity to run all the ovens, microwaves and urns. Once the supply was uprated, we then found there was not enough water pressure to flush the toilets. Our farm, which is listed, hadn't had any money spent on it over the years as Derek's parents had paid for it and whilst it had a lovely air of 'going back in time', when it rained a lot of the roofs were like sieves. It was one thing after the other and I marvel how we had got through. Nikki was going to have to find work as well, but said she would help as much as she could with the animals in her spare time.

Now Derek and I had to go to our parents and tell them what was going to happen. It's not easy to tell people that you have failed. Sadly, Derek's father had died from Farmer's Lung, a chronic lung disease caused by the dust and mildew spores in hay, but he still had to explain to his mother. Maybe the worst part was carrying on every day as if nothing was happening, knowing that eventually all the staff – cleaners, shop assistants, animal carers, maintenance and the ladies in the tearoom – people that we knew as friends as well as staff, would all have to be told in the first week of December. You just felt sick as soon as you woke up in the morning and it was still there when you shut your eyes at night.

We still had our own problems with paying back our loan from the bank, which had grown over the years. Dad's health had continued to go downhill and it was on one of my visits that both my parents wanted to have a serious word with me. They had both thought about our position and asked that if we were happy to do it, they wanted to sell their flat and have the tearoom made into a downstairs home for them. They would be near us all for help if ever needed. The money left would be what my sister and I inherited so

I could have mine straight away, which would help pay off the bank. It would help Mum who was really finding it difficult to cope with everything that needed to be done. Derek was as happy as I was for it to go ahead. So their flat was put up for sale.

* * *

Nikki was working hard on the Auction and Ball that we were holding at the Webbington Hotel. We were going to call it a Celebrity Auction as we had Valerie Singleton, Kate O'Mara, Andrew Lynford (who was appearing in *Eastenders* at that time), Clinton Rogers (our local senior BBC journalist) and Chris Sperring MBE from the Hawk and Owl Conservancy. There was to be a main auction of about ten items and a silent auction of items which Nikki had approached companies and shops for, so there were over a hundred! They were placed around the room with clipboards so that people could keep bidding against each other through the evening until it closed at midnight. After the three-course meal, the celebrities took questions and chatted with the audience. With an Abba tribute band that was going to appear at a vastly reduced rate, we hoped it would raise a lot of money.

Tickets sold well and everyone worked so hard to make it a success. Indeed it was a huge success and over £10,000 was raised in one night. The euphoria was short-lived as we came down to earth because it still wasn't enough to save Secret World as a tourist attraction, but it just might get the charity through the first few months.

It was only a week later that we told the staff that Secret World was closing and a press release went out. All the staff were amazing. There was more concern for us and the animals than there was for themselves. They were all true friends indeed and were prepared to help in any way that they could. Letters went out to supporters of the charity but they were more likely to have heard it through the media as there was all the local TV crews, alongside radio and newspaper reporters on our doorstep as soon as the news was released.

The press want tears and that was easy enough as they asked pertinent questions. Many pictures were taken of me with Glade, the badger, as we were well known to all the press who over the years had been in covering so many different stories – this was front page stuff. Despite the tears at the realisation that we were now closed, it was such a weight off my shoulders that we could now talk about it and apologise to the staff and volunteers who we felt we were letting down. Totally drained by the end of the day, the phone had stopped ringing from the announcements on the evening news, it was probably the first night that I had slept so well for a long time.

A staff Christmas party had already been organised and everyone wanted to go ahead with it as a farewell party. They even gave us a beautiful cut-glass bowl inscribed to Derek and I, wishing us luck. Words fail me as to how much that meant to us all as a family and mine weren't the only tears shed that night.

The response was amazing. So many Christmas cards came through wishing the charity luck in trying to survive and many donations were received. It was hard over the next few weeks as the animals still had to be cared for with dramatically reduced staff, but many volunteers helped. The fireplaces in the tearoom lay bare and empty. Tables and chairs were packed away and with no heating downstairs apart from the Rayburn, it felt very cold. Derek had already started to log everything for a sale organised in the first week of February. The sale would be for a whole day as all the animals, such as the rare breeds of chickens, sheep and cows, would probably take the best part of the morning. Then there was all the equipment from the tearoom, tools, vintage farm machinery, ornaments – it was endless.

There was quite a lot of shop stock, including some tools that the charity would still need, as well as an old tractor. The charity was not in a position to be able to buy this so we gifted £48,000 worth of stock to them. The thought was that maybe on bank holidays, the charity could still have open days to attract donations and sell shop stock, but that was in the future.

Things were beginning to fall into place. Mum and Dad had accepted an offer on their flat and Nikki had applied for a temporary job for the RSPCA in connection with a research programme looking at having a cage in the sea for rafting birds to recover in, rather than in pools at their centre. Applicants needed to be good swimmers and take a course on handling a boat. So it all seemed very interesting.

Derek had managed to get a part-time job doing milk recording. This is visiting a farm for the afternoon and morning milking, taking samples of the milk from each cow and recording how much milk they produce at each milking. This is done once a month for farmers with pedigree herds who like to keep records for each individual cow. The samples, which Derek had to send off, would tell the farmer what level of butter fats and protein each cow's milk contains. Farmers are paid according to the quality of milk produced by their herd. Derek used to do this with his own cows and was finding the new job very interesting. It was just a shame that it was only part-time and didn't pay very well.

He was also still doing leaflet drops for other tourist attractions and looking at becoming a rep for retail suppliers, having had contact with so many firms in the past. As it was winter, I was doing several talks to groups and societies mainly in the evening, so we were beginning to feel a bit more positive.

A week before the auction, Dad was taken into hospital during the night with another suspected heart attack and I went along with Mum. He seemed settled by the morning and we returned home. I said I would visit him that afternoon as Mum was so tired. Dad was sitting up when I got there and he took a phone call from a friend. He then needed to take oxygen as the effort of it had affected him. On the way out, I spoke to the nurse and she said he would probably need to be on oxygen for the rest of his life. Knowing my father and his thoughts on disabilities, I knew he wasn't going to be an easy patient.

I was staying with Mum so I was there when late that evening we were told to get to the hospital as soon as we could. I needed to contact Simon as he was very close to both my parents having visited them often when he was small, usually when Derek's children went to visit either their mother or their grandparents. Unfortunately he didn't answer the phone but arrived at the hospital soon after us, having picked up the message I'd left.

We saw Dad briefly and he was on oxygen and struggling for his breath. The consultant came to talk to us in the visitors' room and explained that they were going to try to fit a pacemaker to his heart, but Mum didn't pick up on how serious this all was. The procedure was going to take a few hours, so once the doctor left Mum started to talk about going home and visiting the next day. I saw the crash team run past the window and suggested to Simon that we went and got a cup of coffee, before we sorted out what we were going to do. Once outside, I explained to Simon that I thought Granddad was dying and we needed to stay.

We were only back with Mum for a few minutes and a nurse came to tell us the bad news. We went to see him briefly, at peace at last, and someone had placed a flower on the pillow by his head. It struck me how, even though these people deal with these situations every day, they still understand that such small actions show they care.

The next few days were a blur, but the usual arrangements and legal matters were attended to. The auction came and went. A few more thousand pounds were taken off what we owed to the bank.

* * *

The flat downstairs was created for Mum as she still wanted to move in with us. The only difference was that she didn't want to have a second bedroom so I had one of the rooms as my office. It meant that I would be close at hand and Mum could pop in whenever she wanted anything. The only thing was that all the coffee and biscuits that were brought in, and the chocolates every time she started a box, added to my weight problem!

Just as Mum moved in, a cardboard box was dumped near to our front door. It was a neighbour who found the box and, looking very briefly inside and seeing a large black animal, immediately brought it to us thinking it was a badger. When I looked inside, there was the ugliest dog I had ever seen. She had fur around her face and legs but on the rest of her round body the skin was bare and had sores covering it. She was absolutely terrified but allowed me to lift her out of the box.

Taking her through to Mum's flat, we bathed her sores and I made an appointment to go to the vets with her. We kept her away from Mum's Yorkshire terrier, Suzi, as we weren't sure if she had anything contagious. I placed a basket next to the radiator in my office and she quietly lay inside just watching me.

When it was time to take her to the vets, Pippa, as Mum had called her (always dangerous once they have a name) was wrapped in a warm blanket and taken through to Quantock Veterinary Hospital in Bridgwater, who we had been with for several years. It was Colin, one of the partners, who saw us.

'Oh dear,' said Colin, 'she's in a bad way. You don't see many of this breed.'

I was amazed that it was a breed. I thought it was just an unfortunate mongrel that had missed out on the cute factor.

'It's an Affenpinscher,' he continued, 'often called a monkey dog because of its face – ugly.' I agreed on that score. 'I think we need to take a blood sample to see what we are looking at, can you leave her with us for a while?'

'I can, but she's had a pretty upsetting rotten day so I wouldn't want to leave her too long,' I replied.

'No, I can see where you're coming from. I can do tests straight away – about an hour or so?' asked Colin.

'That's fine,' I replied. There was some shopping to do and then I'd be back. Pippa trotted off happily on a borrowed lead.

When I arrived back it was good news – I think! She was suffering from Cushing's Disease, which is an imbalance of hormone cortisol. It could be corrected with treatment and the sores on her back needed to be treated and daily baths using a special shampoo would soften the skin and possibly help the growth of new fur. Well, a dog needing all that attention, I thought, would be a very good diversion tactic for Mother, with all the things that had been going on recently. I therefore returned home and presented her to Mum. I can't say she was thrilled but her soft heart (which is where I get it from) wanted to help the poor little mite. I would help her with the baths, I said. Suzi, her spoilt little Yorkie was horrified with the intrusion, but I think secretly she knew that Pippa was no contest as far as admirers were concerned.

'God, what's that horrible thing your mother has got downstairs,' was Derek's first question when he came home from work. Bless her; she didn't stand a chance – the dog, not Mother.

'God, what's that horrible thing?'

We were still occasionally filming with *Pet Rescue* and they loved the story so came to film Pippa and get reports from the vets, hearing how she had been dumped, probably due to the cost of the veterinary treatment she was going to need. They also wanted footage of Mum taking care of her and Pippa's daily baths. Then to follow Pippa's progress as time went by. Day by day, Pippa did improve and was soon covered in soft downy fur and one of the programmes showed Pippa going to a local kennel for a 'shampoo and set'. She did come back very posh, but they couldn't do much with the face – that was the breed!

* * *

It's funny how when you hear about a national crisis, you can remember exactly where you were at the time when you heard about it. And it was going to happen twice, as far as I was concerned, in 2001.

It was breakfast television, something I do as soon as I get up is to either turn on the television or the radio – I have to have 'noise'. It was obvious from the tone of the presenter's voice that something serious had happened. It was an announcement that anyone involved with farming would dread. It was the first outbreak of Foot and Mouth, a notifiable disease, found in Essex. The last time I had heard that was when I was working as a dairymaid on Pennywell farm in Berkshire, having just left school. It can affect cows, pigs and sheep. I can remember the thick swathe of straw at the farm entrance soaked in disinfectant. No feed reps were allowed on the farm and even the driver of the milk lorry that picked up the churns, had to stop by the gate and wash his boots in a container before he came on to the farm and again as he left. Even though the outbreak was mainly in the North West Midlands, everyone was terrified it would spread.

For the next few days the true horror was going to unfold. Terrible pictures of funeral pyres or animals being hoisted into lime graves were on every single news programme throughout the day. By 16th March, 240 cases had been reported and by the end of March, 50 new cases a day were being notified. It moved from Essex to Devon and then spread to Cornwall and then Cumbria – the Lake District – with terrible financial disasters not only on the farms but the tourism trade too. Whatever we had experienced with our farm becoming non-viable due to milk quotas and having to close our tourist attraction – we had never had to face what those people had to face and our hearts went out to them. Between 80–93,000 animals were killed each week with five new cases reported every day from May to September until it was finally over. Farming has to be one of the hardest industries where your whole life is controlled by nature – weather, disease, whatever is thrown at you.

We knew if we had made it through the winter as a tourist attraction, we would be bound to have gone under with this outbreak and with so many other people suffering, we would never have had as much help as we did. My mother was a great one for believing if something goes very wrong, take stock and look back at things six months later and maybe you will see a reason for it. Perhaps you took a different path that you wouldn't have taken if it hadn't been forced upon you. She had a great relationship with her guardian angel!

Immediately Derek lost his part-time job as all milk recording stopped. Anything to reduce movement in the countryside from farm to farm was stopped. This meant even TB testing of cattle for a year and we were to see the effects of that in future years.

With no restrictions in Somerset, we were hoping that the charity would be able to open just for the four days of Easter and other bank holidays throughout the summer. Many of our visitors were holiday camp people who probably wouldn't even know that we had closed. It would be very different from the attraction but we still had resident badgers, foxes, birds of prey which went out to talks in schools and we thought we could make it more like a fete experience with no admission charge but asking for donations towards our work. Volunteers organised a bric-a-brac stall, tombola, home-made cakes, a catering van in place of the tearoom and, of course, we already had a shop with stock so we hoped to raised more funds to help us survive.

Our large greenhouse where the terrapins were housed was still with us as the Chelonia Group said they would help us with any veterinary treatments that the terrapins might need. It was an easy place to keep tidy and an option in wet weather if we were going to have open weekends. It was a very valuable lesson for people seeing the terrapins, some of them the size of dinner plates, that the tiny pretty ones in pet shops that are only the size of a 50p piece could grow into large terrapins with quite a bite and needing ponds with pumps and filters to keep them healthy.

People always came to see the badger cubs at Easter, and indeed this Easter there were already six cubs in the kitchen crew and feeding times were slightly hectic! For some reason we had gone for biblical names in 2001 so Joshua, Mary, Delilah and Joseph were joined by Noah because he came via ferry (ark?) from the Isle of Wight (a very loose connection). Of course the little cub found in a stream had to be Moses.

This time we were blessed with a lovely sunny Easter weekend – so different from last year – and we were amazed at the number of visitors who came. Some of our volunteers were musical and the front lawn was full of visitors having picnics and being serenaded! The ferrets were still with us so ferret racing was a popular event and the bouncy castle was busy the whole time. We certainly couldn't have done it without the help of our volunteers but visitors were so pleased to be able to come again and there were no complaints that there wasn't enough to see, so we were very pleased.

I have to say that people were still bringing us many casualties, but aware now of the cost and our situation, we found that they would often give us a donation.

* * *

It was only a couple of weeks later that the BBC Natural History Unit rang to say they were doing a series about people and animals and thought it would be good to follow one of our badger cubs. As it happened we did have a late cub in the kitchen but all the others were outside. They seemed to think that was fine as they wanted to show the protocol that our cubs went through and they could follow it with Tessie as she was called (she somehow missed the biblical theme!). They arranged to come out a week later.

By now the 'kitchen crew' as our milk feeder badger cubs are known, had all weaned and were now one of the groups held in enclosures. We had a lovely big grassed enclosure for our resident foxes. These were ones that people had kept as pets and then no longer wanted them for a variety of reasons and of course, by this time, they were too tame to be released. Then behind, was another large grassed enclosure, that couldn't be seen by visitors, so it was where our first family of badgers would go once they had reverted to being nocturnal.

We were well known for our work with badgers. There was the political view that badgers were part of the problem with increasing

Nikki with Doh, the roe kid

Nikki with Robbie the runt

Murray who loved the baby deer

Mr Woo

Our first common seal, Sammy, who loved mackerel smoothies!

One of over 1000 badger cubs cared for at Secret World in the last 25 years

Mum's cockerel, Roger

'Is it safe to come out'?

Rocky, gentle giant

Ducklings hatched in December

Emily, animal carer, launching a
swift on its two year journey totally
on the wing

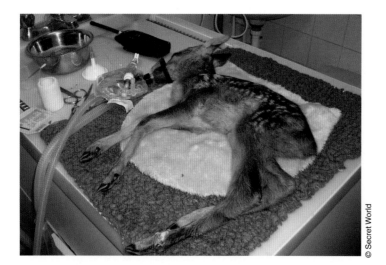

We do everything we can for every animal

New Year's Dip in the Sea at Lyme Regis

Pauline with Freda, the fallow fawn

Yellow-nosed albatross, first time ever seen in Britain

Pauline's grandchildren, Harry and Katie, helping feed the fawns

A juvenile stoat

Bovine TB in cattle and we'd had our own outbreak in our dairy herd. So when I started to do wildlife rescue, I wanted to make sure that our actions as rehabilitators of badgers would be responsible.

Following the science, advised by government scientists and Liz, our vet, who was very interested in this, we were able to create a regime of testing our badgers for Bovine TB prior to release. There was a test for badgers called the ELISA test and although this test was not 100 per cent accurate, it was all that we had. This meant that our cubs were tested three times, a month apart as this disease cycles and we wanted to do all we could to ensure we were only releasing healthy badgers back into the countryside. When we anaesthetised them for the second test, we also tattooed them so that if they turned up later (in a road traffic accident or found dead), we might get the information and know how long they had survived.

With adult badgers, they are returned back to where they came from if they recover, so we're not changing the status of the area. Our badger cubs were formed into family groups and were released into new areas, with the landowner's permission, where there were few or no badgers. If a cub tested positive then we would euthanase it and it would then be sent away for a postmortem to see if the disease could be detected. Sadly, often they would come back negative, but for landowners to have confidence in the cubs that we released, we needed to show our commitment to proving they were healthy. It is impossible to know if a live badger has Bovine TB or not. Considering we are in the South West, which is an area where TB is often found in cattle, we had very few badgers brought into us with the disease. What we really need is a much better cattle test as at the moment only eight out of ten cattle are correctly diagnosed. They are either killed and found not to be positive (a false positive) as suspected, or far more seriously they are a false negative, which means that they really do have the disease but have not reacted to the test, and go back into the herd with the possibility of infecting further cattle.

It was incredibly hard to put to sleep what appears to be a healthy badger, but how can I argue on behalf of the badger if I don't do what the farmer has to do when he gets a reactor in his herd?

Tessie arrived just as we had moved out all the other cubs. She had been discovered curled up in a greenhouse. She was a very pretty cub but seemed small for the age that her teeth were telling us. And her teeth were a real problem; I had never known such a snappy cub so filming with her could be interesting.

* * *

The film crew arrived the next week and the programme *Bringing up Baby* started to be filmed. She was asleep in the cubby hole and then, when ready for her feed, everything had to be filmed. The BBC certainly like detail, so everything from getting out the equipment from cupboards, the milk powder from the fridge, the mixing of the milk, the bottle coming out of the sterilising tub, all had to be done in sequence. Very time-consuming and, more to the point, longer for Tess to wait for that bottle which, as far as she was concerned, was well overdue. By the time I was sitting in the armchair ready to feed her, I had to make sure that my hands were under the cover of the towel and hope that once picked up, Tess would find the teat before my fingers! Success was followed by a camera close-up, which Tess wasn't too happy about but paddling against the towel in a way that would normally express the milk from the mother, she decided that all her concentration needed to be on emptying the bottle.

Even when she had finished the bottle, she would swing her head round in case there was any chance of getting a mouthful of flesh – and it was a good example of how a badger cub is a wild animal and you can't expect them all to be friendly. The next day was a visit to the vet with the film crew, to look at why she was starting to lose her fur and maybe, why she seemed so very small for her age. She was to see Ngaire, a vet at the Quantock Veterinary Hospital.

Warned that she was a snapper, we managed to get the examination without drawing blood. Ngaire explained that she thought it best to anaesthetise her and take some bloods as she wasn't sure what exactly the problem was.

'Is Tessie more bitey after she has had food?' she asked.

'Yes,' I replied, 'now you ask, I think she is. She can be a real sweetie when she's tired and sleepy, but yes, now you mention it, she is more snappy when she wants food and soon after.'

Everything was filmed and I went home with a woozy badger cub, who slept most of the anaesthetic off in the cubby hole. Ngaire hoped to have some more information for me by the next day. The news wasn't good. The blood test showed that Tessie had a liver shunt. This meant that a blood vessel was bypassing the liver so blood still containing protein, sugar, bacteria and toxins was reaching the heart. This would cause stunted growth and seizures (similar to her being snappy). We had a chance, as she was so young, that maybe we could sort it with a diet and medication but the long-term outcome was not good as this could be genetic and get passed on through to other cubs.

'Let's just see how she goes for a while,' said Ngaire, and I agreed.

The next week, Ngaire made a home visit with the film crew in attendance. Little Tessie had lost nearly all her fur and was really not very well. I was syringe feeding her now and the new fibre diet meant she was no longer snappy, but things were not looking good. She had a hot water bottle to lie against to keep warm. I wanted to know if we were being fair to her and Ngaire felt that the next 24 hours were going to be critical. Even the film crew had tears in their eyes, she had been such a little fighter. Ngaire would come the next day and we would leave the decision until then. That evening I sat with her on my lap stroking her head as she snuggled against my arm. I was willing her to slip away during the night so that we wouldn't have to make decisions.

The following morning, I looked into the cubby hole, half hoping she would be dead. I had got up several times during the night but she had been sound asleep so I hadn't disturbed her. To my amazement, a little bit of cooked chicken mixed with bran had disappeared from her dish. This little badger, that looked more like a Vietnamese piglet than a badger cub, was sat looking at me with bright eyes.

'Are you feeling better?' I asked as I removed the board, and she padded out. Yesterday, she couldn't be bothered to even walk. 'Well,' I said, picking her up, 'looks like you want to continue the fight.'

'How is she?' Derek asked as he went to put the kettle on.

'Amazingly, she seems a bit better.'

'Oh, great, I suppose we'll be back to badgers biting our feet – I thought that was over for the year,' he moaned, pulling his face to show he was actually joking.

Both Ngaire and the film crew were pleased to see the improvement. Within a week Tessie was put out in one of the casualty pens at night to play as she had now turned nocturnal and it's amazing what a mess one badger cub can do in one night, especially as you got to the point of barricading the fridge and moving the armchairs so

that she couldn't climb on to the shelves where I keep all my ornaments and where the kettle lives for teas and coffees. Those little
claws are very good at opening doors and drawers. However, the
routine was that first thing, I would open the pen and she would
charge back up to the house, up the stairs and into the cubby hole
for the rest of the day.

I can remember some years ago coming into the kitchen to see
with horror that the badger cubs had managed to climb up on the
shelves. It was bad enough that several of the ornaments had been
knocked off on to the tiled floor so few had survived. But all the
brown marks over the walls and along the shelves made me cringe
at the thought of having to clean it all up. In my line of work anything brown is always considered to be only one thing! I was
pleasantly surprised to find what had happened was that one of
the cubs had knocked over the caddy and stuck its wet snout in
the coffee, so all the brown stains were coffee. I was much happier
now!

The film crew were able to follow the different families of cubs
that we had at the Centre through their protocol of testing and
marking. Tessie, although having survived, was far too tame now
and Ngaire warned that the condition was probably congenital
and she would pass it on to any cubs she may produce in the wild.
'To be honest,' said Ngaire, 'she is unlikely to live more than six
months even though she seems better now.'

The decision was made to put her in with our resident badgers,
Glade and Nippy. Foxglove had sadly died in the winter and we
were moving the badgers up to one of the courtyard pens as the
barn that they were in was going to be sold to clear our debt with
the bank. We have a yearly check-up with our vets for our resident
badgers, giving them the yearly vaccinations that they need. Every
year we comment on the fact that we were told that Tessie would
probably live only for six months – she is now thirteen! Nippy
was quite old by now and it was lovely to see Glade playing with
Tessie in the artificial sett. It is a very rare occasion that we keep
any animal that cannot go back to the wild. It is only after a lot of
thought that we do, our badgers certainly act as ambassadors for
their species – one that is rarely understood.

* * *

It was during the summer that falconer Jeff Prince asked us to take
on a small kestrel. She had been taken from the nest by some

youngsters and kept in a canary cage. She was confiscated by the RSPCA but by that time she was incredibly tame. Due to the bad diet she was given she was very small for her species. As a falconer, Jeff has to keep birds hungry to make them return for the food. This kestrel, Amber as she was called, was so small that to make her hungry could almost be life-threatening so Jeff couldn't fly her.

She was lovely for our talks and a species very rarely seen in captivity. We still had Sage, our barn owl, that had been given to us fifteen years ago and he was very popular with the visitors. It was the same year that we also gave a home to a tawny owl called Twinkle. A lady rang from Portishead to say that she had a tawny that she no longer wanted. It was an owlet that she had picked up eight years previously and had hand-reared herself. She had trained it to the gauntlet but not had her out in recent years. She had now moved away from the house but her son still lived there. I explained that we would only be able to give a home to Twinkle, if we were able to use her for talks for schools etc. and would need to have a look at her first. I was somewhat confused after she had given me the address, when she mentioned that we would need to take bolt cutters with us.

'Why would we need those?' I questioned.

'Oh,' she replied very matter of factly, 'we lost the key to the padlock of her aviary a few months ago.'

That meant that no-one had been in to clean the aviary out or to clean her water dish and that the tawny would have had no contact with anyone at all. She was just having her food posted through the mesh.

Colin Seddon went to have a look at her for us and brought her back the same day. She was so friendly and talkative and it was obvious that she wanted to be near people. Some of our volunteers got to work and soon we had a block of aviaries for our birds that were used for talks. Twinkle, Amber and Sage were very pleased with their new aviaries. They were sited where our visitors could see them, which were different from the aviaries that we had for wild birds which were kept within areas that had limited disturbance.

Twinkle would always call as you passed her aviary, even in the day. She was happy to be on the gauntlet and loved going to schools. We were all pleased that she was now with people who loved her.

* * *

For some reason the project at the RSPCA was halted, so Nikki was a free agent again. The committee realised that whilst our aim is to care for wildlife, if there is no money it cannot be done, so Nikki, with her university qualifications in media, was taken on as our fundraiser. She had already been doing a lot in her own time.

We were still doing filming with *Pet Rescue* for different stories and they were with us in September just catching up with extra voiceovers and link pieces that they needed to complete the programmes. We had all gone up to the kitchen for a drink and Sam, one of the film crew, glanced at his phone and said urgently, 'Turn the television on!'

I can't even remember who did switch on the television but the image of the plane going into the side of the Twin Towers is as clear now as it was then. We all watched speechless, as I'm sure many, many people did. It was beyond belief that anyone could plan such a mass disaster. With our wonderful world of communications, people were actually talking to those still trapped above the fire in this building.

Then came the total collapse of the towers and there aren't any words that can describe our feelings let alone those who lost loved ones within those buildings. Anyone experiencing that crime, as many of us did, through the immediate media now available to us all, will always remember 9/11.

* * *

We were surprised to receive a letter from DEFRA inviting us up to London to join in with a meeting discussing rehabilitation of badgers. Simon, myself and our vet, Liz, were to attend. The RSPCA had been asked to attend too, together with the National Federation of Badger Groups (NFBG – now known as the Badger Trust), the NFU, British Beef Association, many other farming representatives as well as scientists involved with the tests and vaccinations that are current.

When we arrived and as the debate started it was quite clear that the aim of the meeting was to stop rehabilitation of badgers. There was a belief that hundreds of badgers were being reared and then released all over the country. We were able put the real figures to them. At the most there were probably less than 100 badger cubs taken into care nationally each year. Probably 20 of those wouldn't survive. Most of those remaining would then be formed into family groups of anything from five to eight cubs in each group. So we were looking at 10 to 12 groups being released in a year – hardly a statistic worth worrying about in comparison with thousands and thousands of cattle movements around the country.

Whilst we couldn't speak for other rescue centres, we explained our policy of adult badgers always going back to where they belong and the testing regime that we put our cubs through, even though this was done voluntarily. They were very surprised at the amount of work and effort we took endeavouring to release only healthy animals and found it quite difficult to argue against what we did. What they also realised is that if you made rehab of badgers illegal, it would just be done under cover. Just who is going to take a small defenceless badger cub into a vet to be put to sleep? Better that the procedure is responsibly followed. We were therefore tasked to go away and write up a protocol. This we duly did and it became a policy quoted in Parliament. Despite the fact that we were the leading charity in the creation of the protocol, with the agreement of the RSPCA and the NFBG, it was still a voluntary procedure that you hoped other wildlife centres would also follow.

The Randomised Badger Cull, which was still carrying on, was extended for another year because of the Foot and Mouth outbreak. So there were still some years to go before any results would be given out and badgers were still thought to be the culprit.

* * *

It was late September and I walked into the kitchen with the shopping to find Nikki and Mr Woo already there. Despite the acquisition of Mrs Woo, there were still times when it was perfectly normal to see Mr Woo sitting in the armchair eating a custard cream.

'Oh, hello,' I greeted them, 'you're back in the kitchen then?' I questioned Woo.

'Only for a short while,' pleaded Nikki, 'and I promise I will sweep up any currants – but guess what?'– I wasn't to be given any time to guess – it was far too important to wait.

'I've got some really exciting news,' secretly lowering her voice. 'I'm sure I saw something moving around in Mrs Woo's pouch – wouldn't that be cool?!'

I laughed, 'Absolutely cool!' I teased. 'The visitors will certainly enjoy seeing it next year, if it survives.'

'Are you still hearing your saucepans rattling in the cupboards?' Nikki asked.

It was a bit of a joke that I kept hearing rattling of saucepan lids. They were in the cupboard under the sink right next to the armchair where I usually sat so I picked up the noises more in the evening but never saw anything when I quickly opened the cupboard door. We had got in touch with the rat man. Usually we had trouble with mice, especially in the autumn, as once the weather starts to get colder, they migrate into our thick walls that are hollow so you can't always see them but the droppings cannot be denied. If we saw one mouse, the rat man cheerfully told me, there will be another 30 mice running around in your walls. So we did have to put bait down and when they died, we would have a dreadful smell in the room until they rotted away. I must admit I had seen a few quite large droppings and hoped it wouldn't be rats, as Derek absolutely hates them.

We chatted as I put the groceries away. Cold meats and yoghurts in the fridge, cereals, soups, biscuits and cakes in the cupboards and veg plus some cooking apples under the sink were all put in their respective places. Nikki was full of the auction that we were planning for this year. She was following the theme of James Bond and had noticed that a local cinema was showing the recent James Bond film and they had a huge life-size cardboard cut-out of Mr Bond himself. Nikki was going in to see if she could have the cut-out once the film moved on to the next location. Knowing Nikki's skills of persuasion, I had every confidence in her getting it.

The next morning, we had all finished breakfast and I was washing up. Opening the door under the sink to find the washing-up liquid, I saw four apple cores – they had been large cooking apples the day before. I then knew who was living behind that cupboard. It had to be a glis glis. Obviously one at least had survived and come in ready to hibernate. They don't eat cereals so he wasn't going to be affected by the poison put down for the mice.

Over the next few days, I did catch a glimpse of his fluffy grey tail disappearing over where the drainpipe went through. But after a couple of weeks he was not to be seen. I pondered if he was now sleeping through to the spring as dormice do, somewhere in the roof. Would I see him again next year, I wondered? I'd just have to wait and see.

* * *

Simon walking through reception with the life-size cut-out of James Bond under his arm was proof indeed that Nikki had got her prize! The next week was really busy itemising all the auction items ready for the main and silent auction. Tickets had sold well again and 270 people were expected at the event. Tim and Margaret, two volunteers, were to start the intricate table centres and bidding cards that followed the theme of the evening have set the standard of all the detail that went into making this event a success. The room at the Webbington Hotel does look a little bit like a hangar at an airport but once all the decorations were up, it became a magical event. Great pain was taken in sorting out the table plans, making sure that people would get on well with the guests they had been put with. It was shown last year how important this was – having put someone with his second wife on the same table as his first wife and new partner.

There was so much going on with the silent and main auction, the dinner, dancing and casino that the evening just flew by. It was lovely to see everybody in evening dresses and suits. Nikki and Simon made such a good couple. Each of them working so hard to make the charity a success, I could see that they would be completely capable of running the charity, when I was too old.

So many people had come from all over the country to support the event that there was a lot of catching up to be done once the evening was over, and the bar remained open well into the early hours. Eventually I had gone back home to check the animals but Derek, Nikki and Simon had stayed over. Derek having arrived in his dinner suit for the event had forgotten to bring a change of clothes and was the only one so poshly dressed for breakfast!

* * *

Everybody wants to be home for Christmas. Simon and Nikki were up at Nikki's parents and with not quite so many animals to look after, I was quite capable of doing the afternoon feeds, allowing staff and volunteers to be home in time for the celebrated Christmas lunch. We hadn't had any call-outs on Christmas day, which was just as well as Derek had gone down with a heavy cold and really wasn't feeling very well. Halfway through Boxing Day, I had a telephone call from a couple in the village of Woolavington, which isn't very far away from us. They had a young Alsatian in their garden and didn't know what to do. They couldn't take it indoors as they had a dog of their own. I said not to worry, that I would go and collect it. From previous incidents, I knew that the dog warden wasn't going to be on duty on a bank holiday and the police, although they are actually responsible for stray dogs (hence RSPCA will not attend), do not have any kennels these days to keep them in.

I told Derek where I was off to and took the van. On arrival the dog was still in the garden. He certainly wasn't young but quite happily allowed me to put a lead on him and climbed into the van with me. Once I got home I rang the police and explained I had the dog and where it had been found. Hopefully, having lost the dog, someone will ring the police to tell them they have lost it. I gave him some food and rather than put him in a room with our dogs, I asked Derek if he could have him with him, while I did the afternoon feed. Derek is not a fan of Alsatians so the affirmative answer was given somewhat grudgingly.

I was just crossing the yard from checking the casualty pens, when I saw Derek standing by the door. 'Can you come and get this dog,' he asked, 'I don't like the way he keeps looking at me.'

I rolled my eyes. 'Two minutes and I'll be there,' I said. I wondered if I took him back to Woolavington on a lead he may take me to where his home was. I collected him from Derek, who was relieved to see the back of him.

It was already dark. My first move when I got to Woolavington was to go in the pub, which was absolutely packed, in case anyone recognised him. That was a mistake. Trying to break away from drunken conversations, I managed to get outside. Keeping the lead loose, we meandered up the hill so that I could see some shops. To be honest, I didn't realise that they were there. Beside one of the shops, there was a telephone box with a man inside. He had just finished his conversation and opened the door, yanking the phone off the wire, obviously very cross and possibly drunk. Oh, dear, I thought, I'm quite glad I've got this large Alsatian with me and I pulled him in closer to me.

The man slightly staggered and then saw me. His composure changed immediately as he strode over to me. 'What the f**** hell are doing with my dog?' he snarled.

The dog didn't show any sign of recognition so I put my hand out and said, 'Hang on, I don't know that this is your dog. It has been reported to the police so I have to know where you live and your details before I can hand him over.'

'I live just over here,' he signalled, and fell into step with me as we walked towards his house. 'I've had an effing awful Christmas. I had a quarrel with my missus, I threw the table through the window and now she's cleared off with the kids. The bloody dog disappeared during all the fuss.'

By this time we had reached the gate into his back garden and we went through. He was quite right, there was the dining room table half in and half out of the lounge window. There was another dog which came up to me and the two dogs did know each other so I was happier leaving him with the chap once he had written down his details. That family hadn't had a very happy Christmas. He did thank me for looking after the dog.

Quite glad to get away, I went through the gate and was walking down a path trying to remember how to get back to where I had parked the van. A huge man came up towards me. Dressed in leathers with chains across his chest and face piercings glinting under the street lamp, he appeared quite menacing. "'Ere,' he grunted, 'you 'aven't seen an Alsatian dog, 'ave yer?'

I waved behind me, 'I've just taken him back.'

The man charged at me, grasping me under my arms and swung me around in a couple of circles. He placed me back on the ground. 'You're a f**** angel.' And he was gone.

Back home I flopped into a chair opposite Derek watching television. 'I have decided,' I said, 'that I never want to do domestic animals!'

* * *

I found out recently that my sister thinks exactly the same as I do. When I pack away the Christmas decorations, I always wonder where I will be this time next year. Little did I know how much I didn't want to be there.

4

A rocky road
(in more ways than one)

The year started with an enquiry from the Charity Commission. They wanted to know why our appeal was for Secret World, when our charity was called the Bluebell Sett or the Bluebell Sett Trust. We explained that most people knew us as Secret World and all the accounts showed a clear record of everything that came into us, but we did despair a little bit. I started the charity called the Bluebell Sett in 1993 but once we put the base down for the rehab block (with the money won from *Animal Country*) it meant that the building was on our own private property so the charity had no financial security with regards to owning the building.

We approached the bank to see if they would allow us to sell the orchard, where the building was, to the charity, but because we had a mortgage and it would devalue the property, the bank said no. It meant that strictly speaking, we couldn't build any aviaries or casualty pens within the farm buildings with charity money. Eventually, after a lot of discussion with the bank, solicitor and financial advisor (at a huge cost personally to the Kidners, I might add), the way around it was for the charity to rent Secret World and so a lease was drawn up. The problem with that was that the Bluebell Sett needed to be a trust in order to rent property. It was best not to close the first charity as if there were any legacies left in that name, it wouldn't necessarily go to the new charity of a similar name. So the second charity, the Bluebell Sett Trust, was started.

The Charity Commission now wanted us to start a third charity called Secret World Wildlife Rescue to make things clear! Anyone starting a charity beware – three lots of charities means three lots of accounts and bank accounts besides many other complications. Eventually, with new rules, all our charities were incorporated into one charity but not before a lot of personal expense had been accrued on our part. We had split the property into four lots so that the charity could hopefully, in time, afford to buy the land. The work at Secret World would then be secure, no matter what happened to me, and that was my lasting wish.

The Long Barn, on the extremity of our property, was sold as a residence and at last we could say goodbye to the bank and the mortgage. We had a consultant fundraising advisor who had come forward to help us free of charge and the charity was feeling more secure – things were looking up.

Our open weekends were very popular and were a way of attracting supporters as well as fulfilling the mission of our charity which is to 'Prevent British wildlife suffering needlessly and inspire in everyone an understanding and love of wildlife and the countryside.'

Nikki was organising extra attractions. The cake stall with one of our more flamboyant volunteers, Chris, brought people in for his wide selection of cakes that 'his ladies' at the W.I. baked for him. They were all cut, bagged and labelled by Chris on the day before and there were some really unusual cakes, such as beetroot and chocolate. I always describe him as a mini-Pavarotti, with wonderful colourful shirts and cravats and a straw hat complete with daisy to protect him from the sun. Vera and Joyce were two elderly ladies that accompanied him, all of them travelling over an hour to reach us and then worked really hard – it was and still is one of our best fundraisers.

Daphne and her friend were going to continue doing the bric-a-brac stall for us, despite the fact that last year she had managed to sell my kitchen clock! I had done a Wildlife Care Course prior to the open day and had taken my kitchen clock down and put it at the back of the Visitor Centre so that I didn't overrun on my sessions. Unfortunately, this was followed a few days later by an open weekend and the bric-a-brac stall was sited underneath the clock. I hadn't got round to bringing it back upstairs and by the time I remembered, it had been sold!

A local dog training group contacted us and said they would like to have us as their charity of the year. They were called Canine Capers and had offered to bring their dogs on our open weekends as they did dog line-dancing. Well, in for a penny in for a pound ... The Wolf Trust were going to bring their wolves on our Nature's Hunters weekend at the end of June. Even though they were coming from Reading, they had heard of us and wanted to come and help raise funds, which was great. Also, the Chelonia Group were going to bring different tortoises and turtles to our July open weekend. Different attractions each time meant that visitors could come to all the open weekends if they wanted to as the displays and animals, other than our residents, would not be the same.

* * *

There was indeed a tiny head now visible from Mrs Woo's pouch and local papers had reported on the arrival of Baby Boo, so Woo fans were bound to visit over the coming Bank Holiday.

It was another Easter where the weather was kind to us and it excelled the previous Easter weekend in visitor numbers and donations. The theme for the badgers this year was weather conditions and this was started when our first badger arrived during a storm and was named Gale. She was only a couple of days old and had been found by an open drain, very close to death. There had been plenty of coverage about her as there had been severe storms and the media just love stories that emphasise the dramatic effect of the stormy weather. It was also the photo taken by Richard Austin with her held in the palm of Nikki's hand, a really super photo, which appeared in national papers as well as local. So Gale, Drizzle, Puddle, Storm, Sunshine and the twins, Bright and Breezy were the stars of the weekend.

A lot of people love badgers, as I do. Sadly quite a few of the cubs that we had in during 2002 had to be put to sleep as they were reactors to the test. The badger and the cattle test is looking for anti-bodies. Testing positive can mean that they have the disease, but it can also mean that they have come in contact with Bovine

TB and have created their own immunity to the disease – the very animals you want to leave behind. There is a great deal of heartbreak to this situation, but these are the best tests available, so little can be done to improve the situation. The RBCT trials were later to show that there was a huge increase in the incidence of TB in cattle because TB animals had remained with their herds while all movements were banned in 2001 due to the Foot and Mouth outbreak.

Bovine TB also increased dramatically in cattle in more areas after there was no testing through 2001 and, stupidly, many cattle were moved around the country to replace the 600,000 that were killed due to the Foot and Mouth outbreak. Moved, I might add, before the government caught up with the TB testing of herds.

* * *

We have to buy in dead chicks for our birds of prey and other wildlife that have to be given whole food as part of their digestion process. It's not something that we like doing as these are the 'waste' product of rearing laying hens. The breed of birds used for laying hens is a light bird so that they don't eat so much food but still lay the eggs. This means that sadly the male chicks are all killed a day old, as they will never fatten for food. They are sold as a food source to zoos or pet shops. Fortunately for us these arrive dead and we just spread them out and bag them up in quantities that we will use and then they are frozen down.

The usual order had arrived, and I had gone to bag them up and to get them out of the way as quickly as possible, a job that none of us enjoyed doing. I started to work and within a few minutes, thought I heard a noise. Dismissing as just something outside, I continued. Then I heard it again, louder this time and definitely a 'cheep'. One of the chicks had to be still alive. Going through them quickly, I very soon found the source of the noise. A yellow fluffy chick with his eyes partly closed was definitely breathing but was very limp. Rushing him upstairs and putting him one of the incubators, I left him – hoping the warmth would revive him. Half an hour later, he was up and pecking about.

'What are you going to do with him?' one of the volunteers asked.

'I don't know,' I replied 'It's one thing when they come in dead but ...'

'He's bound to be a cockerel,' the volunteer continued helpfully.

'Yes, but ... Well, let's just wait and see if he stays OK,' I said placing a small dish of water and food inside the incubator. The chick went straight to the food and started to eat, little knowing how close he had come to the happy coop up in the sky.

He did continue to thrive and eventually became a very attractive cockerel. My mother named him Roger. It was really nice seeing a chicken around in the garden, I missed seeing our rare breeds that we used to have. A home was found for him with six ladies that had space in their hen-house but much to our horror, they were certainly no ladies and beat him up. A rather bedraggled cockerel returned, but he was really happy to be home and cock of the roost. My mother had a special house made for him just outside her bedroom window. She was then able to check that someone had remembered to shut him up for the night. Woe betide us, if he had indeed been forgotten! He was even given a bell with a string attached for him to ring when he wanted food. I think my mother had thoughts that he would behave like swans on the moat around Wells Cathedral. A chicken does have quite a small brain.

Simon had trained hard all through the winter and managed to get over a thousand pounds in sponsorship to do the London Marathon. Both Nikki and Derek went up to follow him around the course and to cheer him on at different points. Nikki was in awe – if there was one thing she didn't do, it was running. They all run with Flora emblazed upon their T-shirts as they sponsored the event. Simon did say that by the time the hundredth person had shouted 'Come on Flora, keep running' the joke was wearing pretty thin. He managed to complete the run in a very respectful time of 3 hrs 50 mins (which he did manage to reduce to 3 hrs 31 mins in the second marathon he ran) and the sponsorship meant that we could revamp the old rare breeds pens as hedgehog pens.

AXA, the insurance company, sent local employees out on a team-building day and they were able to build the new fences and metal line the pens so that they were 'hedgehog' proof. It gave us the proper facilities to put the hedgehogs outside once they had recovered from illness or injury. We could then check that they continued to put on weight and behave naturally prior to being released. There were eight pens in all and Andrew Lynford came down to officially open them for us on the Whitsun Open Weekend.

I wasn't exactly looking forward to him coming down as he

had been in touch with me recently to ask if we could take his two cats for him. He was loath to lose them but with his career being more successful he was hardly at home and he knew they would be 'far happier' with us. I had been slightly hesitant as we did already have ten cats (!) on the premises and thought they might fight. So it was with the proviso that they would go back if things didn't work out.

Nikki enthused over them (and Andrew) when they arrived and she took them through to their lounge. Nine cats lived downstairs and just one white one lived up in our flat. Gem, a tabby cat, and Dill, a lovely tricolour long-haired cat – minus a front leg and a tail, lost in an accident that happened before Andrew adopted them – seemed quite happy in their new surroundings. They were content in with Nikki and Simon and rarely came in contact with the other cats so it appeared to be a success that wouldn't affect me. That is until Simon's half brother, Barry, turned up with his family – Kelly, his wife and three children, George, Lizzie and Anna – to stay for a week with Nikki and Simon, complete with dog, a Great Dane called Rocky! It was like having a pony in the house. Gem and Dill soon deserted camp and came into our flat. The shock was such that the return of the cats to their flat never happened.

Simon was absolutely smitten with Rocky the Great Dane and, being so like his half brother, Barry, could get him to do anything. When a dog weighs eight stone, it does help if you can control it. Rocky loved the freedom while he was at Secret World. The family lived in the town of Lowestoft so the only place he had real freedom was on the beach. Barry worked abroad in Saudi Arabia, so it was only during his home time that Rocky really got romps around. The only thing with dogs that are a huge size is the slobber factor. When excited and running, Rocky would occasionally shake his head as he ran and the slobber would do full circle around his head – nose, ears, face, the lot got covered and sometimes you just wished that when he saw you, he wouldn't come over to say 'hello'. The stationary stance then required a really good shake which did indeed remove the slobber from his face, but if you were standing too close ...

Derek had had a pretty rough time with his jobs over the past year. The milk recording never really got off the ground, the rep jobs were for areas where there was little trade and whilst he was still doing some delivering of leaflets for different attractions (and

Rocky's slobber would do full circle around his head

ourselves but we weren't paying him!) he really wasn't bringing in enough money. He'd spent a soul-destroying month or so trying to sell British Gas and was far too soft and kind to do what was required of him – and probably too honest. He'd done some time in the shopping centres and was then moved on to calling at houses. Most of the houses, to be fair, were empty during the day but he came back one day having spent the afternoon with an elderly gentleman trying to help him decide whether he ought to go into a home or not.

'I just hate it, hate it. The pressure you are meant to use to make people sign the contracts, well,' he sighed, 'it's just not me.' He was almost in tears. There was Simon, Nikki and I still doing what we loved, and he had given up everything.

'Just hand in your notice,' I said. 'It's really not worth it. Something will come up, I promise,' and I hugged him.

He didn't need much encouragement, the next day he handed in his notice in the morning. Mother's Guardian Angel was at work as that very same day, in the afternoon, Dan Medley rang and asked him to go to work with him in a company called Leisure Marketing, which was all about delivery of leaflets advertising local tourist attractions. He already knew that Derek had contacts with several attractions and would bring those to the company. A very happy Derek came home that night. It was what he deserved.

The next day wasn't the best day for Mr Woo because we had decided that it was necessary to have him neutered. The last thing we wanted was a group of wallabies. Nikki was obviously going along to soothe his brow, and even Simon had fellow feelings, and thought he ought to be there too! Just the same as dogs with these operations, there seemed to be little pain involved with the aftercare and Woo made the most of a night indoors at Nikki's insistence – just in case he had a sudden relapse.

'Why does he have to sit in the armchair?' Derek sighed when he came into the kitchen for a coffee. 'His currants will be all down the side of the cushion and ...' The complaint stopped as Nikki came in and picked Woo up and the two of them curled up on the chair to watch television. 'I give up,' was the passing shot, as he went down to the front room to watch television.

I hadn't really thought much about it, but Nikki did seem to spend more time in the kitchen with me. Not that I minded. She had been living with us now for eight years and was almost considered a 'daughter'. We shared the feeding of orphans, cooking and had similar feelings for animals – although I don't think I was quite so soft!

'Oh,' Nikki said, getting up and placing Woo back in the chair, 'I meant to show you something,' and she disappeared. 'Look,' she said coming back in with a magazine she'd seen at the vets. It was advertising that Earthwatch were offering the chance to join their expeditions free of charge to animal-minded people. The spaces were limited and you just had to get the application form off the website. 'You ought to put in for that, you'd be just the person they would give it to,' she said.

I frowned, 'I don't think so.'

'Yes, you are, we can fill it out tomorrow,' and that was that.

* * *

The wolves certainly were a draw on our Nature's Hunters, which was the last weekend in June. There was any amount of people who came and queued for ages to go in and meet the wolves in the huge cage that had been erected. They seem to have fascination for some people, although they get a reaction of hate from people in the countryside, especially as some people have a hope that they will be re-introduced in Scotland. Certainly Scotland was the last place that wolves were in Great Britain, having disappeared from England in the early sixteenth century, but the last one killed in Scotland was in 1684.

They have a similar appearance to Alsatians but with a much larger head and a completely different stance. They are animals that should be treated with respect. Visitors were told not to make eye contact with them and to offer a fist for them to smell before getting too close.

There are many stories of wolves attacking people and children in countries where wolves live in the wild but the majority of these attacks were carried out by animals suffering from rabies, so not behaving in a normal way. Luckily everyone who came to the weekend escaped with their lives!

Sometime later, I visited Wild Wood in Hastings, Kent, where they have wolves. It was an evening visit and we were hoping that they may start howling, a very ghostly sound which we are told can carry, in certain weather conditions, over 150 square miles. It is usually the female that starts the howl and the rest of the group then join in. Our guide said it would be unlikely for them to start howling on a summer's night. Then, in the distance, we heard a police siren and that was an invitation to howl, and we experienced the incredible of sound of their mournful communication.

In the autumn, the charity was able to say that we could afford a seclusion pen for birds of prey. This is made completely out of panelled wood with strong netting over the top. This allowed the larger birds of prey like buzzards space to fly and build up condition. Without any netting sides, they wouldn't damage their feathers as they would do if they kept flying at the wire trying to escape. Every time we created another pen or enclosure, it would be in use straight away. Within a few months, we would be wondering how on earth we managed before we had them.

Space is so important to give animals the room outside in the natural climate so that they can build up muscle condition, waterproof feathers and, in grassed enclosures, the ability to forage naturally prior to their release. Moving from intensive care, wildlife casualties need that time to be completely fit before they are released and thoroughly checked to make sure they really are ready to go. Yet these are the facilities that many centres just don't have. This can be from lack of funds, space and sometimes just because the necessity isn't realised.

Debbie, bless her, has been around for years. She joined as a volunteer in the 1980s and then became our Centre Manager. Debbie then left to go to Australia for a year out with her husband Mike, but returned to us and then left again when she had her first child, Harry. Even then she would come back and help at times. Charlie was born and after three years she returned part-time so she has seen many things during our time at Secret World. If ever anybody was totally dedicated to Secret World, it's Debbie and I'd trust her with my life. She has always had a love of bats and a lot of the time had cared for Himmy and Bertha, two Noctule bats that were resident at Secret World. Many people have changed their views of bats – probably the species most endangered in our country – by meeting them and hearing all about our resident bats.

I had never realised how long bats can live – the Great Horseshoe can live up to 25 years! Noctule bats are really placid and although they are one of the largest species of bats found in Britian, their head and body length combined is only 4–5 cms long. Debbie had noticed that Bertha's stomach was swelling and it was with great concern that she made an appointment to see Liz. By now Bertha had to be at least 16 years old. She was still eating well and behaving in her usual way. A tearful Debbie returned to Secret World. Liz thought there was some kind of blockage but she was going to see what she could do. However, the prognosis was poor, if she needed to operate on something so small, the hardest thing would be gauging the anaesthetic. Debbie was not to be consoled, she was sure that it was the end for Bertha. She went to her desk but the box of tissues was nearly empty by lunchtime.

Eventually the call from Liz came through but Debbie refused to take the call and asked me to take it. Hesitantly I listened to a very upbeat Liz. 'Well, Mrs Kidner, I am very pleased to say that we decided to open Bertha up and she had fibroids in her womb. I am probably the only vet who has carried out a hysterectomy on a bat but she has recovered from her anaesthetic and is ready to come home!'

Debbie, as you can imagine, was delighted and Bertha lived for a further year.

* * *

Just before Christmas, it was obvious that we hadn't taken Mr Woo to the vet soon enough as both Mrs Woo and Baby Boo had little heads looking over the edge of their pouches. Roo and Sue were the new additions to the Woo family. Needless to say, Roo was taken to the vet to be neutered sooner than Mr Woo.

Simon and Nikki were away for Christmas again and had planned to spend New Year in Edinburgh. It was the telephone call that I received soon after Boxing Day that was such a shock. Simon rang to say that he and Nikki were splitting up. I felt physically sick and went out in the rain to take the dogs for a walk and cry. I just hadn't seen it coming. I had failed both of them because neither of them had spoken of any concerns. They were both so pivotal to the charity and I loved them both dearly.

The next few days were hard for everyone as Nikki collected her things and even came back to wind up all her paperwork and get it straight for the next person. I don't know how she managed it as well as saying goodbye to so many animals that she loved. It was also so hard for Simon in the glare of everyone at Secret World knowing about his personal life. Suddenly Secret World was a different place.

I was completely shattered by what had happened and was still finding it hard a couple of weeks into January. I was talking on the phone to Jean Thorpe, an amazing woman, who does rehab of wildlife in Yorkshire all on her own. She also fights continually against all persecution but particularly badger digging and baiting. Sadly, this is still so evident in her area despite the law supposedly protecting the badger and its sett. She's a hard-hitting, 'say it as it is' kind of person. I was wittering on about Nikki having left and how much I missed her and how hard it was for Simon when she said, 'I know how you feel, my partner was diagnosed with cancer at the beginning of December last year and he died even before New Year's Eve.'

It was my wake-up call. What on earth was I doing? Hard though it was, both Nikki and Simon were healthy and quite able to move on, even though there would be a lot of heartache. I had nothing to compare with that kind of loss. My heart went out to Jean. She was a fighter then and she's a fighter now, what I do pales into insignificance.

* * *

A very plain-looking envelope arrived for me at the end of January. I had won one of the places in connection with the Earthwatch projects. I was off to Sri Lanka to study the Macaque monkeys. I was thrilled – but also, a little scared.

With the help of Simon I planned my three weeks in Sri Lanka. The flight stopped halfway at Dubai and arrived in Colombo, the capital of Sri Lanka. I then had four days to visit the Pinnawala Elephant Orphanage before meeting up at the Tamarind Tree Hotel in Colombo. From there, mini buses were to transport us to Polonnaruwa for the 14-day expedition.

It was the first time I had really travelled very far and certainly not on my own. Simon had brought me up to the hotel to stay overnight before catching the first flight early in the morning. I'm sure I'm not the only one that keeps waking up during the night because you are so afraid of oversleeping. There was no cause for concern as I was awake immediately the alarm went off only to realise that I had a very strong feeling that a migraine was on its way. Fighting off the symptoms, I struggled through feeling sick and with strong waves of pain but by the time I had reached the airport, it had all started to subside and was probably due to the disturbed night and a mixture of excitement and dread.

The first flight was to Dubai where there was a waiting time of two hours before the next flight took off. I'm pretty lucky in the fact that I can sleep on a washing line so by the time I had fought my way through the plastic-wrapped meals, been amused by people exercising in the aisles and probably (knowing me) snoring whilst asleep, the flight was soon over.

Dubai airport was amazing. Goodness knows what it looks like outside the airport but bright lights and gold were the overall impact of this opulent place. Men in white robes called *thobes* with headscarfs that varied from white or red and white check. These are called *guthras* and are kept in place by a black rope called an *egal*. Evidently in days gone by, these ropes would have been used to tie up their camels. The robes were so white with no creases or marks. Otherwise most men were in suits and it was easy to see the holidaymakers with their skimpish and colourful clothes. The local women seemed to glide with their long black robes and faces hidden by their burkas. With signs for prayer rooms, it was a different world and the contrast showed how easily we must offend their very strict lifestyles.

Glittering decorations, fountains and beautiful statues were everywhere and the two hours waiting time was spent window shopping and seeing so many things that were way beyond my income. It did me good to see how much I could live without! I was soon on my connecting flight and was surprised to see that I was the only white person on the plane. I was to find out later that the fight was full of Sri Lankans returning home to their families. Certainly they were loaded with toys and parcels. Many of them go to Dubai as servants, sending their wages to their families. They are allowed to travel home every so often. For many, it was a way of surviving. I was looked at with suspicion and soon came to understand how it must feel to be a black person in a group of whites. At one stage one woman shouted at me, but I couldn't understand what she was saying so I turned away, feeling very alone. I was glad when the flight was over.

On arrival in Colombo, as I came out from the plane the temperature was so hot it was almost suffocating and pungent smells of spices filled the air. Entering the air-conditioned airport was a relief and we went through the arrivals section and collected our luggage. As I came out to the arrivals suite, men were held back as they fought to catch my attention. I had arranged to be met by someone from the hotel that I was going to and the policeman, seeing me being bombarded, checked that I had someone to meet me. With his arms protecting me from the crowd, he found my contact and I was taken through to the car.

Roshan was a tall man with a lovely smile, he shook my hand and bowed, directing me into the back of the large car with a driver. I was to find out that his name was Banduka. We had over two hours to travel to Pinnawala to the hotel near to the Elephant Orphanage. Colombo was a very busy town with three-wheel taxis called *tuk-tuks* honking as they drove along. Men on bicycles with their wives sitting on the cross bar with a baby in their arms and another youngster on a child's seat at the back showed that transport was very different to ours! Stalls decorated with fruit and vegetables of every kind in baskets, spice shops, shops with colourful clothes, filled every gap in the streets. It was a mixture of old and new, with modern vehicles driving through handcarts and even some being pulled by cattle. Roshan spoke English easily and told me how Colombo is their capital and that it is a busy city.

From the city we went through countryside along dusty roads with cattle grazing on the side of the roads accompanied by cattle egrets. It almost looks like every cow had an egret of its own – benefiting from the egret taking the ticks and flies from their backs and legs. Trees and shrubs formed most of the countryside beside the stone buildings that were homes with no windows, just shutters and roofs made from leaves. Washing was strung on lines between the trees. Washing of bowls and cooking equipment took place outside where a standpipe was the only supply of water yet all the people were in bright, colourful and clean clothes.

There was an excited shout from the driver, who slowed down so that I could see two elephants grazing in the distance and I was told how dangerous they can be, so to get out of the car for a photograph was not a good idea. The tall palm trees were laden with coconuts, which were sold on roadside stalls where an elderly woman hoped that you would stop for a drink of the coconut milk or to eat the coconuts. There were other stalls almost every half a mile with every fruit you could think of, with no other sign of people living nearby, that you wondered how on earth it was worth their while to have such a large variety of food if they were only selling to passing vehicles. Young boys waved bunches of flowers, hoping you would stop and even getting so close to the car that you were concerned that they were going to get run over.

We stopped half way for a cold drink and something to eat. The heat hit you outside the air-conditioned car – and me not being very good with heat, was wondering how I was going to survive! The tea shop was filled with the smell of fresh bread and I was delighted to pick a small loaf with a cold drink – I love fresh bread. A few bites in and I found curry! I was soon going to find that curry is on the menu for breakfast, lunch and tea.

As we arrived in the small village, several wooden shacks were laden with all manner of souvenirs for the many visitors wanting to see the elephants. The car turned down a dusty lane and pulled up outside the hotel covered with many plants and climbing shrubs full of colourful flowers. The river was in the distance and as I got out of the car, there were cries of excitement. Looking back down the lane, a group of over 40 elephants were on their way down to the river for their afternoon visit. It was an amazing sight with so many elephants, some with babies by their side, walking down the road. One elephant had a front foot missing and was finding it hard to keep up with the others. Roshan explained that it had lost its foot in a trap by bad men who try to kill the elephants, but it had been brought to the orphanage where it had recovered.

Quickly putting my luggage in a lovely cool bedroom, I made my way down to the river to see the elephants enjoying the water and rolling in the mud. The restaurant by the side of the river was full of visitors enjoying the view but also enjoying some ice cold drinks. I was glad of my sun hat and already my shirt was wet with sweat. I took some photos and just enjoyed the scene but I felt sorry that the elephants weren't allowed to go too far and were kept near to the side of the river for the tourists. The elephants were brought down twice a day and within half an hour were on their way back up to the orphanage. As I returned to the hotel, Roshan met me and arranged to take me up to the orphanage in a couple of hours, giving me time for some refreshment and a sleep.

I took a cold shower and was glad of the fresh lemonade placed in the room. I was really worrying that I wouldn't be able to manage out in the sun. It would be expected of us to spend time outside during the day to monitor the monkeys when we went to Polonnaruwa.

Roshan was waiting for me when I got downstairs and explained that I would be safer if I visited the orphanage with him, as a woman on her own would often be bothered by sellers. We entered the orphanage and by now the elephants were being fed. They were held in place by chains around their legs and I must admit I felt sad that they needed to be controlled in that way, but then they are very large animals. You could take photographs but had to pay if you wanted to be standing alongside them or touch them – and even more money if you wanted to feed the orphans with their bottles.

Talking to Roshan, it would appear that any elephants causing problems or injured would be brought to the orphanage and there didn't seem to be a programme of returning them to the wild. It was questionable that with the loss of habitat, there would ever be anywhere for them to go. I felt very uncomfortable about the whole thing but then one has to remember that tourism is very often the only way that wildlife will be looked after and survive in these countries that we visit. It's so easy for us with our lifestyles to question what other people do until you realise how little many of them have. They have the stark choice between surviving or saving the wildlife and luckily we are never placed in that position.

I had a full day planned for me with an early start. Yet again it was Roshan and Banduka that were to take me around. In my conversation as to why there were two of them, I was amused to learn that it was for their safety rather than mine. Ladies of a certain age (and roughly the age I was) come to Sri Lanka looking for 'love and attention' and it can prove difficult for those not in the trade! It was still quite cool when we left at 7 a.m. and we wound our way up to the tea plantations. As we went out of one area to another, the car was stopped and Bandura would go into a small building where there would be a shrine and it was customary to offer a prayer for safety in their journey.

It was an amazing sight of green hills covered with tea plants with women carrying the baskets on their backs. The ziz-zag roads carried us further and further up, with children waving bunches of flowers as the car passed, hoping we would stop. As soon as we passed they ran down the steep sides to hopefully catch us on the next bend. We eventually reached the Labookellie Tea Factory where a guide took me and several other visitors around explaining how the tea is grown, picked and dried for high-class tea. The dust at the bottom of the grading trays were made into tea bags and sold to Britain! A party of school children were visiting and they giggled at the sight of white people and asked if they could have their photos taken with us. It seemed strange that white faces were still an oddity for these children from the villages.

I couldn't believe when I got back to the car that I was to hear English voices as the commentary of the latest cricket game came over the radio. Here was I, thousands of miles away from home and Derek with his cricket and I was going to be stuck in a car listening to it in Sri Lanka. Roshan asked if I minded. 'No, of course not' was my reply – not realising that this was the signal to visit Roshan's cousin who had a restaurant nearby with a lake – and Sky TV! As we arrived, one of the young men at the restaurant offered to take me out in a boat on the lake, which was lovely. I was told it would give them time to cook my order for lunch, but knew that this was also a ploy to give them chance to watch some of the game. I knew another man just like them!

When we left to make our way towards Kandy, we went through a small town and Roshan offered to take me into the market. I was so glad to have him with me as different people constantly called and asked me to barter for their wares; every step of the way there were men trying to help you up steps, or encouraging you to go into their shops, but with Roshan just waving his hands, they moved away. Baskets of grain, fruit, clothing, pans and dried fish made a smell that in the heat was almost overpowering. Men were cooking on the pavements and constantly called out, beggars held out their hands and children peered nervously from curtains of material that were almost used like walls to divide their sleeping quarters. One thing certainly made me think of England – pigeons strutted around picking up any grains of rice or food that had been spilt although I think there was more chance of them ending up in a pot than being fed!

We then moved on to Kandy to see the Temple of the Tooth, Sri Lanka's most important Buddhist relic. This is where the revered tooth is held within several gold caskets securely held behind glass with two monks each side to safeguard the relic. Offerings or prayers are held at 6 a.m. and 10 a.m. and also 6 p.m. daily. We had to remove our shoes, which were given to minders at the temple's gates. Shoulders and legs need to be covered as a sign of respect and we slowly made our way through the many chambers with local people coming to give prayers and to bring flowers. There were so many flowers in one area that the perfume was almost sickening. The whole visit through the temple took over an hour and for most people coming to pray, it would be a two-hour session. These people come every day as part of their religion and their way of life. The beauty of the gold décor and Buddha figures seemed incredible because of its size and intricate sculpture which dated back to the seventeenth century. The Tooth itself is believed to be from the funeral pyre of the Buddha in 543 BC.

The day was drawing to an end as I was then taken to a theatre to see Kandyan dancing with colourful dancers and beating of drums. Athletic dancers portrayed different animals with very detailed headdresses and many kinds of masks. Darkness was drawing in as we left Kandy with lights reflecting around the lake. Moving into the quieter areas, the small houses with their stone walls and roofs covered in coconut leaves had an eerie blue glow. I then realised that it was the reflection of television screens. They may not have everything but already the television had entered their world!

The next day was not so busy but we did visit a spice garden and I was once again able to see the group of elephants making their way to the river. We called in to a smaller place which had three elephants and offered rides on them. They were also chained. Two of them weaved from side to side – 'dancing' their owner explained, but it was more like synchronised behaviour of an animal constrained from leading a normal life. I caught up with some sleep as I was still trying to get my body clock in sync with the new regime. During the day, when I went down for lunch, there was a traditional wedding held in one of the rooms. The costumes were beautiful, braided in gold and bejewelled so heavily that they must have been quite heavy to wear. It was easy to see who the bride and groom were as they stood on the decorated platform with flowers strewn across the floor and with so many others in really lavish costumes it must have been a very rich family.

Soon it was time to go back to Colombo. It was an early start as Roshan and Banduka were to take me back to the Tamarind Hotel in Colombo in time for midday. No wonder the people of Sri Lanka believe that we are rich as the journey from the airport to Pinnewala, return journey, three days' dinner, bed and breakfast and the tours with the car and Roshan as my guide cost a total of £53!

At the hotel, I met up with my fellow travellers – three Americans, three British, a German and Japanese. Everyone was friendly and we met our guides and soon were in two minibuses on our way to the sanctuary. It was a five-hour journey with a stop for a drink, which was very welcome. Roshan had already explained that the temperature in Polonnaruwa would be a drier heat and easier to cope with, so I wasn't quite so worried. When we arrived at the camp, it was very basic. The toilet comprised a hole in the ground with feet marks either side to squat! A tap and bucket were provided to swill the floor down with a huge spider in the corner so not a place frequented all that often. We were staying in two small units a few hundred yards away from the main building. Each unit had three double bedrooms. I was sharing the unit with Mary and Val from Kendal, Yokio from Japan and Carla from the USA. They were all good company and I had managed to get one room to myself having admitted to snoring!

There was no air-conditioning in the rooms but we did have fans and mosquito nets to cover the beds. The sink in the bathroom was hanging off the wall and the taps didn't turn off easily so we just hoped it would last our stay! A big bin of water was next to the shower in case the water stopped running which can often be the case, but it was a normal loo. We were told that the electricity was quite temperamental too – all good fun! The main camp was just a few hundred yards away and once unpacked, we returned to the camp. The short distance was past a few houses and walls covered with beautiful tropical flowers. Small squirrels (five-striped palm squirrels) scampered through the branches of the trees and flashes of colourful birds passed overhead. The small squirrels looked very much like the chipmunks that we used to have.

Dr Wolfgang Dittus welcomed us to the monkey camp. He had been carrying out the research at the centre for over 30 years. This is one of the longest research programmes held into understanding the nature of primates and their societies.

We talked about the problems that monkeys face, loss of habitat, stealing food from houses with no windows and being attracted down to the roads for rice which the taxi drivers put out for them so that holidaymakers can take photos. Due to a corrupt government, people were being allowed to build their houses within the forests and the reserve areas were slowly reducing. With the presence of people, garbage was becoming available to them and some people even knowingly fed the monkeys. Once monkeys knew that people would give them food, they classed humans as subordinates within their groups and could become aggressive towards them. The monkeys would climb over the roofs and remove tiles so were becoming a nuisance.

Farmers would lace rice with poison as the monkeys came and ate their crops. With the ever-decreasing areas of forest being lost, food resources were becoming less and monkeys were moving out to other residential or farming areas. The monkeys would eat caterpillars, weaver ants and termites in the forest so were playing a part in ensuring that the langurs had the supply of more mature leaves that were part of their diet. Everything plays a part in an eco-system.

Apart from Dr Dittus all the field research assistants, cooks and office staff came from local communities so that they could pass on the importance of the survival of the macaques. They explained the reason for all of us having to bring khaki-coloured clothes was that the monkeys accepted us if we all wore the same colour as the staff at Monkey Camp. We were in the dry zone so the heat was easier to cope with than it had been in Pinnewala, but even so we were to be sensible and tell someone if we were not coping with the high temperatures.

It was time for dinner and because they had found out it was my birthday and also Angeline's, one of the guides at the sanctuary, we had a birthday cake after a lovely meal of curried vegetables, fresh bananas and lime juice to drink. We had already met Ukka and Malini who were to cook some amazing meals for us during our stay. Despite all the different sounds of creatures that take over the night and creaking branches as some made their way through the trees, with so much information and such a full day, within minutes of getting to bed, I was asleep.

Our first day was easy with rising for 7 a.m. breakfast and the rest of the day spent learning about the monkeys and what we were going to have to do to monitor them. We were going to work with both the macaques and the langurs. Part of the morning was taken up by going out in the two minibuses with our guides, Sunil and Chameera, as well as Dr Dittus. Different species of trees were pointed out to us and it was going to be important for us to recognise them as it would be part of what we needed to record as we followed different monkey troops around.

We were excited at the sight of the monkeys and the vast remains of temples that would just suddenly appear as you rounded a corner. The roads were wide, dry and dusty and each section was named so that they could be identified on our data forms. By 11.30 the heat was very strong so we returned to the camp for a 12 noon lunch and then it was siesta time until 2.30 when we met for iced tea (yuk) and biscuits. The stone seats were the coolest to sit on and we soon learnt that dipping our hats in cold water or just wetting our hair made the heat easier to bear as we went out for our afternoon sessions.

As we travelled through to the temples where the monkeys roamed we went past what to me looked like huge lakes but in Sri Lanka are called 'tanks'. The amount of water in them would vary from nothing to being full and we had followed a wet season so they were full. Families were making the most of the water to bathe and many women were washing sheets and towels from hotels and spreading them out in the bushes to dry.

There was lots to learn with map reading, trees and also how to identify individual monkeys but the leaders were very helpful and made it all fun. Each of us was given a card which had two side-view faces and a frontal face of a monkey, where we could fill in identifying marks that would help us find the monkey we were to follow. On the back of the card we would enter whether they were female or male and particularly if they were an alpha animal and comments on their general appearance and the shape of their 'toque', which is the head of hair that grows in a circular whorl on the top of their heads. The name comes from a popular kind of hat that was worn in the sixteenth century in England. The females tend to have red faces with blue eyelids, black lips and ears and have golden brown fur. The males are twice the size but don't have the red faces. They have long sharp canine teeth that are used as lethal weapons in battles against other males.

We had split into groups to follow different troops and we needed to keep with them until they decided on which tree they were going to sleep in, so we would know where to find them the next morning. One of the predators of the monkeys is the leopard. He had two ways of catching monkeys. One way was to rush at a group if they were foraging on the ground. This would cause confusion and they would quickly try to escape up into the trees but often one would lose its balance and fall to the ground, soon becoming a tasty meal. The other way was for the leopard to lie in long grass and hold its tail upright slowly waving the tail from side to side. Ever inquisitive, monkeys will eventually become fascinated and slowly approach. Once close enough, the leopard would pounce. Slowly, slowly catchy monkey – I wonder if that's where the saying comes from?

Back at camp, the water wasn't running so we all swam in the tank that was near to us. Evidently in drier times they would play football out there! Dr Dittus gave us a lecture on his work in the evening. So many things like the loss of territory, the persecution by farmers, the feeding by humans causing problems and the very territorial way that the groups live is so much like the badger. Then it was a case of washing clothes out by the tap near the tank in the dark and leaving them to dry.

It was quite magical with the crickets noisily making their presence known and the whooping of the monkeys that carried through the night. I found my way back to the unit by torchlight. I considered myself very brave until a sudden rustling above startled me! Luckily my torch beam picked up the slow movement of a Slender Loris, another primate, making his way through the tree above me. His large black eyes accentuated by rings of black fur around them made him look like large bush baby.

The head of the shower had now dropped off – although the sink was still clinging to the wall – so it was a case of just standing under the pipe and enjoying the cold water. I was soon ensconced in my bed under the mosquito net hoping the insects were definitely outside the net and not trapped inside with me!

The next day was typical of most days. Breakfast at 5 a.m. and then out to find the sleeping tree. The two women from England were complaining that the lecture the night before should have been held earlier in the evening to give more 'us' time. They seemed to find most things to moan about. There were five of us with the guides. We were encouraged to look for the monkeys once we found the tree and moved under the canopy to see if we could see them as the sun started to rise. We then thought it was raining as water trickled down through the leaves, much to the amusement of the leaders who had stayed back. Yes, it was the monkeys waking up and urinating, so first lesson learnt!

We followed the group once they started moving off and needed to record all their foraging, what they were eating and to note any confrontations with other monkey groups. I was following a macaque monkey called Karen who was heavily pregnant but she still had to keep up with the group. There were nearly 60 in her group and they often went into high vegetation and you had to be careful that you kept up with them. If we got lost there was a call that we had to make so the leaders could find us.

We were all ready to go back once it got near to 11 a.m. and the sun was high. It would then be lunch, siesta, writing out of notes and recording movements before leaving again at 3.30 to catch up with our groups and then to follow them through to the sleeping tree. Sometimes they had travelled quite some way by the afternoon and one of the leaders would go around on a motorbike to find the group, which then meant walking quite long distances.

On one day, the group were late in finding their tree and it was 6.30 p.m. before they finally climbed and settled so it was getting dark on the way home. As we made our way along the dusty road a large wart snake crossed the road, it seemed to be about 6ft long. Even though the water was still not running, none of us were too keen on swimming in the tank that night! Even though, on another occasion, we saw a large monitor lizard nearly two metres long close to where the tank was that we swam in, the heat and the days of no running water, meant that swimming was still the better option.

Another night I found out I had been sharing my bed with a cockroach – really pleased not to have found it under my pillow until I got up! It was quite an active research programme and two of the Americans did pull out halfway through the project as they found it too physical. Often when the monkeys went into dense vegetation it was quite difficult to fight your way through and the times of the sessions were controlled by the actions of the macaque monkeys. Occasionally they rested around the temples and you were able to spend time just watching them as they interacted. It was up to us to record whether they were preening, eating, sleeping and many of the females had tiny babies clutching them tightly on their fronts. The juveniles would play together chasing around the trees and gliding from one branch to another. Chasing the adult's tails was a popular game. On this day we were to see Karen with her new baby, which seemed so tiny gripping tightly to her body.

Once on the move, they did go at speed and it wasn't always easy to find them in the afternoons if they had covered a lot of ground. So on some days, you were walking for long periods of time until you found them. The troop would have a dominant male who would often be challenged by other males in the group. An aggressive confrontation between groups was very noisy with bared teeth and the eventual winners of the confrontation would usually gain the feeding ground which had caused the dispute. However, males fighting could cause a lot of damage with their sharp teeth, and deep wounds and scars could often be seen on the males particularly.

Just occasionally we would see the larger monkeys called langurs. They seemed to be far more secretive than the macaques. Despite their size, if they were resting against the trunk of a tree in the canopies, it was easy to miss them. They too live in social groups that can vary from five to fifty but each time we saw them they were only in small groups. Langurs have light grey fur with black faces. They can digest mature leaves which the macaques cannot do so they don't really compete for food. When there is an altercation with another group of langurs, being much bigger animals they crash through the trees, breaking branches as they go making a loud 'whoop-whoop' noise.

I was really glad that we weren't told until the end of the course that the huge termite hills that we passed nearly all the time were often the homes of either cobras or rat snakes. I really loved the rain when it came, as it was so totally drenching in such a short time and yet most of us felt it was a relief from the very strong sun.

We had two free days within the period when we were at the sanctuary, and we were taken to amazing historic places. One organised day was a 4 a.m. rise to be in time to get the minibuses to Sigiriya. An argument broke out with the English as we had to pay for the tour in with our expedition. Since the two Americans had left due to the project being too energetic, we could have all fitted in one minibus. So Val and Mary said we didn't need the other minibus and should get a refund. The minibus driver tried to explain that it was a bank holiday and even if we didn't use the minibus, he would have to charge for them. So at this unearthly time in the morning Dr Dittus was contacted to sort things out. I felt very ashamed especially when Tokio asked me if all English were so difficult. To which I replied an emphatic 'No'.

It was good to be on our way and the wonderful scenery allowed us to forget the difficult start to the day. Sigiriya was a spectacular rock fortress built in around AD 480 by King Kasyapa. It was so high on the rock that the fortress was impregnable. The palace was built at the top of the rock with 35 terraces layered from top to bottom. With so many steps to climb it was important to get there before the sun was really beating down. The king would be carried up to the top by sitting on a throne resting on a platform that would be carried shoulder high by the servants. On each level, there was a space to the left of the stairs so that the servants could rest before climbing the next series of stairs.

Once we had got past the majority of the terraces, the final climb was guarded by two huge stone lions. The palace at the top of the rock oversaw the wide expanse of land that belonged to the king. At the top there was a swimming pool, several ponds and when the water was released, it forced the water to plummet through ancient pipes that fed fountains in the water gardens at the bottom of the rock below. The whole of the rock was surrounded by a moat. It was unbelievable that such a building could be created so many years ago without the technology and machinery now available to us. It was built no doubt at the cost of many, many lives.

Where the visitors were dropped off from the coaches, there were several souvenir stalls with men constantly vying for everyone's attention, lots of beggars trying to get tips and regrettably some with trained monkeys to attract people to them. You had to be careful with the monkeys around the attractions as they had learnt that they could get food from tourists and could be quite nasty and bite if you got too near and had nothing to give them.

We were then to move on to Dambulla where we visited the Cave Temples. This is an amazing collection of five caves containing so many images of different Buddhas. At one time many were gilded with gold. In total there are 153 Buddha statues and many people go and leave gifts of flowers which they lay in front of whichever Buddha they want to grant their wishes. There would be one for travel, another for love, another for kindness – each and every one of the statues for different ways of life. The setting was so tranquil that you could imagine the monks living in what really was palatial surroundings. There were many steps again to see everything in the caves and a very tired group of people returned to Monkey Camp, not looking forward to the early rise the next day.

The other free day was spent exploring the small town near to Monkey Camp and the variety of shops with their wares from food and flowers to lengths of material to make the wonderful coloured saris that many of the women wear.

All too soon we were at the end of our time with the research project and I found the whole thing fascinating to experience animal work in such a diverse country. The group members were dropped off at different locations as some people had added time onto their stay at the end of the project whereas my extra time had been at the start of my journey. Many were going to explore the southern end of the island where the beautiful beaches can be found and, if you're lucky, a chance to see the leatherback turtles that make their way on to the beaches to lay their eggs. There is a fine line between tourism and protecting wildlife and many of the locals are paid for identifying these nests so that they can be protected from people walking on them or placing their sun beds on top and causing damage.

When these tiny turtles hatch out, usually at night, they have to make their way to the sea before other predators can swoop and eat them. Some new hotels with outdoor lighting confuse the tiny turtles that should be drawn to the sea by the moonlight. Young turtles going the wrong way are far more likely to be eaten or will die the following day in the heat of the sun. If these tiny hatchlings make it to the sea, there is enough food within the egg yolk that the turtle absorbed as it hatched to start him on his way to the deep parts of the sea. Nobody knows where they go as they disappear at this stage and will then be seen as two-year-olds. Even by attaching radio tracking devices to their shells, it is thought that the devices have failed due to the pressure caused by the depth these tiny turtles go down to. There is so much that we still don't know about the world that we live in. Some species of turtles can be 15 to 50 years old before they reach maturity and start to breed. Once they come ashore, they will return to the same nesting place each year but tourism is one of the main reasons put forward for the huge decline in these animals.

Some of the group were going backpacking which was certainly frowned upon by Angele, one of the leaders, especially when she found out that they had pencils and crayons to give the children in villages that they were to visit. She was cross that by visiting these villages and giving such things to the children, it was making them unhappy with what they had. She said it caused discontentment with their lives in places where amenities are far and few between. Angele believed that tourists should keep to their special areas and not upset the lives of these people who had very simple needs.

As I travelled back to Colombo, in a way I could understand what she meant. Burger King and fish and chip shops could be seen in the old city and I couldn't help thinking that by visiting places to see other worlds and traditions, do we in turn destroy the very thing we come to see by our standards, wants and needs?

I had two nights booked in the Galle Face Hotel, which was very much a colonial hotel and where, at some time in the past, Sir Winston Churchill had been a guest. The hotel was a world away from its surroundings with air-conditioned facilities throughout. Staff were in white uniforms and the restaurant spread outside into the gardens alongside the Indian Ocean. In the evening the sun went down, offering a beautiful backdrop to the palm trees and tables with people enjoying their drinks in the cool breeze after a hot day. With the piano playing, you could imagine you were back in the 1930–40s.

The following day, I walked from the hotel along the sea front and it was a weekend day. The park stretched out from the hotel for quite a distance and families were out enjoying themselves with kites flying and romantic couples sitting quietly under umbrellas in the hot sun. It was so hard to walk on your own without someone trying to get your attention and you really had to be quite rude to them before they would stop pestering you. I was glad to get back to the safety of the hotel where staff were on guard to keep non-paying guests out.

Later that day I made an attempt to get to Viharamahadevi Park, which was only a couple of roads away. To walk across the busy roads was an education as buses just weave their way in and out of the traffic, *tuk-tuk* taxis were blowing their horns with impatience at traffic lights. Even if you were crossing on the yellow crossing, meant to be for pedestrians, one car may have stopped for you but another would cross while you were still in the road! I did manage to get to the park as I wanted to see the Indian flying foxes that frequent many of the large trees there. These bats roost in large numbers that can be anything from tens to thousands in a group, which is called a camp. I could see the trees almost black with the number of bats hanging from the branches. The amount of guano underneath the tree was a very good indication of how many bats were roosting there! Again, whilst it's a sight that some tourists like to see, these bats fly out at night to the agricultural land on the edge of the town where the mango and banana plantations are. Such large numbers looking for food in these plantations can cause a lot of destruction. But on the other hand, these bats do expel waste that pollinates and dispenses seeds, so again play their part in the eco-system. I didn't stay long as so many men were trying to tell me all the different kinds of trees or were wanting to help me up steps or just asking for money. Arriving back at the hotel, I found again that my bed had been turned down and a beautiful flower lay on the clean sheets.

So within hours I was in a plane seeing the last of a beautiful island as I started my long flight home. It was a departure with mixed feelings. I had been given a wonderful insight into the way other people live, to see the variety of animals in a country where Buddhism seems to be a tranquil and simple way of life. How much damage do we do when we visit these countries and yet how much does wildlife only survive because of tourism? All I know is how lucky I was to have had the opportunity to visit Sri Lanka and sincerely hope that a balance is found so that much of its beauty and wildlife can survive alongside progress that all people yearn for, without sometimes realising the cost.

* * *

It was with mixed emotions that I arrived home, but I was so glad to be back.

5

The end of an era

One of the things I promised Nikki was that I would build a Woo pen for the Woo family. I managed to take up some money and build a large enclosure around the pond that we have at the farm. The pond was created when the farmhouse was built in the sixteenth century and the bricks would have been made with the clay. With high fencing and an electric wire across the top it was a fox-proof enclosure, so we were able to move our poultry into the pen for safety as well.

There was a Woo shed so that they could shelter from the weather, but with several trees in the pen, most of the wallabies just naturally shelter under these. Softy Mr Woo, of course, soon worked out that there was a heat lamp in there during the winter so he would be seen at night sprawled out under the heat with whichever chickens and ducks had also found the comfy facilities.

The double gate to the enclosure was opposite the small original Woo pen and we were able to 'jump' them across by using lines of people with material stretched between them either side of the gangway. It all went smoothly and it was lovely to see all five of them springing around. We have French windows in our lounge at the bottom of the farmhouse that faces out to the pond area and you can also see over to the orchard. It was on one of our open weekends that Derek stood surveying the scene. 'If you had told me a few years ago that I would look out of here and see wallabies and dogs line dancing, I would never have believed you!' was his remark. (Perhaps if he had known what was going to come to pass, when I attended the interview to be a housekeeper for him, I wouldn't have got the job!)

I attended one of the meetings held in London on the progress of the Randomised Badger Culling Trial. It was quite heartening to hear that they had stopped the reactive culling of badgers – that's culling of badgers on farms where there were Bovine TB outbreaks in cattle herds – because the research had clearly shown that this increased the incidence of the outbreaks. The control area and the pro-culling area would continue as planned. This was put down to the perturbation effect which so many find difficult to understand.

When badgers live in areas where there is a high incidence of Bovine TB in cattle, there is a risk that they may also be infected but also a certain number of badgers that will create their own immunity against the disease. When you kill badgers, you upset the family clans that would normally remain in their own territories. The remaining badgers will flee and there is a breakdown of their territories and they roam further. These animals, with a natural immunity, can become infectious caused by the stress of fighting badgers in the new territories. As this creates a vacuum, badgers from outside will move in, but as they are animals naive to the disease, a higher percentage of the badgers will become infected.

There was a lot of science explained to those who had attended: farmers, representatives from farming bodies such as the NFU and others from wildlife groups such as the RSPCA, wildlife trusts and badger groups. Most of the science was presented in the morning and it was heartbreaking to hear the first question of the afternoon which was, 'Why can't we kill badgers then?' and you just wondered where they were in the morning, when it was all explained to us.

They had a facilitator who was at several of their meetings and he knew my position and feelings. 'So, Pauline,' he asked coming over to me, 'what will you do if the science proves that badger culling works?'

My answer was, 'If indeed the science proves that badger culling works, then along with everyone else who wants to see us rid of this disease in our countryside, I would not fight against it. But we're a long way from that at the moment, aren't we?'

That was what I truly believed.

* * *

We do get a lot of call-outs to swans. Many are when members of the public see them with fishing tackle attached to their necks or beaks. Almost 80 per cent of waterfowl brought in to us are injured because of discarded fishing tackle. Hand on heart, I can remember when our children were young and went off fishing down by the River Brue, I gave no thought to what happens to the hooks and lines that they took with them.

Fishing is a wonderful sport that crosses the generations and often fishermen get to love wildlife because of what they see while they are waiting for that nibble on the line. In time they can actually 'read' the situation of what is happening under the water and change their line and actions when they know that a large fish, like a pike, is patrolling the swim. We really do need to get the message across to youngsters, just as they start to go fishing, that there is a code of responsibility for their actions that otherwise will cause terrible suffering to wildlife.

Many times injured swans are on wide waterways, ponds or rivers and it is really difficult to catch them. I can remember an unfortunate incident when Derek and I, together with Leigh, who was another animal carer by then, were called to a badly injured swan in a river down on the moors in the late afternoon. Derek and I had driven our car and Leigh was in the Secret World van. The swan had literally broken its wing and it was folded up the wrong way on his back. He must have crash landed to have caused such a fracture to what are almost the strongest bones in its wing. We were losing the light because it was still early spring and the grass was crisp to walk on, showing that temperatures were dropping to freezing point.

We tried using swan hooks and extended nets but it was pointless because the swan just ducked under and went to the other side. After a while we had attracted quite a bit of attention and Derek was deep in conversation with someone who had a couple of canoes. Derek agreed to use the canoes and they were quickly brought over to the river with experienced people paddling but, sadly, two people rather precariously standing at the end of each canoe with a net – Leigh and Derek. I have to say that Leigh was not getting to grips with the situation as he was wobbling backwards and forwards to gain his balance. The paddler quite rightly was not moving the canoe until he was ready, whereas Derek was in full flight and getting nearer to where the swan was. Unfortunately, reaching just a bit too far to net the swan the obvious was about to happen.

Derek suddenly found that he was out of the boat and, whilst he has no specific religion, he gave a tremendous impression of walking on water. There was no hand of God by his side and he disappeared under the water. Thankfully, he was near the edge and was able to get himself out on to the side. Both Leigh and myself looked at each other and knew, without any words being said, that this was no time to laugh. A sopping wet, shivering Derek went to sit in our car. He had hoped that he would be able to turn the engine on to get some heat going but the ticking noise when the ignition was turned made it clear that the car was going nowhere.

Luckily the swan was soon caught and Leigh drove the van with Derek beside him, shivering uncontrollably, trying to get close to the heater. I was sitting on a badger cage in the back. Now, Leigh's excuse was that he was driving fast to get home as soon as possible to warm Derek up – brake, accelerate, brake, accelerate round all the bends of the roads on the moors. I arrived home, feeling dreadfully sick and vowing I was never going to get into another vehicle if Leigh was driving! Derek had no sympathy for me, it was my fault we went in the first place. He went off to have a bath.

* * *

The summer was kind to us and all our open days were very fortunate with the weather, which did make a lot of difference to the takings. One main difference in the house was that, with great despair, the 'Shetland pony' had come to live with us. Simon's half brother had decided that it would be best for the whole family to live in Saudi Arabia. The children's education would be paid for and they would have more time together as a family but the only problem was the Great Dane, Rocky. The children were sure that

Rocky would love living with Uncle Simon and with both parents telling the children how happy he would be living in the country-side, his fate was sealed before Simon was actually asked!

Simon did like him and they were to become real buddies. Rocky adored him but an animal that size is something that not everyone is happy about and Simon often forgot, just walking around with him on open days, that for children coming face to face with a dog as tall as you or even taller could be quite terrifying. Rocky did once disgrace himself at the cake stall by swallowing a complete coffee and walnut cake in two gulps. He was just the right height for people sitting eating a beef burger with their elbow on the table holding it. As they finished what was in their mouths, Rocky walked past and took the beef burger with him. Not many visitors wanted it back after it had been in Rocky's mouth – so Simon did have to pay out for quite a few replacements.

The only problem with Rocky (apart from his size) was that he would chew his paws for no real reason and really worry them until they would bleed. The answer to that was for him to wear an Elizabethan collar which just about scooped up anything in his way, but he was a very gentle giant.

* * *

We are very fortunate that the Burnham Area Rescue Boat (BARB) assists many of our rescues. The members are great because they are giving up their own time but it is also good practice to launch the boat and manoeuvre. With an engine, we have far more chance of catching swans or ducks before they manage to take flight.

Sometimes we are able to get the fire brigade to respond, which is a great help. We were called out to a tawny owl that was in the car park at Sand Bay, just on from Weston-super-Mare. A kite had got away from its owner and the string was trapped high up between two trees. During the night, an owl had flown through and managed to get itself tangled in the string just by the tip of the feathers on one wing. It was left dangling by its wing and had been there until daylight. The fire brigade responded very quickly and met Graeme Thompson, who was one of our response drivers. As soon as they arrived, they realised that they couldn't do anything to help because there was nowhere for them to lean their ladders against, so a fire engine with a turntable and hydraulic lift was called down from Bristol. They were about 45 minutes away but once they had arrived, they soon had Graeme in the pod with the fireman who manoeuvred themselves on the extending ladders over to where the tawny owl was. Graeme immediately covered the owl with a towel, stopping any further stress to the bird, and gently detached her from the string. The firemen very kindly removed all the string from the two trees so that a similar thing didn't happen again.

Graeme soon had the owl back at Secret World. Luckily there was no damage but the female owl was exhausted. On assessment we found that she had a brood patch (a bald patch on the chest where the bird pulls the feathers out so that when she settles on the eggs or chicks, they are close to her skin and are kept warm), which told us that she was either sitting on eggs or looking after quite young chicks. It was important that we got her back to her territory as soon as possible. Leaving her to rest for a couple of hours in a quiet and warm pen, we then checked that she could fly well enough and got her back to where she was found as soon as it was starting to get dark. Placing the tawny onto a post and hold-ing her wings against her, we gave her time to realise where she was. Then slowly, taking away hands, she flew away immediately and we hoped she had returned soon enough to save her family.

* * *

As we went into the autumn, Ronald, one of our oldest resident foxes, died. He was thirteen years old, which is the kind of age that a fox will live to in captivity. In the wild their chance of sur-vival is much less and the average age for a female fox is 18 months and a male only 15 months. It is the same with most species that roughly two-thirds of wild animals die within their first year. Their first year is the hardest. They have to learn how to hunt, to become streetwise with regards to traffic and other human dangers. They have to find their own territory and usually become part of a social group, but they will have to prove their strength when chal-lenged by other members of the group. Life in the wild is hard and they need to be 100 per cent fit to have a chance of survival.

Ronald was a firm favourite with staff and volunteers. He was a very gentle fox and allowed others to join the group without any aggravation. He had been an adult when he came to Secret World. His owner was going into prison and we were asked to take him on. We had no idea of the conditions he had been kept in, but he looked well. He arrived without a name so consequently he was named Ronald after the train robber!

Sage, our barn owl, was also starting to show his age. He was now 17 years old and was spending his time indoors in my office where he had a cage, but the door was always open so that he could come out and fly around. However, he was soon back in the cage sitting down one end near the radiator. Sage came to us in 1986 at the age of two. He was hand-reared from a chick by a young lad called Peter. Peter kept him in his flat but also took him out in his car and flew him in the countryside. Consequently, Sage was used to having his leash tied to the door handle and he would sit on the back of the passenger seat watching the world go by. It did cause a bit of confusion and double-takes waiting at the traffic lights from people in other cars alongside.

Sage was totally imprinted, would happily sit on your shoulder for hours and loved being indoors. There are many stories about Sage that have happened in his lifetime, getting lost in London and being arrested by a policeman amongst them, but the one that caused me the most embarrassment was the story of Sage with the bank manager many years ago when we were still living in the ground floor of the farmhouse. The bank manager was coming out to us for a meeting and after making a cup of tea for him, we went through to the front room where I had forgotten Sage was sitting quietly on top of the bureau bookcase. It was probably one of those horrible meetings where we were asking for a loan to get through the winter. Helping the bank manager to take off his coat, I hung it over one of the dining room chairs. Seeing a new person and just to be nosey, Sage flew a circle around the room and then settled back to his roost. I asked the bank manager, Tony Curtice, if he was alright with him in the room as some people can't be near birds that can fly close to them, but Tony was happy for him to be there. At the end of the meeting, I helped the bank manager back on with his coat. To my dismay, during his quick circuit, Sage must have gone to toilet and it had landed on Tony's coat, making a white stripe down nearly the whole of its length. It was one of those moments when you think, shall I say anything or not? Somehow the moment passed and he was gone. Luckily Tony did take it in his stride, because we did get the loan and it was an in-joke forever afterwards.

Sage eventually died overnight and whilst I wished I had been there, I was so glad that I didn't have to make any decisions. It was only three weeks later that someone phoned asking us to take their barn owl which they no longer wanted and that's how Zazzoo became our second barn owl, but he was never the same as Sage.

* * *

Only a month later, I had been asked to take some animals to a meeting of mentally challenged students near Wells. Orlah was a veterinary nurse with us at the time and she had agreed to come with me. I had got caught up with another problem and we were late getting ready so everyone helped collect the animals that we were going to take with us. Twinkle was boxed and put in the boot of the car, together with a hedgehog in a carrier. We were going to take some ferrets, which one of the girls went to collect from their shed, and the other animals we were going to take were the bats. By now Bertha had passed away but Himmy had another noctule friend, Nora, who was a juvenile now. Nora was a noctule baby bat that Debbie had hand-reared but she refused to fly. The bat was named after Nora Batty from the programme *Last of the Summer Wine*. They both lived happily together in the big bat cupboard in my office but when they went out the bats often chattered whilst being on the move. They were put in a soft material bag done up with an elastic band and then in a cardboard carrier which was placed in the boot with the other animals.

I came out to the car with the last things such as projector and slides and put them on the back seat. 'Everything is loaded,' said Orlah.

'Great,' I enthused, 'then let's get going.' As we drove along, we could hear the bats chattering in the boot. 'They always make a lot of noise when they're travelling,' I mused, 'they're not fighting, they're just chatting.' But as we went on, I did become concerned that the noise didn't abate. We were nearly there and on a narrow road with someone following us quite closely so I was loath to stop until there was more room.

We pulled in at the Centre and I immediately went to the back of the car and opened the boot. I felt physically sick. Whoever had put the ferrets in the boot had put them in a cardboard carrier, something we would never do as they can push through the corners of the top flaps. We would normally have put them in a plastic animal carrier so that they cannot escape. Both the ferrets had been running around the boot and had got the bag out with the bats in and had been playing with them. Quickly checking the bag, I looked inside to find that Nora was already dead and Himmy was just drawing his last breath.

It was one of those situations that if you could only turn back the clock, you would change things. I should have checked the boot before we left. I should have stopped the car earlier to see what the noise was about, but their chattering was something I had noticed before and hadn't thought anything of it. I just wanted to go home and have a good cry. With people waiting that wasn't an option, but I just didn't want to be there. We got through the talk but the journey home was horrendous, done in total silence. I knew that Orlah, like me, was blaming herself for not checking. It was just as if, since Nikki had left, slowly all the animals connected to when she was at Secret World were all now coming to the end of their lives. The arrival home meant that the whole sorry situation had to be explained to everyone. My tears were saved for when I got into bed, I felt thoroughly miserable.

* * *

Debbie was busy getting ready for the Annual Auction and Ball. The theme for this year's event was Las Vegas and we had sent out invitation letters using titles from Elvis Presley's songs. Explaining to them that this year the Auction and Ball was being held at 'Heartbreak Hotel' (the Webbington), we were hoping they would put on their 'Blue Suede Shoes' and come to 'One Night' and bring their 'Money, Honey'. They can 'Surrender' themselves to a fantastic night with a three-course meal, auction and dancing 'Until It's Time For You to Go'. If they didn't come they would be 'Indescribably Blue'. It's 'Now or Never' so they needed to book their tickets soon – just to give you an idea of our efforts to attract guests!

Debbie found out that one of our volunteers was a member of the Harley Davidson club. Steve told us about the event that they do every October. He was offering a ride as an auction prize and the lucky winner would be able to go on the back of one of the Harleys and be part of 'Hogging the Bridge' with the Bridgwater Chapter. He explained that they would have to wait until the following year to have their auction prize but it sounded amazing and Derek and I went to watch. Over 3,000 bikes were taking part to drive over the Severn Bridge on the M48 between England and Wales.

Riders from all over the world meet at the Aust service station at 10 a.m. on a Sunday. It is an incredible sight with all these bikes, some fantastically decorated and in great humour, even a dog riding pillion complete with its own leather coat and goggles. At 11 a.m. a horn is blown which signals the start of the ride over the 40-year-old bridge. The sound of that many Harley Davidsons all starting at the same time has to be seen and heard to be believed. Because it is a charity ride they all pay £10 to be part of the ride and all the funds are then donated to local charities.

We went to look over a wall from above the old Severn Bridge to see the bikes as they made their way across and it was an amazing sight. A young family were watching with us. The young boy and girl chorused together, 'Nanny and Granddad haven't gone over yet,' excitedly jumping up and down.

'How on earth do you know who is who?' I joked.

'Easy,' said the young mother, pulling a face, 'Nanny and Granddad have a mauve Mohican stuck on their black helmets, haven't they, kids.' They all laughed.

When we went back to tell Debbie all about it, we all agreed it had to be one of the main auction prizes. 'I wonder if they would bring one of the bikes along and we could use it as a photo opportunity – guests would love to have their photos taken on a Harley!' said Debbie with more and more ideas filling her head.

By the time the auction was due to start, Debbie had managed to get the hotel to allow us to drive the Harley Davidson bike into the function room and had persuaded Simon to wear the famous white suit with shoulder pads complete with sunglasses, wig and sideburns. Every year we do a special intro at the start of each of the Auction and Ball evenings. We now had the special 'opening' for Las Vegas event. 'Elvis' rode into the function room riding pillion on the Harley to the music of 'All Shook Up'. Elvis was in the building!

* * *

'Elvis', or should I say Simon, had decided to spend Christmas and the New Year in Bali with a group of friends. I marvelled as he disappeared into the airport with a small bag (I can never travel light) and a huge surfboard under his arm. I think he was just happy to get right away for a couple of weeks.

Like a good son, he rang me on Christmas Day to wish Derek and I a Happy Christmas. His holiday was going well, they had found cheap accommodation and the weather was fantastic but he

Elvis was in the building!

had broken his surfboard so thought he might go travelling for a few days. It was lovely to hear from him and know that he was okay.

Naturally, on Boxing Day, I immediately had concerns as soon as I heard the news. This was the day that there was non-stop reporting of the largest tsunami ever seen, with hundreds of thousands of people killed in Indonesia, Sri Lanka and India but it also affected Malaysia, Thailand, the Maldives and the Seychelles. Bali was further around so I was sure he would be okay. Well, I hoped he'd be okay. From that day onwards I had several phone calls from friends and relatives asking if he was safe. To be fair, I thought he was bound to be. I doubted Simon would have even heard about it where he was, but that little niggle at the back of my mind was working overtime.

Anyone knowing Simon would know that his holidays are legendary. From falling asleep and missing connection flights, writing a car off in France by driving on the wrong side of the road (yes, you are right, that was the third car written off!), to losing credit cards, cash and phone stolen by guides in Mexico and as for mobiles ... well, I wouldn't like to guess how many he has lost, including one that had been put in a bag with a soft banana which managed to erode the face of the phone (I was amazed that he got insurance on that one).

Six days later and I still hadn't heard from him and there were now reports of over 200,000 people killed. The guy who does our designing rang to see if I had heard from him and I said no and that I was beginning to panic. 'Oh, I shouldn't worry too much,' said Steve, trying to ease my mind. 'You know Simon, he's got to be the only person in the world taking his surfboard on holiday and missing the largest wave in history!'

New Year's Eve and it was the phone call I'd hoped for. He was blissfully unaware of the tsunami and hadn't travelled far. A very happy mother enjoyed the evening celebrations. However, the day before he came home he rang to say he had some coral in his leg and could I get some antibiotics ready for when he got home, which was going to be late evening. Luckily the doctor did give me some. When Simon got home, the delay of treatment and the pressure of flying meant that his leg was twice the size of the other and very red and inflamed. He started his antibiotic course straight away and went into the doctors the next morning. The doctor told Simon that if he hadn't started the antibiotics the night before, he was very close to developing septicaemia.

Children may be in their thirties but they still worry you. I'm told it continues throughout life – how many of us would have had children if we'd known!

* * *

We always go into a new year knowing that at any moment orphans may arrive, but January usually passes before we see any. Otter cubs and leverets, however, can be found at this time of year. Hares will breed all year round but January to October are the likely months for births. Many people do not realise that rabbits and hares are completely different species.

Born with fur, eyes and ears open, these very pretty leverets are often just left in dips in the ground called 'forms'. The female may even sometimes leave them as singles dotted around in a field so that they are less likely to be predated (mainly by foxes). They will produce between two and four youngsters and will only feed them once a day, at night. The female will let her milk down in five minutes and then will be gone. The development of mobiles with cameras means that when someone rings us, concerned that they have seen a 'baby rabbit' all on its own and in the same place for the last few days, we can get them to send us a photo. Often it is a leveret and can be left alone as it is perfectly natural for them to be there.

Hares were introduced into Britain by the Romans. If seen

boxing with another hare, it was thought to be males fighting for supremacy but in fact, it's the female telling the males she's not ready – brilliant! Compared with a rabbit, a hare is much larger and has very long ears with black tips. They eat mainly grass shoots and cereals so food would be available to them all year round on small farms growing many different kinds of grains and crops. But the larger cereal farms leave them with nothing to eat in late summer and autumn and with no crops to hide in.

The adults rely on speed to outrun their predators as they are capable of reaching 70 kph (45 mph). Hare coursing is illegal but sadly continues all too frequently using lurchers and whippets. Hare numbers have declined substantially since the beginning of the twentieth century with most of the deaths due to large farm machinery and pesticides.

Young hares, leverets, are completely different from their 'cousin' the rabbit, which are born blind, naked and deaf and are reared in a part of the warren. Rabbits were also first introduced to Britain by the Romans. The dominant doe will have the best breeding chamber in the warren. Rabbit families can consist of just a pair or as many as 30. With the ability of each doe to produce anywhere between three and seven kittens every month it is, maybe, fortunate that the rabbit appears on the diet sheet of many mammals and birds.

Rabbits were a common source of food for country folk years ago but in 1953 someone introduced myxomatosis, a horrible disease that causes blindness, through swelling of the head and eyes – the rabbit becomes listless and loses appetite, develops a fever and can also get pneumonia. Death can be as quick as 48 hours or they may suffer as long as 14 days. The hand of man has much to be ashamed of. This disease, brought in purposely to this country, meant that by 1955, two years after its introduction, 95 per cent of our wild population of rabbits were dead.

This had the knock-on effect of reducing the numbers of, particularly, buzzards but with all the things that we mess with, it was years before the loss of rabbits was found to have been a significant reason for the loss of the Large Blue butterfly. The grazing of rabbits does protect certain habitats such as chalk grassland, heathland and sand dunes. These are prime places for the Large Blue butterfly which also depends on the grubs of the red ant for the survival of their larvae. The Large Blue butterfly was first seen in 1795, by 1979 it was extinct. Luckily, thanks to a lot of work by Trusts, the Butterfly Society and volunteers, the butterfly has now been re-introduced back into our country and they can be found in Somerset, Dartmoor and Gloucestershire.

Rabbits, themselves, have managed to gain some genetic immunity to the disease, but we still see rabbits coming in suffering with these terrible symptoms and there is little we can do for them. How long before we wake up to how much our actions often risk the very survival of our world?

We had three leverets brought in to Secret World in January. They had been found soaking wet and muddy. The heavy storms that we had been having must have caused a swell of water which carried the poor little things down into the road. Luckily, they were found when someone noticed them in the road and brought them into us. We have a 'mad' woman working for us called Marie as an animal carer. I say 'mad' in the nicest of ways as she is very much for animals to the nth degree. No animal in her care would ever be underfed, in fact unless we keep an eye on her, most would be dragging their stomachs on the ground! She is fantastic with swifts and leverets. We contacted her as soon as they arrived, and although she was off duty, she came in to take them home.

All wildlife needs to be cared for in a different way to domestic or farm animals. Especially creatures that are predated for food. When a human picks them up, as far as they are concerned they have been predated and are going to be killed and eaten. So they produce natural anaesthetics that close down their bodily functions and eventually die. This is why it is so important to place wildlife casualties in a box to make it dark. That way they start to feel secure and there is more chance of them surviving. Even larger animals such as badgers or deer will respond to being covered up, and feel secure because they cannot see all the movement around them.

Leverets especially are very nervous animals and do much better away from all the hubbub at our Centre. Marie keeps them in her bedroom and there the only intrusion is when she goes in to feed them. To start with she will try several feeds a day while they get used to the taste of the milk and they build up a bond with her. Usually, within a couple of days, they are keen to feed large amounts and she can copy what happens in the wild and just feed them once a day. As each leveret baby looks the same, Marie will mark two with a spot of white tippex – maybe one on the head, and another on the back. That way, she can tell each animal from the other and keep a record of their growth rate by weight, how much they take in each feed etc. and their progress.

All three did really well, although one remained smaller than the others all the way through. Marie doesn't usually try to sex them as that type of handling is completely unnatural. Marie talks to them so that they recognise her and finds that getting down on her knees with her behind up in the air, resting on her arms, she can rub noses with them. The mental picture, I fancy, is quite odd but if it works ... By the time the leverets were ready to come to a shed here at Secret World, Marie's bedroom was more of the appearance of a hay barn! After two weeks, natural food needs to become available and once they've reached the age of four weeks they should be completely weaned. Marie tries to transport them to us using the same container they have had to hide in so as to cut down the stress.

Placing them into a new place brings its own risks but it has to be done to give them more space. Even so, the day after Marie had placed the little ones in their new home, the smallest of the leverets was found dead. These are the times where support from other animal carers helps you deal with these things. Marie naturally blamed herself that she had lost that one because of the move, but being the smallest one there may well have been something genetically wrong with it. Even so these things are crushingly difficult to come to terms with after you have spent so much time trying to get them to survive.

The best time is actually letting them go, and with any wildlife casualty, that's when you can say that you have really been successful in rearing an animal. Marie took them back to the farm where they were found. Again taking them in the same container, she had waited for a lovely sunny spring day. By taking them back to where they were found, she knew it was hare country and they should have all the food that they needed. Sitting quietly by the animal container with the door open, the two juvenile hares came out and grazed around her. After about ten minutes, one of them pricked up its ears and bolted. Running in the typical zigzag fashion as they do, within seconds it was darting into a hedgerow so it could hardly be seen. The second quickly followed but in a different direction. Closing the carrier, and silently wishing them both luck, Marie went home.

* * *

Our Rehab block was finally completed and we wanted to have an official opening. It was now four years since the little girl, Millie

Havercroft, had died. At the time our future was very much unknown so I couldn't offer anything in memory of Millie. It made sense that this building, mainly used for weaned orphans making their final recovery and reverting to being wild prior to their release, be named after Millie, who was such a young person when she lost her life. It was to become known as the Millie building.

Her family were thrilled when we contacted them and the whole family were invited to the opening event. I hoped that enough time had passed for them to be able to cope with such an emotional occasion. They had since had another little girl and we gave all the children life membership of Secret World. The day went well and the Havercroft family were so pleased to have such an important building for so many wildlife animals to be named after their little girl, Millie.

The block now consists of two small pens, one preparation room/kitchen, a small indoor aviary, three large pens with attached grassed enclosures, a special deer unit with padded walls so that if the deer run the walls, they won't hurt themselves (this room could also have all the light from the window blocked out and the electric light could be turned from white to red). There is a very large aviary which is part indoor and part wire, often used for very young fox cubs and three further pens at the end of the building that could be isolated in the event of disease. The complete length of the building, which is approximately 40 metres long, has a corridor. This can be used to run badgers, foxes or swans to assess their ability of movement prior to release. They could then be turned back into their pens from the corridor by using boards. We are lucky to have such a facility although it is not a suitable building for care in the winter as there is no heating but spring/summer/autumn are our busiest times.

* * *

One of our most unusual rescues happened that summer. A lady was following a car and as she drove, she thought she could see the exhaust pipe about to fall off. She was really keeping an eye on the situation as the last thing she wanted to do was to drive into the exhaust pipe if it did indeed fall, and she gave herself more space between herself and the car in front. She was unable to catch the attention of the driver as it was quite a fast road. You can imagine how surprised she was when the thing did drop off the car and she immediately braked, only just managing to stop before she ran over the eight foot boa constrictor that lay on the road, very still. The car in front carried on unaware what had happened. Putting her hazard lights on, the lady rang the police and they were very soon in attendance.

Luckily one of the policemen was not afraid of snakes and bundled a very woozy snake onto the back seat. I believe the other policeman who was driving, was not quite so 'au fait' with the situation and managed to get to us very quickly. One of our carers, Ellie, was used to dealing with snakes and was quite happy to accept the casualty, although many of our staff would not have been so forthcoming! The snake, very shaken from his ordeal, had some broken ribs and a few friction burns. Ellie's dad, Richard West, is very knowledgeable about reptiles and soon the snake was kitted out with a vivarium and enjoying the warmth. Rest was the best thing for him.

I have to admit, there weren't many volunteers wanting to help with his care. He was in good condition and we hoped through the press that we would be able to find his owner. Evidently snakes have about 145 pairs of ribs so how many he had actually damaged, I don't know. I just know he was a very lucky snake to have escaped with his life. If the following car had been unable to stop and had driven over him, then he would have been dead.

Noah, the boa, as he was named, had straight vertical pupils to help him see in the dark and depending on the size of the prey, they can go a considerable length of time between meals – weeks sometimes months. Like all snakes, they use their tongue for smelling and they don't have external ears, they just rely on ears internally to pick up on vibrations to know when things are moving around them. And they don't have eyelids so it's very difficult to tell if they are asleep! They do have a special ocular scale that will protect the eye from dirt.

Boas don't have venom – not that it made it any easier on the staff, when it came to getting him out. Most weren't happy about it! But they don't actually squeeze their prey to death, they just constrict every time the animal breathes in, so that they basically suffocate their victims.

Noah was a very quiet snake and recovered well. We did indeed find the owner, who lived in Glastonbury. What we believe had happened, is that Noah had escaped from his owner's house and gone under the next door neighbour's car. The neighbour had already been out that day and the exhaust pipe was probably nice and warm. Wrapping himself around the exhaust pipe, the boa probably thought he was on to a good thing. Once the car was on another journey, things started to get too hot and the snake just had to release himself from the exhaust pipe.

Just prior to his owner collecting him, Noah did actually escape from his vivarium. There was a panic on to find him – not only our concern for him and to get him back for his owner, but our cats and Mother's Yorkshire terrier were just Noah's kind of sized meals that he might be attracted too. A very relieved Ellie found he had climbed up into the roof of the barn and Noah was duly returned to his vivarium and eventually to his owner.

* * *

One of the things about living close to the moors and on the flat land between the Quantock and Mendip Hills, is that occasionally we are used as a practice flight area for the jets from Yeovilton. There is usually three of them that scream across the sky and are so low that you just naturally duck. It used to be a nuisance when we had the cows as they got very jumpy if you were milking at the time and certainly many of the animals, poultry and the wallabies around the farm would run to escape from the noise.

It was after one of these flyovers, that one of the staff called us to go and look at Mr Woo as he was hiding in the hedge in the Woo pen and looked as if he was hurt. Both Simon and I went to look, he was dirty from running through the undergrowth, with blood down his back leg which was at a horrible angle – it was clear that he had broken his leg. Wrapping him carefully in a blanket, we rang through to the vets to say we were on our way with him.

Simon was driving and I was holding Woo. I could see from Simon's face that he was as upset as I was.

'I know it's silly,' I said, 'but whatever it costs, I want to do all we can.'

'Yes, I know,' he said, 'we will.'

The rest of the journey was silent.

Liz was waiting for us when we got to the vets. Taking him straight through to the scrub room, I laid Woo on the table. We both then got a real look at what was wrong with him and we knew there was no hope. His hind leg was completely broken with the main bone sheared through the skin. Fragments of bone were around the wound. Liz started to say, 'I can't—'

I shook my head and said, 'I know, at least we're both here to say goodbye.'

Woo just lay against my arm and I was stroking his front paws – my God, everything, everything that I loved so dear was going. At last, as the deep anaesthetic started to work, he just slowly closed his eyes and his breathing stopped. I carried him home, still wrapped in the blanket, still someone special, not just a body, and I wasn't the only one with tears running down my face as we went home.

We think that Woo must have been frightened by the jets. Wallabies thump their back legs like rabbits and he was probably going fast and slammed his legs down on one of the large granite stones in the pen for the leg to shatter and shear through in the way that it had. As you come out of our front door, straight ahead in the front garden is a fir tree which is where Mr Woo lies. He was such a character and has to be one of the animals that I hand-reared that will never be forgotten.

* * *

On 18th September many, many people were celebrating. Hunting with dogs was banned. It was passed in the Houses of Parliament: 356 votes for the bill and 166 against. It was meant to be a successful day and at long last save animals from being hunted until, through exhaustion, they give up and face their fate. At least everyone thought that this archaic sport had finally come to an end. No longer would deer, foxes, hare and mink be mauled and torn apart by dogs.

Future years were to prove that people can still act against the law quite openly.

6

Silly dares

With more animals coming in, we had to keep ways of getting funds to do the work. Sponsored events were good because people could get others to help them raise money, so we were coming up with different ideas. Dan Medley had sold his business, Leisure Marketing, to Take One Media which meant that Derek had a new boss. Not that he was as happy with them as with Dan, but Derek knew he was getting near to retirement age so was happy to stay on. He was also enjoying working in a job with weekends off, allowing him to play cricket in the summer, and the holidays were more than he had ever had when farming or with the tourist attraction. There's a lot to be said for working for someone else when, once you've finished work, you can walk away with no problems or responsibilities.

Dan went to work as General Manager at Wookey Hole caves. Debbie and I came up with the idea of doing a 'Sponsored Sleepover' in the caves. By the time we had called in as many favours as we could the 'sleepover' was complete. It was going to be in October so that by the time we had assembled in the restaurant at Wookey Hole caves it would already be dark. The Wolf Trust was going to be there and the evening started with a walk around the grounds with the wolves. We had to split the group into two and the others were getting a talk with Debbie showing them the bats and owls that we had at Secret World. (Wookey Hole caves are actually the home of a roost of Greater Horseshoe bats.) This was to be followed by walking up to the cave entrance by torchlight.

As we entered the cave, the Greater Horseshoe bats would be pointed out and a little further on, Bill Harrison, a clairvoyant, was to talk about the spirit world. Halfway through the caves there is a particularly large cave with a huge lake with lights shining through it, showing just how clear the water is. Water drips almost constantly from the stalactites and rivulets ran over the rock surfaces, but there were enough flat, almost dry, surfaces for us to sit or sleep on after ghostly stories had been told. At 4 a.m. we were to go through the rest of the caves and finally back through the grounds, by which time a full English breakfast would be ready for all of us at the end of the event.

Dan, bless him, would be with us all the time and with Simon as our first aider, it meant we had all aspects covered! We went to make sure that everything was going to work alright and did think that we would need some duvets in the cave in case people wanted to sleep, at least that would make the floor a bit softer for them to lie on. The huge problem that I had was just how far away the toilets were. When you reach a certain age, visits to the bathroom do become a regular thing during the night. Everything else seemed fine.

The days went by and we had almost thirty people booked. Every night, each time I went to the loo, I thought this is going to be terrible if I can't get to the toilets in time. My closest secret, never told until now, is that I resorted to incontinence pads (and I'm pleased to let you know, they were not necessary!).

Debbie was busy signing people in. Simon and I drove down near to the entrance of the cave with the transporter full of the duvets that we get donated to us for the animals – but obviously washed! It took seven trips up the long path to the entrance and then down into the large cave which was halfway along – some of it ducking to miss the low ceilings – with Simon marching ahead with no concern for his aging mother. Come to that, I don't think I had realised how unfit I was either.

We then returned to the restaurant to meet everyone. The wolves had arrived and were being held on heavy chains. I must admit they didn't look as sleek as when we had seen them last at the Centre but I put that down to moulting. With me casting glances at mirrors that were around to ensure that the said pads were not increasing my usual beam, we gathered together. The press were there and one particular photographer was from the *Weston Mercury*, you sometimes wonder how much of the press release they have read before they arrive to take the photos.

In the usual chat of this photographer, he started. 'Right, come along everybody, we want to get a nice photo for the paper with everybody involved. We want the brave people at the back, and then the Wookey Hole Witch would be lovely in the front, yes, and someone from Secret World with an owl. Pauline, we must have you in the front too, and you,' he beckoned to someone holding one of the wolves on a leash, 'if you'd like to bring your greyhound over too ...' He was quickly corrected.

Other than that, there were no calamities. I think everyone really enjoyed themselves and it was a huge thank you to Wookey Hole for allowing us to hold the event there which raised £1,500.

From the sleepover, the next emphasis had to be the Annual Auction and Ball and this time the cruise ship had called into Hawaii. Guests could come dressed up as people on the cruise, naval uniform or come as the islanders. The naval uniforms and grass skirts were the most popular choices. But from that lovely warm idea of a holiday theme, I yet again had come up with another dare!

This sponsor was for a dip in the sea on New Year's Day. No wet suits and the dare was to at least get your shoulders wet. As with all these things, people are very good at imparting information from – 'Oh, the sea is only a few degrees under what it would be in the summer,' to 'You have to wear goose grease,' to the best, 'I heard someone had a heart attack doing that'. Derek was not to be drawn on the subject; he thought it was all very silly. The one proviso I had put in was that we would do it at Lyme Regis as there is always people around, even in the winter, and it was a sea that I knew. I can remember thinking at Christmas, I wonder if I will still be alive this time next week.

Of course, in the end it wasn't too bad. The local pub allowed us to use their skittle alley to change into a variety of costumes. I was in an old-fashioned man's swimming costume with stripy material and straw hat. Debbie was in her glory dressed as Andy Pandy. We got to the beach and there was just six of us (can't understand why there weren't more!). Luckily Richard Austin lives in Lyme Regis and he was there to take photos. Allan, one of our volunteers and a keen canoeist, was launched to stay in the sea – to drag us back if we were swept out to sea. (I'd already told him which one to go for first if we all got dragged out!)

We had plenty of people watching us. Six people in outfits and carrying swim rings on 1st January were bound to catch a few people's attention. Once we were on the beach it was just a question of all holding hands and running into the water. When you actually start running, it's not a good idea to hesitate – get it over and done with, was my thought. The photographer, Richard, was calling instructions of 'Great, just all splash together, kneel down so that the waves come over your shoulders, great stuff' and the proverbial 'Just one more, yes, good, one more,' until Debbie in her high-class voice shouted, 'No f***** more, I'm bloody freezing!'

Although one to always do a dare, Debbie said she hated every minute of it. I must admit I found it exhilarating and have done it most years on the days between Christmas Day and New Year. I'm not the only repeat performer either. Some of us just like pain! I must say, the hot meal afterwards was very welcome.

I say that and yet Debbie did something I could never do. She ran the London Marathon. The training she had to do, either before her two young boys, Harry and Charlie, got up for school or in the evening, was true dedication as far as I'm concerned. I did try. I read that you should run at one speed and then do short bursts of faster speeds. I attempted this sound advice only to find my 'short bursts of speed' were the same as my slower speed and I'm afraid I gave in. Once Debbie has decided she will do something, then Debbie will do it and, as usual, it was all for Secret World.

The day came and sick to death of pasta and scared stiff she wouldn't make it, she joined the thousands of people at the start. There are so many people there that it takes a considerable amount of time for an amateur to reach the start line as all the professional runners go first. I can always remember a comedian talking about hitting the wall, which they reckon is almost towards the end, just as you're feeling that you can't do it, and where all the crowds do their part by encouraging the runners to keep going when they see them flagging. The comedian said there were so many people waiting to run that he hit 'the wall' before he'd reached the starting point!

Patrons

"Secret World Wildlife Rescue represents the rare mix of a pragmatic, common sense approach to the care of wildlife coupled with ethics and morality. Any wild creatures that have had the misfortune to need a helping hand are conversely very fortunate if that hand is extended by Secret World."

Simon King O.B.E.

"Secret World shines as a light in the dark when it comes to the welfare of our wildlife. The remarkable hospital and its staff and volunteers define excellence and expertise and their passion and commitment are extraordinary. And they make a difference, which is why I urge you to support them in any way you can."

Chris Packham

Patrons

"Whenever I'm asked who my wildlife heroes are I always say that it's people who dedicate their lives to saving wildlife – passionate people who give up their normal lives to dedicate themselves to making a difference. Not for financial gain, not for fame, but because they just love animals. Pauline at Secret World is one of those people. I've filmed at Secret World many times over the years and have always admired Pauline and her team. Whenever I've visited she'll be lovingly hand-rearing orphans in her kitchen. The work Secret World does in rescuing, rehabilitating, educating and campaigning, is completely amazing and will always have my support. I'm honoured to be a patron."

Michaela Strachan

"I am pleased to become one of the most recent patrons of Secret World Wildlife Rescue. By engaging the public in learning about British wildlife, Secret World helps them to reconnect with nature and encourages the protection of its heritage. I'm really looking forward to seeing their new Learning Centre completed so that groups visiting the site can explore their work further."

Martin Hughes-Games

Patrons

Lloyd Buck

"Having spent most of my life flying birds and watching wildlife, I have been fortunate enough to turn what was my hobby and passion into a career. I felt very honoured when Pauline asked me to become a patron for Secret World Wildlife Rescue, as I know the huge effort that Pauline and the team of staff and volunteers put in on a daily basis, all year round, which is hugely successful at giving many species of birds and animals the chance to make it back to the wild. In particular, starlings and many other garden birds are currently in decline, so if we can all acknowledge this, and do what we can to help by putting up bird boxes, bird feeders and adapting part of our gardens for wildlife, we will be giving all these birds the chance to stabilise their numbers, and adapt to a rapidly changing world. Most importantly, please support the work of Secret World in any way you can."

"As a patron of Secret World for the past nine years, I have been able to see how hard all the members of staff and volunteers work to save every kind of wildlife casualty – right down to a tiny baby bat. Their ethic of every animal being important to them gives all the animals that come through their door the best chance of returning to the wild. Please support them in any way that you can – help save a life!"

Anthony Head

"I have worked with animals for many years and am fascinated by the care that is given to wildlife at Secret World Wildlife Rescue. Having recently been asked to become a patron, I am proud and honoured to accept and hope that all of you reading about Secret World will donate as much money as you can to support the extraordinary work that goes on at this centre every day of the year."

Sarah Fisher

Anthony Head & Sarah Fisher

Patrons

"I am a huge fan of Secret World and I think they do marvellous work looking after wildlife."

Jilly Cooper

Mike Dilger

"Having seen first hand the devastation wreaked by the recent floods in the southwest, I'm only too aware that it's not just the human residents that have been suffering. A vast array of wildlife has been either drowned or made homeless as a result of the unprecedented water levels and Secret World is one of the very few organisations that has been willing to stand up for and look after these misplaced animals. It's not just the 'wild' victims of the floods that Secret World has helped. For the last 30 years this fabulous charity has rescued and rehabilitated thousands of animals needing help as a result of man's, often inadvertent, actions. I therefore encourage anyone who has ever had fun fox spotting, derived a buzz from badger watching or simply taken delight from the discovery of a deer to support Secret World's work to redress this imbalance and ensure as many animals as possible are given the second chance they so desperately deserve."

Patrons

"I have been a patron of Secret World since 2000. Each time I visit, it is good to see how much this charity has grown and developed. Yet it still has the ethic that every animal is important to them no matter how small or common the species may be. A team of dedicated staff and volunteers work tirelessly round the clock to make sure every rescued animal survives and Secret World now helps over 5,000 casualties every year. Each day they will rescue, rehabilitate and release British wildlife and the charity runs purely on donations. By buying Pauline's fourth book, *A Place of Safety*, you will have helped towards the funds desperately needed to ensure that this work continues – and hopefully enjoyed the book too!"

Valerie Singleton

"Secret World is the coming together of People and Wildlife, the very human adventure at the forefront of nature conservation. The sick or injured animal in the hand is to me the symbol of caring and the essence of how we can begin to put things right. The dedication of Secret World's staff and countless amazing volunteers is a testament to them of their individual passion for life, and for wildlife. I have always been proud to be a patron of Secret World, and hope it continues to make such a major difference for wildlife and for people."

Chris Sperring M.B.E.

"When I think of Britain, I think of her countryside. That green and pleasant land of my childhood. All tumbling hedgerows and lush woodlands, teeming with flora and fauna. But as we continue to encroach on the natural world we must look to the likes of Secret World to preserve and protect it for generations to come. Their dedication to maintaining the beauty and diversity of the world around us is as impressive as it is essential. They are true guardians of nature."

Rhianna Pratchett

'Rhianna Pratchett is our latest patron, and her father, Sir Terry Pratchett, is a great supporter. The whole family love wildlife.'

Sir Terry Pratchett

Sir Terry Pratchett charmed by the starlings!

Other celebrity supporters

"Secret World Wildlife Rescue is doing vital work to repair the terrible damage caused by the thoughtlessness and cruelty of mankind. Luckily, there are thousands of people who care desperately for the well-being and safety of all creatures, wild and tame, and with their support this valiant charity is calling for mistreatment of wild animals to be considered a crime that can be pursued in the courts. Through education and encouragement the world will learn that all creatures are pretty much the same under the skin, and deserve kindness, compassion, freedom from fear and our protection at all times."

Joanna Lumley

Tom Heap

"Pauline is a tireless champion for our wildlife: not only running a dedicated and innovative casualty clinic for the creatures of the South West, but also understanding that the animals' long-term welfare depends on persuading us humans they matter. She has a warm, personal approach – rearing baby badgers in her kitchen – but doesn't let this love for animals descend into narrow sentimentality. She has both empathy and authority. The amazing story of Secret World proves her talent."

Debbie was there wearing her black bin liner to keep herself warm until they reached the starting point and then she was off. All credit to her; she did the whole 26 miles. It was another challenge that she had done to raise money for the wildlife that she loves so much. But in her usual blunt way of speaking, when she came back to work, her comment was that 'I won't be bloody well doing that again!'

* * *

With huge excitement, our first charity shop was opened in Burnham-on-Sea. Simon worked hard finding cut-price fitments and spent a few days in different charity shops, courtesy of other charities, to find out how they marked things, rotated stock and attracted volunteers. Everyone had helped with the decorating and a lot of the animal carers got caught up in the first few days to man the shop until there were enough volunteers to assist the manageress who was paid staff. It was still quiet on the casualty front as the baby birds hadn't started arriving yet. The best person to send was Marie, because she always ended up buying items so that the shop always took the most money on her shifts!

The shop was soon attracting lots of donations of clothes, ornaments, shoes, videos and books to name but a few things. It was another way that people could donate and help us find the money we needed to help wildlife. Equally, lots of supporters were coming in for the odd item and a browse around. So many townsfolk kindly continue to support it to this day; many of them know that whenever they need us to help with a casualty, we will always be there.

We usually only get up to about ten fox cubs a year, which is quite different from other centres which are close to big towns or cities and get much larger numbers. This year we seemed to be forever taking young cubs in, and soon we had nearly fifty. It seemed to be the case that because hunting of foxes had been banned, everyone was out shooting them irrespective of whether the vixen was in milk with dependent cubs or not. If there was one good thing about hunting, they did stop at that critical time of year. Better to let them have cubs and then there would be more foxes for them to hunt in the winter. We had enough accommodation for the cubs while they were small, but as they grew they would need more space. We were going to need more grassed enclosures to turn them into once they were weaned but still unable to defend themselves. We were to put out an immediate appeal for donations to build some enclosures for them and also for landowners that would be happy to be release sites for our foxes.

The response was amazing. We needed to build six large enclosures with a central corridor to use to catch them in when it was time for them to be released. Not only did we manage to get the funds needed but the pens were up and ready for us to use in a matter of six weeks. Two of the main contributors were Chris and Elaine Fairfax, who run the Animal Friends Insurance Company. These are amazing people who wanted to do something for animals and they started up this company for anyone wanting to insure their pet. All the profits from this insurance company go to many animal centres, not only in this country but worldwide.

Foxes are close to the hearts of Chris and Elaine and they both came and saw the groups of foxes being released into these lovely pens. With logs to climb over, long grass to hide in, shelters for when the weather was bad and short grass to forage for worms when it rains, they were perfect enclosures for our foxes. We are very lucky in that we do have twelve acres of land to spread out into.

Some farmers often believe that they need to keep shooting, snaring or poisoning foxes as otherwise we would be overrun with them. After Foot and Mouth in 2001, when no-one was allowed in the countryside to shoot or hunt, the following year most wildlife centres had fewer fox cubs because foxes breed according to the food that is available to them. If their numbers remain fairly constant, there is no need to breed more. Animals know that to keep breeding in territories where you only have so much food, you're either going to have to keep the numbers down or chase the weaker ones away when food becomes scarce. Something humans haven't learnt yet.

We were very fortunate with release sites too. We always like to release where we know landowners will put food out for the foxes until they are able to find food for themselves and don't need to come back for it. It is much harder to gain data on how successful fox releases are, but we do have some sites where people have said they have stayed around for a long time. Others disperse quickly.

* * *

When the first little bundle of spotted fluff arrives, we know that the herring gull season has started. Nearly everybody who lives in

Burnham-on Sea will have a pair of gulls nesting on their roofs and soon after, there will be complaints from people being dive-bombed as they go into their gardens to hang out washing or just to reach their cars. This only happens occasionally but it is under-standable that people become scared because they are such big birds and they do have large beaks.

There will always be people who take matters into their own hands but the sickening discovery of six gull chicks in a carrier bag thrown out of a car on the moors, as far as I am concerned is horrendous and callous. Two were dead by the time someone found them but the other four did survive. They are ravenous ani-mals as they grow and their diet consists partly of fish which means that the fragrance of their pens takes some putting up with. Once they are out in our water paddocks with lots of grass around, they are less of a problem.

It's always amusing when, on open days, we take a tub down from the hospital room with some tiny gull chicks inside to show the visitors. 'Aren't they sweet,' is usually the comment – until they find out what they are. Still, as far as we are concerned, every animal is important to us so they will be looked after in the same way as anything else that finds their way to our door.

By this time we all carried radios which makes it much easier to find each other, to contact someone if there are queries regarding the animals and also it means that we can tell if someone has gone off site – and come to that, when they return. It was pay day and everyone had received their payslips. A resident from Burnham-on-Sea came in with an adult herring gull. It was still alive but he thought it had been shot. He had heard his neighbour firing at the gulls on his roof and wanted us to confirm the gull had indeed been shot. The entry and exit holes on the gull's body were obvi-ous and there was nothing we could do for the gull other than to put it to sleep. He went away very angry.

Within a quarter of an hour he was back with another gull that had been shot and the man's neighbour had been really abusive to him when he picked it up. The poor chap was really upset. I rang through to the police and reported that someone was shooting at gulls within a residential area and gave the address. Because it was a firearm situation, the police were very quick in responding. The man was given a warning and the policewoman who had attended the incident asked that if she was to contact Secret World, would he be prepared to let us go up and rescue the chicks. With no adults to look after them, the chicks were now a welfare problem. The man agreed and gave her his mobile number so that we could contact him as he was now going out, and wasn't prepared to wait around.

The call came through from the police asking us to attend and to get the gull chicks down. Simon radioed through to me asking if he should ring the fire brigade and I said yes. The next radio message was that the fire brigade were unable to help. Debbie in her fundraising office joined in the open call saying she knew someone with a cherry picker who was near the house mending streetlights so it was left with her to organise. Eventually Debbie radioed to say that her friend had contacted his boss, who had agreed he could go, so he was meeting Debbie at the house. I tried to ring the man's mobile just to let him know what we were doing but got no reply.

I met up with Simon and suggested that he went with Debbie. I wasn't sure that she was good with heights and I had concerns that the owner of the house might return, and he didn't seem to be a very nice person. So Simon and Debbie went to rescue the chicks. It was half an hour later that a call came in to say that the cherry picker was now stuck and wouldn't come down. Simon and the operator were up in the sky and could someone now ring the fire brigade to see if they would now come to rescue Simon and his friend. This was all put over the radio with great mirth from the rest of the staff. Lisa, who was our vet nurse at the time, radioed to say there wasn't any hurry, Simon had paid everybody that day, so not to worry too much!

The operator's boss had to come and mend the cherry picker and in the end, the platform was lowered, rescuing the operator, Simon and two herring gull chicks. Even the local press heard about it and photos were taken of the situation and the final rescue. In mending the cherry picker, a small amount of hydraulic oil was spilt on the drive, which the boss said would wash off with some soapy water.

It was later that evening that I had a really abusive phone call from the man in question. He was furious that his drive had been spoilt and that, not noticing the oil was there, he had walked on it and gone in the house, ruining his carpets. I did say that we had been told the oil would wash off, only to be met with a torrent of bad language. I wasn't really interested in speaking to him as he was not to be placated. I suggested he got in touch with our insurance company, which luckily covers us for such situations.

Would you believe that he didn't get any compensation for his carpets (that part of the story had probably been fabricated) but he got £2,000 for a new drive. How many wildlife rescue groups would even think that it would be necessary to cover yourself for those kinds of situations?

* * *

During the hot weather and because we have rhynes around our fields, we do get a lot of call-outs to grass snakes. I think a lot of people don't realise how big they can grow and suddenly confronted with a snake that can be anything up to a metre and half long, can be quite frightening. Often they get caught in netting that is laid over some fish ponds to keep the herons out. Grass snakes can usually slide through the netting but if they've just eaten a frog and there is a bulge in their body, then they get stuck. Grass snakes are quite easy to recognise because they are usually a lovely olive green colour but they have a collar behind their head that is quite distinctive. This collar can range from a cream to yellow, an orange colour or even red. They are very passive snakes and rarely bite.

They lay their eggs in compost heaps which eventually hatch out as lots of little bootlace-size snakes. Cats are notorious for taking them into houses as a 'gift' to their owner whose first reaction, if in the kitchen, is to place a washing-up bowl over it (and usually something ridiculously heavy on top to stop the snake from pushing the bowl up and escaping). Grass snakes do two things in defence if they are frightened. One is to pretend that they are dead, which means that they turn themselves upside down and open their mouth with their tongue hanging out. This can be quite amusing because if you turn them back up the right way, they turn themselves back over as if to say, 'No, I'm dead'.

The other defence is to exude a really foul-smelling liquid. This can be quite handy if you are called out to a snake under a washing-up bowl as you really don't know what kind of snake it is under there. Non-indigenous snakes do escape and on rare occasions, it could be an adder. So if you can smell that disgusting smell, you just know it is a grass snake and you can bravely dive for it when the bowl is lifted.

There was one situation where this nearly got me into trouble. A nearby neighbour rang to say she had a snake and could we come and take it away. It was only up the road so I went with one of the volunteers. When we got there, the lady was standing waiting by the front door for us looking very worried. As we went into the house, there was this terrible smell and I so nearly turned to the girl with me to say, it's got to be a grass snake. Fortunately I said nothing, because the lady took us through the house out into the garden, which is where the grass snake was. So the smell in the house had nothing to do with the snake and I have no idea what it was!

On another occasion, it was the usual call, just as dinner was being served. A lady had a snake in her garden and, together with her husband, they were both really scared.

'Was it near a compost heap?' I asked.

'Yes,' she said.

'Well then, it's just a grass snake. How long is it?' I asked.

'It's about ten centimetres long,' she replied.

'Right, so it's really thin like a bootlace,' I questioned, trying to find out more about it.

'No,' she said, 'it's about as thick as my thumb and it's got a big round head.' Well, that didn't sound right.

'OK,' I said, switching off the hotplates and oven. 'You're not far away in Highbridge, I'll come out.'

'Oh, thank you so much, we're really scared,' she said.

It was only a matter of about 10–15 minutes later that I arrived at the house. Both husband and wife were wearing shorts but had donned Wellington boots so that if they were struck by the 'snake' they were protected. They had also locked the back door, which was duly opened slowly so they could peer out and make sure it wasn't out there waiting for them. They both stood on the doorstep pointing to the end of the garden, neither of them keen to come with me.

I have to admit, I laughed when I found this creature that was causing all this fear. 'It's a caterpillar,' I said picking it up. 'It's an elephant hawk moth caterpillar.' Luckily, they could laugh at themselves. It is the largest caterpillar found in our country and it has markings on its body so that if it draws its head into its body, it really does look like a bulbous head. Equally, when it's moving along, the head and upper part of the body can lift making it look like an elephant's trunk. Once it's ready to change into the pupae, it goes underground, emerging the following summer as a very pretty brown and pink moth with a 7 cm wing span, living for just five weeks.

Wellies for protection from snake attack!

* * *

That summer, we had an appeal for our first proper ambulance vehicle. It was kitted out with all the equipment we would need on a rescue. As it was a dedicated vehicle, it was standing ready to go as soon as we had a call-out which meant we could respond quicker, rather than trying to collect things together from various places.

One of the first rescues taken on in our new ambulance was when Simon was called out by a worried neighbour who had been watching the house next to her. She was concerned that no one was around to feed the cats that she knew lived there. Simon had contacted the RSPCA as we don't really do domestic animals and would have no authority to get into premises, if there was reason to believe that any animals inside needed to rescuing. Simon met RSPCA Inspector Hammond at the house.

As it happened, the owner of the house arrived soon after them but admitted she hadn't been home for five days. There were seven cats in the house, which itself wasn't what you'd call tidy. She explained that her boyfriend had left her, leaving his owl behind in the shed in the garden. She couldn't say when the owl was last fed. When Simon went to have a look, a very sorry Bengal eagle owl was sitting on a broken cardboard box in a filthy shed that was likely to fall around the owl any time soon. The girl was happy to sign over the cats to the RSPCA and the owl to Simon. She didn't really care what happened to them so, as far as she was concerned, the sooner they were gone the better.

The Bengal eagle owl was named Ben and joined the selection of birds that we use for talks. When we go to schools, we often take the birds of prey, a hedgehog, possibly the land snails to talk about the importance of slugs and snails in our garden for wildlife but also keen to point out that land snails aren't found in this country. (I've done enough damage saying they hum.) We also had a small snake that at the time belonged to Ellie – one of our animal carers. Snakes are always popular, even people who don't like them will come over to tell you they don't like them! This corn snake was called Ruby. She was quite young so only about half a metre long. When we transport snakes, we advise rescuers to place them in a pillowcase, gathering the top of the pillowcase and then bend it over double and put an elastic band around tightly. If you don't bend the top of the pillowcase over, a snake can push their way through the elastic band, especially if it hasn't been done up very tightly. The pillowcase is then placed in a carrier so that nobody sits on the pillowcase without realising there's something in there!

Debbie and Ellie were off to a school in Weston-super-Mare to do a talk to the children. When they got there, they realised that the snake had escaped. The maintenance man kindly took as much of the car apart as he could, but the snake could not be seen. Ellie and Debbie drove the car back hoping the snake wasn't going to come out while they were driving and slide by their feet. When they got back, they parked the car near to the office which has a long, low, tiled roof. Because it was autumn, it got quite cold at night, so using an extension lead, they put a heat pad on the floor in the passenger seat. The hope was that the snake would find the warmth and decide to go to sleep on it.

After a few days, nothing was found and for a month nobody was in a hurry to drive the vehicle anywhere. Soon, it was forgotten about and the car was used as usual and we just had to accept that Ruby had escaped but where she was, we really didn't know.

A call went out for Lisa, our vet nurse, to go to reception. When Lisa got there, a gentleman had a kitten in a box. He had found it in his garden and was worried that his dog was going to hurt it. Nobody living near him knew anything about it so he thought he would bring it to us. Lisa started to explain that we don't do domestic animals and was checking over the little ginger and white kitten. She discovered a nasty wound to the side of the kitten's neck, which was infested with maggots. Now, because the animal was at risk, we do take them in and pass them on to the correct association once they have recovered.

Lisa took the tiny kitten upstairs and cleaned the wound. The kitten then polished off a supper of cat food and curled up in one of the tubs next to the radiator in the hospital room. Unfortunately, the reason for him being accepted into Secret World stayed with him because he was named 'Maggot'. The scruffy kitten's wound soon healed and he became a very sleek juvenile over the next few weeks. There was no need to pass him on to a cat charity, as a home was found for him with one of our volunteers within days of him being with us. The volunteer was to bring a photo of 'Maggot' (yes, she did change the name!), a very beautiful adult long-haired cat stretched across a very nice settee. He had certainly found a good home.

Our Christmas appeal was 'Caring for the Carers'. It was to modernise the preparation room and to get some central heating into this room and the adjoining offices. Up until then, animal carers had to work in a freezing cold room in all weathers. While the builders were there, we asked Pat, the boss, if he could look at a leak in the roof just above the offices. He took a line of tiles off the roof to walk on the struts to reach the leak. A white-faced Pat came back down and into the office. 'There's a snake up there curled up in your roof, but I'm not going to touch it.' Pat had found Ruby and if you knew Secret World and the huge roofs that we have, it was incredible that Pat had just happened to remove five tiles to find her. Ellie was very pleased to have Ruby back and, placed in a warm vivarium, Ruby was soon moving around.

* * *

When we go into a new year, I always wonder what we will face in the coming year. Will there be weather conditions that challenge the wildlife? Will we have certain species that we've never had before? The stories behind why animals come into us are sometimes quite amazing – either the dedication of the finders in getting to them, or the incredibly slim chance that the animal was even found. In 2006 our first amazing rescue was to happen on the very first day of that year.

7

Raining otters

January 1st is always the time that I take the Christmas decorations down. There is so much to do as there are decorations in the shop and reception, the offices, the staff room, our own and Mum's flat too as she needed help with packing things away. So this was a good day to do it with few staff about on a bank holiday. The phone would be quiet and once the decorations are packed away and it's vacuumed through, 2005 has disappeared and everyone returning work tomorrow, can do so with clear desks. Another year has started.

It was a phone call just after lunch that alerted us that some orphans were coming in. The caller, a local farmer, said they were otters but we have so many wrongly identified animals brought into us, I was not really expecting them to be otter cubs. It didn't take the farmer, Mr Thorne, long to reach us as they lived down on Gold Corner pumping station where the River Huntspill meets the South Drain, only a matter of five miles away.

He arrived with a cardboard box and I went down to meet

him. Peering inside the box, I saw there were two otter cubs that were probably only about six weeks old. Their eyes looked milky and their fur was short and smooth. They were the youngest otter cubs I had ever seen. Evidently in the morning, Mr Thorne had heard crying under the shed at the bottom of their garden, next to the river. He hadn't bothered too much as he thought it was probably mink. The crying continued into the afternoon and he decided to take a look. As soon as he realised it was otter cubs, he contacted the Environment Agency, who told him to bring them to us. I thanked him and took them up to the kitchen.

Lifting them out of the box on to my lap, they snuggled down. They were cold but hadn't been without food for very long. Checking them over for parasites, they were clean and I could tell we had two little girls. It was the first time we'd had more than one otter in at the same time and they were named Splish and Splash. Taking the time to enjoy them, I sat watching the girls stretch their lovely webbed feet and settle to sleep, happy to be warm and safe. Their fur was still short but within a few days, it would become quite long and then they appear very fluffy – protection in case they fall into the water while they are too young to swim.

After an hour I slid the blanket they were asleep on back into the armchair as I got up to get some milk made up with the syringe and teat. We use milk called Esbilac, which is a powdered puppy milk from America. One of the difficulties while doing the slow procedure of toileting, soothing and feeding, is keeping the milk warm so we usually have an outer container with boiled water inside with the bottle standing in it. Once milk gets cold, orphans will soon refuse it so it really is the same test on the wrist that you do for human babies, to make sure it's the right temperature. I also started an incubator to put them in once they had fed.

Starting with Splish, the smaller of the two otters, I toileted her. She immediately started to 'nose' into my arm, looking for food. Just as the badger cubs do, she wrinkled her nose as I gently syringed some milk into her mouth. But by the time the second syringe was offered, her tongue curled around the teat and sucked so that the plunger of the syringe was pulled in and I didn't need to apply any pressure while she took about 13 mls. She decided that was enough of this strange milk and slid down on top of her sister who was still asleep. Bringing Splash to the top of the pile, I did the same with her. Splash was a stronger cub and immediately wanted the milk. She wasn't bothered that it didn't taste the same. Her thick tail thrashed with her enjoyment of the milk. Twenty-five mls was polished off quite quickly and she then literally fell asleep still with her tongue around the teat, comfort sucking but without actually taking any milk.

I gently picked them both up together and placed them in the incubator with the same blanket that they had got used to, so that it smelled familiar.

It was quite magical to watch them. Badgers usually sleep on their side with their body curled in a foetal position. Their head is tucked in between their front paws. Otters seem to flop over each other more and don't curl up so tightly. We are so lucky to see this kind of behaviour, watch young animals – a thing that many people never ever get to see. Simon came home having been away for the New Year and came in to see the new orphans. 'Aren't they great,' he said. Although he's not as 'hands on' with the orphans, he enjoys seeing them as much as I do.

'Great time-wasters,' I replied, aware that the decorations still had to be packed away.

'And why shouldn't you enjoy them?' he said. 'You do all the night feeds!'

I smiled. Both he and Derek understood me so well.

I knew I had a two-hour window before the cubs would need feeding again. Once they start taking larger amounts then the feeds can be less often but, at the moment, it's all about building up confidence and a bond with the youngsters. Going back to the Christmas decorations, although it was still only late afternoon it was already dark. The front doorbell went again and when I went to answer it, there was Mr Thorne standing at the door with yet another box. 'Not another otter cub?' I asked joking.

'Yes,' he replied to my question, 'and a very lucky little fella too, but he's soaking wet.'

Mr Thorne had gone out to feed some cattle in the next field on his tractor. Because it was dark he had the headlights on and they just picked the cub out in the field. He must have started to try and find his mother.

'Thank you so much,' I said, 'how lovely that they will be all together.'

Taking him up into my kitchen, I found a warm towel to dry him. It was a boy and what else could he be called but Splosh! He was a little bit bigger than Splash and much stronger. Adding him to the incubator there were grunts of disapproval at the new cold addition, but nosing him, they soon became an otter scrum. Splosh searched for the heat under both the others and they were quite content to use him as a mattress.

When it was time for the next feed, I thought I would try them with a bottle. Balancing all three on my lap, each one took voraciously, ranging between 100–150 mls. One by one they would fall asleep on the teat, once they had had their fill. Orphans very often spend their first 24 hours after their rescue asleep. They know that they are safe after the fear of being alone and these guys were no different. Putting them back into the incubator, there were squirms, stretches with those wonderful webbed feet and yawns. Splish, Splash and Splosh – absolutely magical.

It was fantastic the next day when we moved them into the cubby hole to watch them. Still unable to walk properly, they spent most of their time on their back exploring their feet with their mouths and each other's tails that thrashed around while they tried to catch them. When they did try to walk, it looked very unsteady and they shook as they tried the first steps. How Splosh had managed to get so far was a mystery. He must have been very determined. They were easy to feed and as very young otters, slept most of the time. But at feeding time it was easier to get them all on your lap and sort them out one by one. Bottles were now being emptied very quickly and rounded tummies showed that they were doing well.

A couple of days later, Richard Austin came to take some photos of the cubs together and he always comes up with different ideas. He arrived with a large salmon that had cost him £25. None of the cubs were in the least bit interested in solid food at this stage but the picture he wanted was the three cubs peering over the salmon. This he managed to achieve and he went away very happy with a photo that he was almost sure would hit the national papers – and he was right. The salmon was left behind as he had no further use of it. This was much to the pleasure of Simon who washed it off and had it for his tea!

To watch the trio as they grew was a real pleasure. Ellie who was with us then as Animal Care manager helped with the rearing of the otter cubs and we were able to film a lot of their behaviour. With three young otters, we decided that perhaps now was the time to see if we could raise enough money to have the facilities to see these cubs through to their final release. We wanted to have a grassed enclosure that was going to have to be about 30 metres square to give them enough space to play in. We wanted to give them a pool for swimming in and a volunteer called Alan Gory was going to help us install cameras to monitor the otter cubs and even install cameras underwater so that we could see them swim.

With many supporters who love otters, we were able to raise enough money for the pen to be built and so work started. Splish, Splash and Splosh were growing fast but were still in the kitchen. They explored the kitchen while the cubby hole was being cleaned and soon were playing with the water in the dogs' water bowl. It was quite noticeable that Splash and Splosh were always together and Splish was more of a loner but they still snuggled together when it was time to sleep. Simon had placed a small trout in the dogs' water bowl and was filming Splash and Splosh trying to get it out. They hadn't learnt how to close their nostrils and a lot of snorting and head shaking was taking place in the vain attempt to catch the fish. It was a good job that the kitchen floor was tiled as we ended up with more water on the floor than in the bowl.

It was time to start the swimming lessons in the bath. A careful eye had to be kept on them as the water got deeper as Splosh and Splash were bigger than Splish and stronger. The fun and games chasing each other under the water could sometimes get just a bit too powerful and Splish would be jumping up at the side of the bath wanting to come out. They were so fast and the amount of time that they could spend underwater was amazing. The squirming and excitement once back in the kitchen was brilliant. We left dry towels on the floor and they would each put their chins on the ground and using their back legs, push their way across the towel. Then they would go over on their backs wriggling their bodies from side to side. Then it was up for a circuit around the kitchen, often jumping over each other, before returning to have another squirm!

Once we were sure that Splish could stand her own ground, it was time to move them out to the Millie building away from Ellie and I who had done the bottle feeding. Now, instead of fleeces, a warm kitchen and towels, they had logs, a large water container so that they could bath whenever they wanted and wooden boxes with straw for bedding for them to sleep on. These had been made by Graeme, one of our volunteers. The boxes were very heavy duty and were waterproof and insulated to keep them warm in the cold weather and cool in the summer.

The only concession for their first few days was a couple of blankets to 'squirm on'! It has to be said that for the first two days, the blankets were the subject of comfort but soon the young otters became used to their new boxes. Now aged about 8–9 weeks they soon became nocturnal but we were still able to see them on the infrared camera and monitor their behaviour. By now they were eating trout, minced beef and dead chicks.

The new pen was eventually finished and by this time the otters were five months old. The pool indeed had an underwater camera which I could watch from my kitchen. We transported them in their boxes that they slept in. The boxes had been designed so that a wire mesh door could be bolted across the entrance and it was less traumatic to take them in their home that they knew. Setting both the boxes down in the long grass, we took away the mesh doors and added the tunnels which fitted on the boxes and waited. Three heads popped out of an opening but no one was coming out in the new strange surroundings. We had all secretly hoped that they might come out and take a swim in the large pool but the tentative peep out and then going back in, was the kind of behaviour we really wanted to see. If they didn't revert to being wild, we weren't going to be able to release them.

Waiting patiently in the kitchen, it was just as dusk was arriving that the beautiful image of an otter swimming under the water came on the screen. Shouting to Derek and Simon, we all watched. The use of their rudder-like tails was fascinating with a stream of bubbles following them in their wake. Romping around the sides of the pond, they were diving and playing with each other. They glided, easily missing each other in the clear water. There are images that remain in my mind that I felt were truly mesmerising and that had to be one of them.

There was still another 10 to 12 months of care for those guys – a very expensive period for the charity. When you realise that otters in the 1970s were nearly extinct due to pesticides being washed from the land to the rivers, it has to be right that we help otters if we can.

* * *

Every year, when the fawns come into the kitchen, I always have my dog, Murray, to help with them. An Alsatian cross Doberman, he was a lovely softy and being the same size as a deer would often be a comfort to fawns when they arrived. The fawns would often nudge him for food and I could sometimes offer a bottle from the other side and they would start to suckle.

Murray came to us as a puppy and had been very ill with sarcoptic mange. Someone had stolen him from a gypsy having seen how poorly he was and taken him to our vets. Recovering from the parasites which had left him almost bald, I was talked into having him by Becky, one of the girls at Quantock Veterinary Centre. I loved him dearly and over the years he had been a gentle giant to many orphans. Now at the age of 12, arthritis in his hips was making his life really tough and he was no longer enjoying life. It's one of those things that you can't bear to have to make that kind of decision, but there comes a time when you know that you are being unfair.

I had asked Dom, the vet from Quantock, to come and put him to sleep for me. I didn't want to make Murray do the journey and I think it's kinder to let stay them at home. Dom agreed with me that it was time and holding his head, I said my goodbyes. As Murray had got older, he had become my shadow. In younger years, he would be out with the animal care staff following them around in their daily chores, but as time had gone on, he could no longer keep on the move. Eventually, even when I got up in my office, he gave a look of, 'Where are you going now?' as he strained to stand up and follow me.

I buried him in the front garden with a cherry tree to mark the place. This was the garden that he would walk a distance of about four metres away from my office to lay on the grass and enjoy the sun. I'd lost my shadow.

He would have loved the next fawn which was to arrive just a few weeks after he died. It was a young fallow fawn that had been found hanging up by her back leg in a wire fence. She was so lucky to have been rescued as it was a couple of children that were out with their mother taking the dog for a walk that found her. Their father was a vet. The dog had disappeared in the hedge and the children were trying to find it. One child saw the fawn through the hedge and saw the maggots on the part of the foot that was caught in the netting and she thought the fawn was dead. She ran to tell her mother and being children of a vet, the other child wanted to see it. Resigned to having to look at a 'dead' fawn and the dog having come back, the mother allowed them to go and see. As soon as they realised the fawn was alive, they rang their father and he came out to cut it from the wire.

The fawn must have tried to jump over the fence to follow her mother and caught her back leg between the top two strands of wire, which then trapped the leg as she hung from the other side. She had been there for at least two or three days which we could tell by the size of the maggots that had started to eat away at the wound. One strand of wire had cut into the hock of the back leg and the other had cut across the ankle of the same leg. The vet took the fawn home and cleaned the wounds, gave her some antibiotics and then rang to see if we could take her.

When she arrived, her leg was badly swollen and the foot was knuckling under. The most important thing was to give her some food and stabilise her. Fallow fawns are nowhere near as shy as the roe kids. This is because they follow their mothers around, whereas the roe will be left lying up in long grass until their mother returns to feed them. She really was a pathetic looking thing but already a lot bigger than the roe although she was only about two weeks old. She was named Freda because we 'freed her' from a fence. I know it's awful but it did actually suit her. Freda was quite happy to nudge into my neck and eventually take a bottle of milk. She settled in the cubby hole with some fresh browse hanging for her to nibble or hide under but I didn't put up the board. As long as I was in the kitchen she was fine. Tomorrow was the day with the vet to see how much of a chance she had for getting any of that movement back in her leg.

Liz already had all the details when we arrived at the vets. Freda had sat quite happily on my lap as Simon drove – I had already become Mum. She trotted behind me into the vets, swinging the back leg that appeared to have no movement. Although Freda was quite calm, Liz wanted to mildly anaesthetise her so she could get a really good look at the leg and to take some x-rays, to make sure there was no damage to the bone. There was certainly no movement on either joint and Liz had concerns about the foot being knuckled under. I have seen this in fawns and calves before so was not quite so worried about it. The decision was we would give it a go and the leg was bandaged, trying to bring the foot forward with a little bit of pressure. It was, however, going to have to be constantly checked and re-bandaged. It was going to take time. With her leg completely covered from top to toe, Freda was oblivious and took over the duty of being my shadow.

It was okay to take her for walks so, like my other fawns, every day we went around our Home Ground, the large field attached to our farmhouse. The hedges and trees that had been planted for the Millennium were growing well (although I have to say a few small trees were stripped by the local deer – marvellous, you try to create a wildlife habitat and the wildlife eats it!).

Derek was not a fan of Freda, but to be fair she didn't bother him very much. It was just the fact of coming in and finding a deer in the kitchen, quite happy sitting on the carpet chewing her cud, that was at times hard to swallow. Freda was so good when she had to go into the vet and would stand quietly, allowing Dom or Liz to take the bandage off and re-apply as long as she could suck my neck for comfort. This was fine – it was just the red marks around my neck could lead to embarrassing questions – especially at my age. Slowly the foot was coming forward and limited movement was coming back on the hock. We allowed ourselves to be optimistic.

* * *

It was a lovely summer and Derek was able to play most of the games booked for East Huntspill cricket team. As captain, he had to make sure that there were enough players for the two teams on the Saturday. Fridays, therefore, did seem to get rather fraught with phone calls from players saying, yes they could play or, no they couldn't, with Derek's mood swinging from good to bad, depending on whether he still had enough people to play.

He came back from one match telling me that the rest of the team were hoping to go to Australia to see the Ashes at Christmas. What did I think? I said I thought he would have a lovely time! There was no way that I wanted to go and put up with hot weather and with everyone talking about cricket. Equally, Mum was going to be on her own so it would be unfair for me to go. Happy that I didn't mind, Derek started to make plans for the big holiday.

* * *

The Randomised Badger Culling Trial (RBCT) came to an end and a meeting was held to discuss the findings. The meeting was held in London. It was not what the farming organisations wanted to hear. As I mentioned earlier, the reactive culling of badgers, where badgers were killed on farms where there was an outbreak of Bovine TB in the cattle herd, was stopped two years earlier as this was found categorically to make matters worse due to the movement of the remaining badgers. What they had found was that in the areas where as many badgers were removed as possible, the incidence of TB in cattle reduced by about 27 per cent. However, in the zones around the cull area the increase was almost the same, slightly more so as in fact the 'edge effect', as it was called, cancelled out any reductions from the internal area.

The Independent Scientific Group knew that this was going to cause a lot of complaining so they had all their data peer-reviewed and they also carried out an exercise to see if culling of badgers by the farmers instead of professional operators would make it financially viable and they found that this still remained non-viable. There are three statements from the conclusions of the RBCT by the Chairman of the Independent Scientific Group, Professor Bourne, which stay in my mind and these are:

Point 9: *'After careful consideration of all the RBCT (Random Badger Control Trials) and other data presented in this report, including an economic assessment, we conclude that badger culling cannot meaningfully contribute to the future control of cattle TB in Britain.'*

and

'... substantial reductions in cattle TB incidence could be achieved by improving cattle-based control measures.'

and, maybe the saddest of all the conclusions:

Point 13: *'The ISG recognises the difficulties faced by Government in implementing control strategies without full industry cooperation. It is unfortunate that agricultural and veterinary leaders continue to believe, in spite of overwhelming scientific evidence to the contrary, that the main approach to cattle TB control must involve some form of badger population control. It is our hope that DEFRA will embrace new scientific findings, and communicate these to these stakeholders in ways that encourage acceptance and participation.'*

There was a media frenzy and it was maybe sad that enough wasn't said of the 11,000 badgers that died to prove these figures and at a cost of £53 million of taxpayers' money. All of those badgers, which came from areas of high incidence Bovine TB in cattle, were given a postmortem and 85 per cent showed no signs of the disease.

As you can imagine, we all rejoiced at the findings. When the trial started in 1998, the agricultural leaders thought this experiment was going to be the best thing since sliced bread. They straightaway denigrated this experiment which was the largest ever held in the world on Bovine TB. In a few years, they and the government were to re-write it but just at that time we thought that at last, the badger, that had been the scapegoat for so many years, had been vindicated.

Labour took onboard the findings and badger culling was stopped by Hilary Benn.

Professor John Bourne CBE MRCVS, chairman of the Independent Scientific Group, quoted that he was reassured that Hilary Benn has taken the scientific route rather than the emotive one. He went on to say:

'Now farmers will realise the strength of the science and will recognise that culling has no part to play. They should now objectively, alongside government, consider the cattle control elements that we all know are absolutely essential as outlined in our report.'

It is so hard to fight historic mindset.

* * *

Two months on and Freda was now using all of her leg. Her movement on her hock and ankle had recovered and the foot that had been knuckling was now in the correct position. It was nothing short of a miracle from such a sad accident. We made arrangements for Freda to go to the Chestnut Centre in Derbyshire. There they had a fallow herd and for Freda, being tame, it meant that she would be popular with the visitors and yet have a fallow herd to live with.

It was my last walk with her around the Home Ground as the next day she was off to Derbyshire. In her usual way she ran ahead, and then returned but this time, she was going so fast towards me that she had to do what I call a prong dance to slow down, when all four legs go down on the ground at the same time. She was showing me that her legs were now so good, she would be fine. Driving up to Derbyshire with Freda, I was to meet Nikki for a few hours as she lived not far away. In fact, one of Nikki's fallow fawns from when she was at Secret World was also at the Chestnut Centre – a fawn called Teddy. We met in the car park and it was lovely to see her again. We had stayed in contact and she was now working for Macmillan as a fundraiser. I remember getting a request for a reference for her and writing saying how lucky they were to be getting her and writing it in glowing terms. There's only one thing Nikki doesn't do, I said in the reference – she doesn't do dusting!

Freda jumped down from the back of the car and Nikki and I walked her up to the reception. My little shadow snorted with excitement at the new surroundings and skipped alongside us, swishing her tail from side to side. Meeting the staff at the centre, they immediately fell in love with Freda who thought all the fuss was great. Now came the hardest part. To walk her to the shed that was nearby where the fallow herd came down to feed and lead her in, knowing that the door was about to be shut as I left her. Freda was going to have to stay. I heard her calling as we walked away and the clatter as she tried to push the door open.

One of the staff was going to take her a bottle to settle her after I had gone. They kindly rang to say she was fine and had polished off her bottle – so much for the emotional separation, but it did make me feel a lot better. I do know that although they never forget you, they move on with the changed circumstances. That's what they have to do in the wild. Within days, she had joined the herd and already had her favourites amongst the staff but to be honest, they all loved her. Perhaps she hasn't gone 'completely' back to the wild but she will not run the risk of being knocked down or shot by poachers. And I dare say, she will have every opportunity of having fawns of her own.

* * *

Mum, I think, was secretly pleased we were going to have Christmas just between the two of us. She wanted to go out for Christmas lunch so we didn't have to do any work and it was all booked up. I was having to do more for Mum as time had gone on and weekly trips to do shopping and hairdressers were the norm these days. The guardian angel was kept quite busy looking for parking spaces every week. We'd taken a couple of long weekends away as she had wanted to revisit places where we used to live and I enjoyed seeing the houses we had lived in. (Simon was quite upset when he went to visit Lowestoft to see the house where he was born to find it had been turned into a fish and chip shop!)

Dad being a policeman in the Kent police force meant that we had moved at least seven times during my childhood until they had moved to Somerset, when Dad retired. We would meet up with Mum's friend, Theo, whom she had known since school days, and it gave them chance to catch up with the news. As they had got older neither of them enjoyed travelling very much and apart from the few times away together, they kept in touch each week by phoning and having a chat.

Derek was busy organising all his packing. He loves the sun and the thought of being in gloriously high temperatures and watching cricket over Christmas was like a dream come true. Thin T-shirts and cricket whites were packed in an overflowing suitcase, although he kept telling me that there wouldn't be anywhere near as much to pack because he wasn't taking me!

With my Christmas totally planned for me, I waved goodbye to Derek as he joined the others on their way up to the airport. Unfortunately, England had already lost the Ashes before they had even got out there, but they were all going to enjoy themselves, come what may.

They flew to Melbourne to see the fourth test (which England lost) and had booked up for a boat trip for Christmas Day to include Christmas Lunch. Christmas Day dawned and it was the coldest day in the history of Australia, with frost on the roads. With hardly any jumpers between them, a fairly uncomfortable boat trip was spent trying to get warm, but I hazard a guess that once the alcohol had flowed, it wasn't quite so noticeable.

Flying on to Sydney for the fifth test (which England lost), they watched the match and then had some time before the New Year celebrations. Derek decided to go to Sydney Zoo – he'd always wanted to see a duck-billed platypus – so he went with Malcolm, another member of the cricket team who had travelled without his wife.

Wandering around, Malcolm saw some pigs and so they went over and Derek was in deep discussion showing off his knowledge of the different breeds of pigs. A lady in uniform came and asked them what they were doing, and Derek explained that they were looking at the pigs. They were both told quite sternly that they were in the children's section, where men unaccompanied were not allowed. Embarrassed at the situation they found themselves

'No unaccompanied men allowed in here!'

in, they hurriedly moved away and took a path that meandered around different enclosures. It wasn't until they realised they were looking at pigs again, that they realised they had wandered into the children's section once more. Looking around for any cameras, the shifty pair made a quick exit and decided that perhaps they had seen enough of the zoo in case they found themselves being arrested.

If there's one thing that Derek will remember from this holiday, it was the incredible display of fireworks celebrating the arrival of the New Year by Sydney Bridge. With everyone's excitement and the jubilation of thousands of people all sharing the experience, it was a night to remember.

* * *

The winter always seems to be at its worst in January with sub zero temperatures, frost and ice. With several cameras, I could watch the monitor in the kitchen either to see a badger basking under the heat lamp in a casualty pen as he recovered from an accident or see the otters going out and breaking the ice on their pond and swimming underneath the ice. I was always afraid they would get trapped underneath it, but they always found their way. Out on the side and a quick shake and they were off chasing each other. Their fur must be so dense to insulate them in such cold weather. In the cold, the fish would be a lot slower in rivers and lakes as they semi-hibernate, making themselves easy prey for the otters. No wonder they breed all year round as the temperature doesn't seem to bother them.

* * *

There had been quite a lot of storms in March and we had received call-outs to gannets. They are beautiful large white birds with a blue beak. They are about the size of a goose and often get blown in from the sea. Just found in the middle of a field they can be quite daunting with their large beaks. Unable to take off from the ground they need to be taken to a cliff so that they can catch the thermals and fly away. Gannets have that wonderful scissor-type action with their wings that changes them from a flying bird to a shape that almost looks like a dart as it enters the sea at over 70 miles an hour. The power is such that they can catch their fish and exit water at fantastic speeds. We always advise rescuers to put an elastic band over the beak if it is a large bird, as these 'bites' can really hurt. You certainly mustn't do it to a gannet, however, as they have no external nostrils because of the speed at which they enter the water.

We had a call from a resident in Brean, a seaside resort nearby, who has contacted us on other occasions for different seabirds that they have found. This one was leaning against the wheel of their 4x4 when they went out shopping. It was still there when they got back so they rang to say they would bring it in. They said they thought it was a fulmar, which is quite a large seabird that has a tube down the middle of its beak. If frightened, it has the ability to emit a horrible black smelly slime from this tube as a defence.

Judith, one of our animal carers, was on duty with me that Friday night and it was her who admitted the bird. Catching up with her later, she explained that she had put the bird in one of the casualty pens. Judith said it didn't look like a fulmar to her so she had looked in our bird book. The only one that it matched was an albatross. We both laughed. 'Well,' I said, 'Leigh is on tomorrow and he's good with identification of sea birds. We'll get him to have a look.'

The next morning, Leigh, Judith and I went to look at this unusual bird. Peering through the small viewing window of the casualty door, the bird stood up and spread its wings and it was obviously an albatross. Excited, we went upstairs and I called

Simon. Leafing through the bird book, we found that a single black-browed albatross lives on a nesting site of gannets in Scotland. For some reason, it must have been blown down here. I rang through to a retired vet, Dick Best, who is very into birds. I only got his answer phone but left a message to say that I had a bird I wanted him to look at and could he get back to me. In the meantime, we assessed the bird and checked its weight by the bird guide. It was a good weight and in very good condition so we were loath to keep it any longer than we had to.

We checked the tide times and found that high tide was at 4 p.m. that afternoon. We got permission to go onto Brean Down with a vehicle and contacted the Burnham Area Rescue Boat to see if they could help us. We wanted them to be under the cliff in case the bird went down into the sea rather than taking flight. Richard Austin came to take photos and I was videoing the event. Placing the albatross into a carrier we travelled into Burnham to meet up with the rescue boat guys. Then we all travelled down to Brean where they launched the boat and we went up on the cliff. Rumours had already got around that we were releasing an albatross and there were at least 50 people on the beach wanting to see it go.

Simon lifted the bird out of the carrier and placed it on the grass. It seemed unconcerned and just looked around. It would probably have never had any contact with humans before and had no fear of us. Simon then just lifted it by placing his hands underneath and the huge wings spread out and it started to rise. In my excitement, I dropped the camera and stood spellbound as within seconds this incredible bird was just a dot in the sky. At least Richard got some really good photos, which helped us identify the bird in the end.

The next morning I got a phone call from Dick Best. 'I understand you've got a bird you want me to look at,' he said, thinking that it may have been a parrot or buzzard.

'We had an albatross in yesterday and thought you would like to have seen it, but we've released it now,' I told him brightly.

'Oh, really,' he said, thinking, she doesn't know what she's talking about, I expect it was a fulmar.

'No, really,' I said, but I could tell he didn't believe me. 'I'll send you the photos.'

'OK,' he said, 'I'll get in touch with the chap in Bristol that records these things and get back to you.'

It was an hour later that Dick rang me back. 'It was an albatross,' he started.

'I know it was!' I said.

'Yes, but Pauline, it gets worse,' he said. 'That wasn't a black-browed albatross, it was a yellow-nosed albatross and has never been seen in Britain before.'

'Well, it might be worth noting that it was much happier when we put it in a grass pen rather an indoor pen ...'

'Pauline,' Dick struggled to make me realise the significance of what he was telling me. 'There are no words in the British language that will explain to you, that you will probably never, ever see another one ... and I missed it!'

I was contacted by a marine scientist on the Thursday wanting more information. Had I kept a feather? Er ... no. Had I taken a blood sample? Er ... no. Had I kept any faeces? It was time to say no again but then to add, 'I'm so sorry, we just didn't realise what kind of bird it was.' Still I was really pleased to hear him say that from our photos and from others taken by someone else, he could let us know that the yellow-nosed albatross was now over 800 miles away and still flying. So as far as I'm concerned, we did the right thing. We did have one twitcher who told us he would have paid us £10,000 to come and see it and mark it off in his book. But could you imagine keeping it in a pen overnight and finding it dead in the morning? It took Clinton Rogers, our local BBC news journalist, months to get over the fact that I didn't contact him!

It was rather sad really because our albatross somehow had got through the equator. Usually with the doldrums, they are unable to glide through. Now that he has, he will have to remain in the Northern Hemisphere as it is unlikely that he will make it back through to the Southern Hemisphere, where he really belongs.

I can remember seeing a programme on television with Carol Thatcher sitting by a cliff in Australia, covered in albatross pairs nesting. She spoke about how endangered these birds now are and that within five years all those birds that we could see would be gone. Many of them get caught on the floats of line fishing and many organisations are trying to educate countries to use floats that remain under the surface of the sea and don't attract the birds. I was saying this to the marine scientist and he said that on one expedition he went on – just on that one day, when the line fishing nets were brought in, over 200 dead birds were on the lines. What a high price to pay for our food.

* * *

Debbie, in her usual defiant manner, had signed herself up for the Steart Swim. This was another huge effort on her part to raise money for Secret World. Burnham-on-Sea is only just 'sea' as it is part of the Bristol Estuary and has the second highest tidal range in the world. This is why people joke that when the tide is out you can't see the sea. Many a parked car that appeared safe on the sand has ended up with the tide coming over its roof before the owner could move it.

The Steart Swim attracts many athletes as you have to swim from Burnham to Steart Island and back but it can only be done on a neap tide to give you time to go both ways. The water is still very cold so swimmers are advised to wear wet suits. The distance is 2.4 km. Debbie trained constantly at the local pool but didn't realise how restrictive a wet suit is and found it impossible to wear so decided to go without. There were over 50 people taking part. These were all being announced by what kind of an athlete they were, until they got to Debbie who was just 'from Secret World'.

The swim was hard but Debbie just managed to get to Steart Island in time to be able to still make it back to Burnham before the tide turned. Determined she was still going to do it, she started her way back. One of the organisers was alongside her in a boat on the way back making sure she didn't drift as he could see she was struggling. Derek had gone to watch, I couldn't because I was with Mum. Debbie's mum was also there watching with Derek.

'Is that her in the water there?' Debbie's mum asked, pointing to a dot in the distance.

'I hope so,' said Derek, 'because everyone else has finished!'

Last she may have been, but she completed the swim and is indebted to the person who kept encouraging her to make it. She never had chance to thank him. If there is one thing that Debbie would never do and that is to give up. She has been an amazing support for me.

* * *

Mum hadn't been feeling well and she was diagnosed with cancer. She tried some chemotherapy but had a bad reaction and decided that she didn't want to have any more. It was an aggressive form of cancer so the time we had together was limited. It's hard to watch someone going through their belongings and to listen to their wishes. Her one main wish was that she could stay and die at home and that was one thing I could give her as long as it was within my power. She was frightened and who wouldn't be when faced with that eventuality.

Mum continued in her own way but when she had an unexpected phone call telling her that Theo had collapsed and died the night before, it was as if her energy had gone. The roles reverse and child becomes the mother. The hardest part for me as we reached the end was controlling the pain.

'Where's my guardian angel now?' she asked one evening.

'Probably still looking for parking spaces,' I replied and we laughed and cried together.

There was three nights of getting doctors out to deal with the pain. We had gone from patches to a morphine pump very quickly and we still weren't on top of it. 'Why is it,' I complained bitterly, 'that an animal can come at one end of the house, in our hospital room, and I can put it out of its misery and yet I can't do it for my own mother.'

'I can turn the morphine pump up,' said the doctor, 'but it will compromise her breathing.'

'It doesn't matter,' I said exasperated. Forty-eight hours and it was over. It's a sobering thought to realise that we are now the older generation and times like this make us realise our own mortality. You take stock and my biggest fear was that I wouldn't be able to make Secret World secure before my time.

* * *

After doing wildlife for 20-odd years, you kind of think you have seen most animals, but Simon was to come back from a rescue in Weston with a common seal. Taking a quick look at him, we could see that he was underweight and had an infected mouth. Luckily we knew Andy and Gay Christie at Hessilhead Wildlife Rescue who have rescued quite a few seals up in Scotland and were a mine of information. Seals are such beautiful animals, I suppose because of their big eyes. While his mouth was so sore, it was easier to mix up a mackerel smoothie which we could gavage him with. Simon luckily had a smoothie machine which we were allowed to use and, strangely enough, he didn't want it back!

The hardest part of gavaging a seal is keeping him still. Their lovely big eyes belie the very large teeth that seals have and so it was definitely an animal to respect. One person needed to kneel with the seal between their legs, holding its head up. Using another syringe or a piece of wood as a 'gag', the seal bites it but is then unable to shut its mouth. Whilst this is the case, it's just a question of guiding the long tube down to the stomach of the seal and then syringing the mackerel smoothie straight into the stomach.

Sammy the Seal as he was named soon realised what we were doing and was very co-operative. With antibiotics, his mouth soon healed and he was then taking mackerel whole. By this time we had found a way of flooding the pen and giving him a dry area he could haul himself out on to. Sammy continued to improve and gain weight. With eight mackerel a day he was another expensive guest! We have a large fibreglass tank that Simon King had made to do some filming of swans. It has a glass panel on one side and filled with water it was ideal to put Sammy in for a swim about during the day.

Simon was passing the tank at lunchtime and Sammy saw him and made a terrible noise. Concerned that the seal was in pain, he radioed with some urgency that the seal was not well. We all rushed out only to find that the terrible noise was Sammy letting us know that we were half an hour late with his lunch! Gweek Seal Sanctuary in Cornwall only deal with grey seals and Sammy was still quite young and needed to go with other young common seals before being released.

They had some young seals at Hessilhead but that was a long way away. However, our fundraisers got in touch with Flybe to see if they would give a free plane ticket to the seal – and they did. Plus a couple of return tickets for Simon and a carer to accompany him, so they were really good. As you can imagine it was a lovely story that the local TV stations picked up. After a vet visit to make sure he was in good health, Sammy was crated up and was on his way to Scotland. When they reached Edinburgh airport, the stewardess's voice came over the speakers: 'Ladies, gentlemen and Sammy the Seal, welcome to Edinburgh airport. We hope you have enjoyed your flight with Flybe.'

In less than two hours, Sammy was in a tank and soon to join other friends. He would be going out to sea in a couple of months. One very lucky seal.

* * *

I was able to go to the International M.bovis Conference with Liz in Dublin. It was fascinating to hear about the problems of Bovine TB in the many countries worldwide. With representatives from all over the world, many in traditional costume, it was a very colourful reception on the first evening. Speaking to an African leader, in a wonderful garment of red and gold, he explained that although Bovine TB had been in his country for many years, their biggest concern was that through infected cattle and wildlife, it was now affecting the lions. This would have a knock-on effect on tourism so now they were having to monitor the problem more closely. Approximately 80 per cent of the human population in Africa test positive to Bovine TB. He explained that the custom of drinking blood and eating yoghurt is part of a custom to welcome a prominent visitor to a village and they have to be very careful not to offend by refusing their ritual. To do so would almost inevitably result in contracting the disease. It was such a simple statement and yet was so clearly showing the value of human life against tourism.

Different countries talked about the ways that they had eradicated TB from their countries. When this was discussed as an international problem in the 1990s Italy, Spain and many other countries took on the fact that the test that we use for cattle is a herd test and any cow testing positive would mean that the whole herd would be removed. In Italy, a speaker explained that many farmers, with the compensation they had received for their lost cattle, had diversified and turned to tourism and started to farm 'people' instead of cattle. Many of the regions in Italy are now TB free.

A speaker from America explained how they had started to give abattoir workers a financial incentive to report diseased carcases coming through. The infection rate of carcases reported increased by 60 per cent. DEFRA admit that almost 20 per cent of Bovine TB cases are found at abattoirs in this country, despite the fact that the cattle have been tested on a regular basis on farms. They had just remained false negatives. To stop a mechanised system and involve yourself in a lot of paperwork, especially if it's near going home time, is never going to be very attractive but if we gave a financial incentive, I wonder if we would find that the reported cases might increase.

In Canada, it showed the problems that they had with the white-tailed deer and how they gave grants to farmers to fence their feeding stations for cattle so that it kept the deer away. The speaker then showed a photograph of deer at the feeding station and that despite the long lengths of wire that were very high to stop the deer from jumping over, the double gates had been left wide open. You can do all the preventative measures possible, but human error will never stop this from happening.

Australia, well they are very gung ho. With many huge tracts of cattle grazing, cattle were corralled into makeshift pens and tested. Driving them in by using helicopters and 4x4s, if odd cattle were difficult to get into the pens, they just shot and killed them. If they tested positive, they just shot them there. With such expanses of land, transportation was out of the question. It was all very cold and calculated but given the circumstances, heat, distance and manpower, there really wasn't an alternative option.

New Zealand would tell their story of the possums. This is a non-indigenous species which carries the Bovine TB disease. Numbers were dramatically reduced by dropping poisoned bait by helicopter. This did cause a problem with the number of domestic animals, such as dogs and cats, that were inadvertently killed. But the possums were disliked by most people because they had been introduced to the country. Even then, with the reduction of the number of possums, they found that the remaining population were highly infectious and the government was having to turn to vaccination.

When it came to England, the Randomised Badger Culling Trial was detailed but more was made of the difficulty with killing badgers because they are an animal that is the emblem of all our Wildlife Trusts and carry such a high profile. It is obvious even in the level of worldwide conferences, politics plays a part and speakers are told what they can and can't say.

* * *

It was time for the otter cubs to go to their release site. As Somerset otters, they were to be released in Somerset. Colin Seddon was to find a landowner who was happy to have them released on his land. Most of the fields around our area have rhynes, channels of water, surrounding most fields and then draining into rivers. This was perfect as Colin could set up a large area with an electric fence around to contain the otters just for a few days until they had got used to their environment. A large rubber water container is put in the enclosure so that the otters can bathe during the days that they are contained. We have a large tube which is used as a feeding tube in their pen. It's just so that we can slide the food inside and the otters can go in after it. This then stops birds like crows coming and stealing the food before the otters wake up. So that was taken to the site and the otters were moved in their houses.

I had videoed them the night before and they sensed that I was there. They kept standing up on their hind legs and then diving into the water in fear, they just weren't happy for me to be there which is great. Now having followed them through their time with us we were going to film the last stage to their final release. Going in quietly so as not to disturb them, the wire gates were placed across the entrance. The sound of spitting as the bolts went across showed that the otters were indeed wild.

Loading them into our transporter with the feeding tube and food, Ellie and Colin took the otters to the site. On arrival, the houses were lifted over the fence and placed in the enclosure. Gates removed (to the sound of spitting again!) but no heads appeared. All was quiet. Because the site was close to us we were able to go every day to do the feeding. There is always the fear that they may bolt at the electric netting and go through. But they were still there that same night and for the subsequent nights until the side of the fence was taken down which ran alongside the rhyne.

The otters were microchipped when they were young. We will probably never know what happens to them unless they get killed on a road and are picked up to be taken to the research unit in Cardiff University. Certainly the food uptake stopped as soon as the otters were released. I feel we were so lucky to have been part of their lives, I know that three very healthy strong otters were released which should stand them in good stead for their survival. But they were free and that's what it's all about.

Note: A video is available which tells the story of Splish, Splash and Splosh and also many other rescues entwined in the story. It runs for 80 minutes and is called 'Raining Otters' of course!

8

Celebrities

A group of ducklings was brought into us by Mrs Williams who ran a garden centre. One of her ducks had hatched out three fluffy brown ducklings and six fluffy yellow ones. Nothing unusual in that, other than the fact that it was December. The duck had done the same thing last year and one by one the ducklings had died with the cold. Two of this year's brood had already died so she had tried to catch them, mother and all, but the duck had flown off.

We were happy to take them on but she wanted them back in the spring. I rang Richard as it is unusual to get ducklings at that time of year. He came to take the photo and because they were still very small, we put them in the sink in the bathroom and it made a lovely picture with the taps and the soap in between. The photo appeared in national newspapers and we got a call from a researcher asking if we would be prepared to take them up to London, so they could have them on the Alan Titchmarsh show. Alan very kindly did the foreword for our photographic book, which we published in 2005. The ducklings were being kept in an incubator so it made little difference to them to be transported. Derek and I went up to London and arrived at the studios in Wood Lane.

As with all these things, it's a long journey with loads of waiting around and a matter of minutes on the screen. But it all helps to promote the work that we do and because we run purely on donations, we have to make people aware of our Centre. We will only do these things if we are sure that it will not upset the animals concerned.

The researcher showed me where I had to be for the quick interview and they had supplied a paddling pool complete with plastic lilies! A matter of minutes before Alan Titchmarsh was coming over to talk to me, we placed the ducklings in the water and the loud *aahh!* from the audience meant he had to explain what was happening. The ducklings loved being in the water, apart from one character who was doing his best to attack a pink lily. Another did a long dive and underwater swim for a few seconds, which the cameras got a shot of so it was all a great success. These appearances do create a surge of interest on the website. Five minutes later and they were back in their incubator and busy preening their wet fluff. They then settled for the journey home and were soon back in the Hospital Room.

* * *

It was a similar situation when we were asked to take a young otter cub up to *The One Show*. His name was Torrent and he was almost as young as the triplets had been so he was in an incubator and still on milk. As his carer, he knew my smell and his life at that early age was just drink and sleep. I therefore had no problem with taking him up to the studio in London. I packed the milk, thermos flask for a hot water bottle refill as the incubator would not be running as we travelled. I also took fresh bedding, towels, newspaper to line the incubator – anyone having a baby will know how much you need to take with you. Derek was concerned as they had given out a snow warning but I was sure that, as I was going to be on the motorway most of the way, I would be fine.

Luckily I stopped off at Reading services, fed Torrent, changed his bedding, had a comfort stop and was back on my way. The programme started at 7 p.m. and they had asked me to be there for 5 p.m. I was just pulling off at Hammersmith which is, at most, four miles away from the studio, when it started to snow. The following four miles took me two hours so that I arrived in the car park at 7.10 p.m. with the researcher desperately trying to find me. Quickly making my way to the studio, I mixed some warm milk and was called onto the set. The time it had taken me to get to the studios meant that Torrent was now ready for his bottle again. Christine Bleakley, Mike Dilger (who I had filmed with before) and James Corden were fascinated to see Torrent settle for his bottle and then squirm onto his back and look at everybody – a lovely shot for the camera. Then it was the end of the show, and the crew asked if I wanted to be put up in a hotel as the snow was falling so fast. I said I would rather get on my way and having finished feeding Torrent, with a fresh hot water bottle in the incubator and renewed flasks, I set off at 7.45 p.m.

I had totally misjudged the situation. I managed to get on to the motorway but that took over an hour just to go four miles. The radio reports were busy saying that even all the hotels were booked in London as people were giving up trying to get home. My satnav suggested I came off the motorway so I did, but I was then caught up in a slow-moving queue with no idea of where I was going. Eventually, two hours later I saw the motorway and decided to go back on, as at least, knowing the M4, I would have an idea of where I was. I was only the next exit on from where I had come off! Lorries were parked on the emergency lane as they had run out of driving hours, cars were abandoned and it took me four hours to get to the Reading services, which should only take 40 minutes. It was now 2.30 a.m.

Turning into the services I could see that articulated lorries were trying to get through the car park because in the lorry park, the lorries were all at a standstill. Quickly feeding Torrent, who was lovely and warm, I then decided to get out of the services but only just in time as I could see that the entrance was now completely blocked.

Driving slowly, I followed the single lane of traffic travelling slowly along the motorway. The snow was really collecting on the other lanes and it was just the odd broken-down vehicle that now and again, we had to drive around. I finally arrived home just after 5 a.m. Even the next day traffic was at a standstill in London with so many people having stayed overnight and now trying to get home. It wasn't a journey I would ever wish to repeat!

* * *

Richard Austin was always looking for that special photo for Valentine's Day. He was chatting to me on the phone and asked if we had a dormouse in care at the moment as he thought that a photo of a dormouse asleep on a red rose would look really good. As it happened, we did have a dormouse that had been brought into us only a month before. A lady had taken her dog out for a walk and thought that he had discovered a ball when he pawed at something under the hedge. It did look like a ball, but as she came closer she could see that it was a ball of moss tightly woven but the disturbance had broken the 'ball' open and there inside was a sleeping dormouse.

Through looking after dormice for Doug, when he was alive, I knew that this is what they do in the winter. Having reached the right weight to survive through the winter, they come down from the branches where they normally live and hibernate in a ball close to the roots of the hedge. The lady picked up the bedding and dormouse and brought them out to us as she was concerned that the hibernation ball had been destroyed. When this happens, we check the dormouse over and as long as it hasn't been harmed, we put bedding of fine hay in a wooden box in a plastic container and keep it in a cold room. They soon weave a fresh nest and settle to sleep. We leave fresh water and a few sunflower seeds and peanuts and check every day to see if any food has gone. Normally they will sleep through to the spring and then we can return them to their original habitat.

When we were open to the public and we had several pens with dormice in, at Christmas time we often showed children the dormice sound asleep and snoring and they would be fascinated. We used to talk about the animals that normally sleep through the winter and not have a Christmas like they did. We would show them the dormice, the bats – Himmy and Bertha – and a hedgehog. Then the children would go and see Father Christmas (Derek) and they were given the materials to make a fat seed bell so that they could make one and put it out for the birds on Christmas Day.

So I really had no problem with helping Richard get his photo. He arrived with his solitary red rose. He had clipped the petals from the centre of the rose so that the dormouse would fit into it. Using a black sheet as a background, I got him to sort out his focus, light and everything else before I even went and got the dormouse. Once he was ready, I went and got the tank, carefully pulled the hay back and gently lifted the dormouse out. He was quite cold as they manage to reduce their heart rate and drop to a low temperature so that they use hardly any energy. I was careful not to keep him in my hand for long as I didn't want the dormouse to start warming up. I placed him on the rose. There was a click, click, click and it was over. Placing the dormouse back in the hay, I moulded it around the dormouse and placed him back in his wooden box and took the container back into the cold room. He never even woke up.

Richard was really pleased. The photo was stunning and he managed to get it into a national newspaper on Friday 13th February. That evening, I was watching the late Jonathan Ross show and he was talking about Valentine's Day. 'Tonight,' he spoke to the camera, 'I am going to show you a beautiful picture.' Lo and behold the screen was full of the photo of the dormouse on the rose. 'Now,' he went on, 'if you haven't remembered to get a Valentine's card for your loved one tomorrow, you can go to my website, download the photo and send it.' Richard was livid but I thought it was quite funny.

That was until the following Thursday when I had a visit from two policemen. They had received four complaints from viewers re the photograph of the dormouse as it is illegal to disturb a dormouse while it is hibernating. This had placed them in a difficult position and it took four hours of police time to eventually resolve the problem that as the dormouse was being rehabilitated, they didn't think that the law applied. But they wanted me to know that I had wasted four hours of police time, for which I apologised profusely.

Not one to miss a trick, I then sent out our photographic book to Jonathan Ross explaining the trouble he had got me in. The next week, the photograph came back on the screen. Jonathan Ross said, 'You probably remember this photo that I showed you last week. Well, evidently Secret World where the dormouse is living were raided [using his w instead of the r] by the police. I do apologise for the trouble I caused ...,' and he winked.

And that's why in that year, our first badger cub was called Jonathan.

* * *

So the kitchen crew for this year were named by the people who found them. The kitchen crew of bottle feeders was nine so it was a busy two months with black and white things charging around the kitchen. Their favourite place to play is in the old fireplace that is full of cones, which are duly strewn across the floor. As the later cubs added don't have to be handled very much, it is better to pick them up very quickly by the scruff of the neck, or otherwise to throw a towel over them to get them back in the cubby hole once it has been cleaned out.

We had been contacted by the agent who represented Johnny Kingdom, someone who is well known by many who have followed his series on television. They wanted to do some filming with the cubs, talk about the protocol that our cubs go through and later in the year see them being released. Johnny is quite a character and drives a very distinctive jeep. With his hat covered in badges and feathers on one side, his appearance matches his reputation. He was a grave digger and a poacher to name but a few of his jobs but he is very much a countryman especially loving his badgers and the red deer.

The film crew came late morning so that they could first of all film the cubs asleep in the cubby hole. The cubs were basically a badger heap, with only one laid on its back further away. Johnny was enchanted when he saw them because even in his long life in the country, he had never seen badger cubs that young. Shirley, his wife, was with him so the kitchen was pretty crowded with the film crew as well.

We all enjoyed a cup of coffee and a chat until it got to the time of the next feed. Most of the cubs by now were weaned but Lilly and Billy, two cubs from Staffordshire, were still having bottles so the board was taken away and the cubs tumbled out into the kitchen. The main problem with filming is all the bags that the cameras have been in and new feet. It's just like putting a new toy in the middle of a room at a nursery. We had moved the table and chairs out to give us more room and soon the cameraman was getting some really nice shots of them playing with the cones. The towel and teacloths were pulled down from the hooks and bundled under their chins as they backed towards the armchair just as they would if they had collected bedding in the wild. Johnny was mesmerised.

There were a few puddles to clean and the cubby hole as well needed attention, with me on my hands and knees trying to clear up but hanging on tightly to the bucket which had the disinfectant in it. Ella, quite a large female cub, managed to fall in so it was a quick rescue and a rub with a towel. One of the cameramen went to stroke one of the cubs. Quickly, I said, 'I wouldn't touch them! That one in particular has only been picked up to feed and you can get quite a nip. They may look cuddly but they are wild animals.'

The one thing that fascinated the badgers was the microphone boom with the large fluffy muffle on it that could, quite easily, be mistaken for another badger. I sat in the feeding armchair having recovered from the quick dip of the drenched cub plus the wet floor. Now this is quite entertaining as although Billy and Lilly were the only ones having a bottle, all the others would have a bottle given half the chance and knew what me sitting in this chair meant. It was a question of scruffing Lilly or Billy who immediately made their way to the chair. Then I had to keep moving my knees from side to side to stop other cubs from wriggling up on to my lap. There would be the occasional successful one that immediately tried to push the cub I was feeding off the teat and I had to quickly scruff the cub and put it back down on the floor.

This totally amused Johnny who was asking questions about the testing that we do and the process that the cubs go through until they are old enough to be released. 'I haven't got many badgers in my wood now, would they be able to be released there?' Johnny asked. 'No, I'm sorry,' I replied smiling, 'they have to go to somewhere away from other badgers as, if we put them into an existing territory, they may be injured by the other badgers.'

'Well,' he said, 'I would love to see them going to their release site in the autumn.'

'That would be fine,' I replied, 'you will be able to see all the work that goes into finding them a new home.'

'I look forward to it,' said Johnny.

* * *

It was not a good year for badgers. Elin Jones of the Welsh Assembly was to bring in an Intensive Action area. Badger culling was back on the agenda despite the RBCT findings. It just didn't make sense. We started a Black and White Campaign to fight on behalf of the badger. Why, after everything that had gone before, were we back to where we had started? I contacted as many celebrities as I could to see if we could start a campaign. A petition was started against the Welsh cull and we wanted to bring as much attention as possible to what was happening.

Together with Wildlife Aid and Care For The Wild, we met in London to protest outside the Houses of Parliament. Several of the staff were with me as we arrived from the tube station complete with photos on placards of celebrities who supported our stance. Chris Packham, Simon King, Nick Baker, Chris Tarrant, Jilly Cooper, to name but a few. We were meeting the ITV camera crew and Jenny Seagrove was joining us for the photos.

Marie and Leigh were with me as we met up with some others and made our way to outside the Houses of Parliament. Marie tugged at my sleeve, 'Pauline, there's a policeman over there that wants to speak to you – and he's got a gun!'

Turning around, I saw the policeman beckoning to me. 'You are not allowed to march and protest outside the Houses of Parliament unless you have permission,' he said very officially.

'We're not protesting, we're just meeting a television crew,' I innocently replied.

'They are placards that you are holding, so I consider you are protesting and it isn't allowed within a mile of the Houses of Parliament unless you have permission,' came back the stern reply.

'Well, where do we go to get permission?' I asked.

'Permission has to be applied for by writing to a special department and then there has to be at least a week for processing.'

'But,' I countered and pleaded, 'we've agreed to meet an ITV film crew here.'

'Madam, believe you me, you are already on camera and if you continue to protest, there will soon be a bigger police presence and you will be arrested.'

'OK!' I replied, and moved off to catch up with the others.

'What did he say?' asked Leigh and Marie.

'He said we would be arrested if we continued to be outside the Houses of Parliament with our placards but let's face it, what do they say? There's no such thing as bad publicity?' I replied and then saw the others that we were meant to be meeting, including Jenny Seagrove and the film crew.

So having let everyone know the situation, we all decided to go ahead with it and with banners and placards raised we were filmed and had photos on the famous piece of grass just outside the entrance of the Houses of Parliament. There were only about 15 of us so, if indeed we had been 'watched by security cameras', they must have felt we were hardly worth bothering with – much to our relief, although I secretly think Leigh and Marie were hoping to be arrested!

It was definitely a success as our protest went out on both local channels and was in the papers too. The one thing that amused me was the report that there were approximately 150 of us. Not sure where the others were, but they weren't with us. As far as the media is concerned, 'It's not really true', does come to mind.

We were certainly going to do our best to protect the badger against culling. Science so clearly showing us that it was a waste of time. The money would be better spent on research for a vaccine for cows and better compensation to farmers. When a reactor cow is killed, the farmer gets paid for the cow, but you have to remember that the rest of the milk production in the cow's lactation period is lost. The cost of the calf that is inside the cow is all part of the farmer's projection in his income and expenses. To grow a replacement from your own stock takes four years and the extra cost of feeding cattle whilst the farm is under restriction can also be another expense. Compensation, however, should only be given to farmers running their farms correctly and with biosecurity against infection in place. Remember, the countryside is mainly 'farmed' and that's where our wildlife lives. Farming and wildlife are reliant on each other, farmers should remember that in the way that they choose to farm and we should encourage them. It may be 'our' countryside but it is also 'their' living.

* * *

Derek was busy getting leaflets out – the spring is always the busiest time for this. Loaded up with boxes and boxes of leaflets, he was visiting so many places each day, making sure that the display stands were full of up-to-date information. He wasn't enjoying his job really, they kept changing the systems and bringing in hand-held computers to record every stop that they made, the number of leaflets they have to put in and it all has to be done in the order they are given. This sounds pretty straightforward but going like Derek does, over the Quantock Hills, there are many places that the signal doesn't get through and until the 'dear little' hand-held computer updated itself, he couldn't move on to the next record. They therefore had to continue with all the paperwork as well as the hand computer until they sorted the teething problems. Very annoying and all extra work. He hadn't left in the best of moods that day and perhaps hadn't been thinking when he drove off from the farm. Making his way towards the M5 Derek wasn't to know that he was about to make the biggest leaflet drop ever. Driving on to the roundabout just before the motorway, the side door of the van, which he had failed to lock when loading, flew open and a series of boxes winged there way haphazardly as he took the bends. Noticing a flurry of leaflets from his side mirror and a sudden draught, he decided to go right around the roundabout, rather than take the exit on to the motorway, in order to

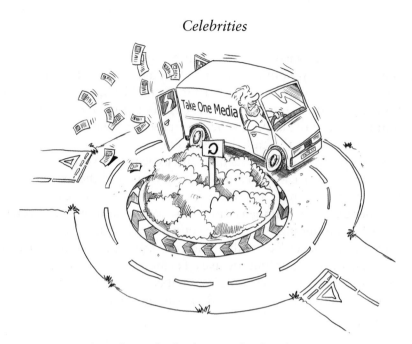

Derek made the biggest leaflet drop ever.

find out what had happened. Derek then realised that he had indeed left a trail of boxes (which he had quite rightly mentioned before that they weren't as securely taped like they used to be) that had spilt and all the leaflets had become a snowstorm.

As with all these things these days, there is always someone around taking photos and within minutes, images of Derek picking up the leaflets, together with the police and a few other people feeling sorry for him, were up on the Burnham-on-Sea website. A very unhappy Derek returned to reload, not amused with all the phone calls he had received from jovial friends.

* * *

Reception took a call from a woman whose son had just been cycling across the moors. He had come over one of the bridges and noticed there were lots of duck bodies in the water, about 20 or 30, which all sounded very odd. I said I would go down and have a look. When I arrived, a small white ferret was running along the side of the road and it immediately came up to me so I picked it up. Not having a box with me, I held on to her and went to look by the side of the bridge. There were easily 30 bodies of chickens and ducks, and several feed bags that were tied with string floating in the water. On the side of the bridge there was a cage half in and half out of the water with another three ferrets inside. They were alive but they were standing on a thick carpet of putrefied bodies of chickens and a dead cat.

I rang back to the Centre and asked Simon to come and join me and to bring a box for the ferrets. I then rang the police call centre and was told they were too busy to attend. I received the same reply from the RSPCA. Simon arrived with the cage and a camera so that he was able to take photos. While we were there, the Environment Agency arrived as the woman had contacted them as well. Simon went back with the cage with the dead chickens and ferrets. I stayed behind until the guys from the Environment Agency managed to hook in the floating bags as I wanted to see if they had anything alive in them. They didn't, thank goodness, but they were full of even more putrefied chicken and duck carcases. There were easily remains of over 100 animals.

When I got back, Simon had got the ferrets into a clean pen. They had emptied the carcases out of the cage but left the cage out by our burning pen. We did a press release with some photos and sent it out to local media to see if anyone would come forward with any information. When our weekly paper came out, a lady in Bridgwater rang to say that her daughter had gone to a house in Bridgwater to buy some ducks. She had gone with her boyfriend and they had seen dead animals. The lad had seen some rabbits in the back of the van. Her daughter had actually bought more ducks than she wanted as she didn't like the way that they were being looked after. She gave me the name and address that had been on a card in a pet shop.

Luckily the story went out in the national papers and a special operations officer of the RSPCA, Rob, saw the story. He rang to see if he could come down to see me and I agreed. When he arrived, I went through everything that had happened and showed him the cage that the ferrets had been in. I had noticed that it had an Exeter market ticket number. Rob took a photo of the cage and asked me not to get rid of it. Taking the ticket number down and the date, he was able to get in touch with Exeter market and find out the name of the person who had bought that lot. It was the same name and address as the one that had been given to me by the woman in Bridgwater.

Rob was able to get a warrant to search the house and arrived there just after midday. He was there until midnight cataloguing animals with a vet, many of which had to be put to sleep as they were in such bad condition, others were taken to the RSPCA centre at West Hatch subject to prosecution. They were unable to connect the man with all the dead bodies in the river, but the man was prosecuted and found guilty of animal cruelty (not the first time, I might add) and hopefully will never be allowed to have animals again.

* * *

Red deer are mainly upon the Quantock Hills and we don't see many of them as casualties or orphans. The male is called a stag or a hart and the female a hind. The young are called calves and definitely do have the long face as we see in the calves of cattle. Deer are ruminants, meaning that there are two processes to eating their food. They have four compartments to their stomach, the first part stores the food and healthy micro-bacteria break down a lot of the food, which is absorbed by the deer. The remainder is the 'cud', which the deer regurgitates and chews. The second section is like a filter and the third part acts like a sponge and draws off excess water before it finally reaches the last section where it is absorbed in the same way as our stomachs work.

The rut is carried out in the autumn, where the males clash with their antlers and fight using their front legs. Once the hierarchy has been set the dominant male will gather his harem, which may be as many as 50 females. Once the mating is over, the males will cast their antlers and they grow again in the spring. They are made of bone and can grow up to 2.5 cms a day. At this time, the antlers are covered in velvet, which is rich in blood and vitamins to help the antlers grow at such a rate. The bone is not solid but is honeycombed so there isn't as much weight to it as you would imagine.

The velvet will remain on the antlers for five months until the bone cells die and the velvet falls off the antlers. Although stags will be seen rubbing their antlers on trees, it is not because it is itchy because by now all the tissue is dead so there would be no sensation. They do rub trees to mark them with their scent and also to strengthen their neck muscles. In captivity, red deer will live up to 20 years but in the wild the average age would be 10–13 years once they have survived their first year. Red deer are the largest earth-living mammal in Britain and are the fourth largest deer species in the world, so a stag with its magnificent antlers is a big size to contend with. Historically, drawings of them have been found in caves 40,000 years old, so a species that's been around a long time!

Usually we might only get one red calf a year. A young male had been brought into us and he was in the kitchen with some roe kids. Although they were nearly five weeks old, the red calf was bigger than them and yet was under a week old. We were just giving Freddie, as we had called him, time to get used to the feeds before we moved them down to the Millie building, where we had a fawn unit. He was very docile because again, like the fallow, they follow their mother. Within two weeks he would be strong enough to join the herd.

The late night bell went and luckily, although it was nearly midnight, I was still up. When I got outside, I met an RSPCA inspector who had been called out to a red calf that had impaled herself on a metal fence post. The Wildlife Unit at West Hatch isn't open after 9 p.m. so the only alternative she had was to get the calf somewhere or put it to sleep. She knew that we accepted casualties all through the night, so brought her to us. The calf was quite lively and was about five weeks older than the little boy that was up in the kitchen. Simon came and helped me move her down to a deer unit in the Millie block. She remained laid down. Covering her head, I was able to clean the wound which was under her front left leg. The wound went right up to the bone and was a horrible star shape where it had split the skin. Packing the wound with gel to keep it moist, I covered it and also gave her some pain relief. Uncovering her head and leaving a bowl of milk in front of her and the infrared lamp above her to keep her warm, we had done as much as we could for the night. The pen had the window blocked out so even in the morning she should be in darkness, which will keep her still.

The next morning she was still quite quiet but I was relieved to see that she had drunk all her milk. When a calf is older, it's more difficult to get them to feed. They aren't so trusting, so hoping they will lap is the best scenario. I made an appointment to take her to the vet later that morning. Simon came with me as she was quite heavy to carry.

Meeting Liz at the surgery, she really wasn't happy with the wound. It was directly underneath the front leg and the continual movement of the leg was going to make the healing of the wound very difficult indeed. Liz didn't think we could take it any further. I pleaded that the calf had drunk her milk and that we did have a younger red deer to keep her company. So the decision was made to stitch as much of the wound together and just to leave a hole for me to manage. We were facing the problem that the stitching could easily break down if the skin died and also whether she was going to let me continually dress the wound every day. But we decided to give it a go. We brought her home still woozy from the anaesthetic and with a huge bandage around her body and the top of her front leg.

While she was a little bit sleepy, we brought Freddie down to introduce him to his new girlfriend. Nuzzling her, he sniffed and then sat by her side. They became inseparable but when we had to take him for a walk to exercise his legs, she would call for him until he came back to her. We managed to deal with the wound on a daily basis, but it was a case, yet again, of someone's neck being nuzzled with the inevitable red marks!

Michaela Strachan was filming with us for a series called *Animals and People* and they were really pleased to follow the tale of the female red deer who by now was called Chaela. Michaela was following a lot of the stories of orphans that staff and volunteers were caring for. She is really nice and she and the film crew would sit and have lunch with the staff in the courtyard.

As time went on we were able to open the door out to the fawn enclosure and just put hurdles against the door so all the fawns could come and see Chaela and Freddie. We still had to restrict the amount of movement that she had and the wound was healing so well.

At last that awful wound was completely healed. The two then went and joined the other youngsters out in their paddock. It was a real success story.

* * *

We are lucky that most of our pens in the Millie block have cameras. These allow us to monitor certain casualties without them being able to see us. Some of the cameras go live on to our website so people can watch what is going on. The camera hadn't been changed yet from in the deer pen when Chaela and Freddie had moved outside.

Judith, one of our animal carers, radioed through to me to ask if the camera was still on.

'Yes,' I replied.

'Oh,' said a little voice.

'Are you alright?' I questioned.

'Yes,' Judith replied, ' I just ducked in there to change from my fleece to a T-shirt because I was hot, and hadn't thought about the camera ...'

'Never mind,' I replied sarcastically. 'If the donations online go up, we might get you to do it each day!'

* * *

We had a group of foxes that unfortunately had become infected with sarcoptic mange. This is an awful illness caused by an infestation of mites that burrow under the skin and create horrendous itching. If it manifests itself over the whole of the body the animal is eventually so ill, it is unable to hunt and feed and slowly dies. The group could quite easily have caught it from a fox in the wild coming close to them in their enclosure. It was a matter of having to round them all up and treat them. The problem with this mange is that it is zoonotic, which means it can be passed to humans. I started to itch a few days later and slowly came to the conclusion that I must have contracted it and I would need to go to the doctors and get something for it.

'And what's the matter with you?' the kindly doctor asked.

I explained that I thought I had contracted sarcoptic mange from some foxes that we had in.

'What do you treat that with?' he asked.

'Well, we usually use ...,' I replied.

He tapped the keys of his computer and read the screen. 'Oh, no,' he said, 'you can't use that, it's for animals.'

I stayed silent, completely bemused.

'Now,' he said, scrolling down the screen, 'scabies and crabs [a complaint usually of the pubic hair], they are all the same thing, this should do the trick.'

Oh great, I thought, I'm now going to be given a prescription for something that no woman is going to want to admit to having.

'Right,' he continued, 'this is a tube of cream. You have to cover the whole of your body but not your face. Sleep with it on during the night, and then shower. You will need then to wash all your bed linen.'

'What about my husband?' I enquired.

'Your husband?' the doctor seemed confused.

'I sleep with my husband,' I said.

'Oh,' he now understood. 'I will make it two tubes.'

I thanked him and left. I decided to go to a chemist where they didn't know me and furtively handed over the dreaded prescription.

In true professionalism, the assistant handed me the bag without a glimmer of a smile. Perhaps my secret was safe.

That evening, I decided not to broach the subject with Derek who had been unaware of the situation but by the time I made coffee just before we went to bed, I had to explain.

'Oh,' he said shuddering, 'I thought I'd been itching.'

'No, you haven't,' I said. 'You're making that up. You would have said if you had. Now I've put my cream on and if you can do my back then I can do yours.' I passed him my tube, which I had used to cover all of my body and yet still had almost a third left.

'There,' I said after he had finished. 'This is your tube, but you might as well use the rest of mine up first but don't forget, don't put it on your face.'

By the time the request came for me to do his back, my tube was completely empty and there was very little left in the other tube to do his back.

There were a few 'bloody animals' and a couple of moans but I thought I had got away without any major complaints. We both got into bed and turned the lights out.

After a few minutes of silence ... 'My legs are sticking together,' came the unhappy voice.

'That's because you probably put too much cream on,' I patiently replied.

'Are you sure we weren't meant to put it on our faces?' came the voice again.

'Yes.' Another few minutes of silence.

'Are you sure we weren't meant to put it on our faces?' came the voice again.

'Positive.'

'I can feel them crawling up my face into my eyebrows and ...'

'One more word, just one more word, and I shall move into the spare room.'

Four minutes later and he was snoring so loud, I couldn't get to sleep.

We both showered the next day and all the bedding was washed and it did solve the problem. But Derek told me when he got back from work that he had been itching 'all day'!

* * *

Johnny Kingdom's manager got in touch with me about the badger cubs. They didn't want to follow the release as very little of the badgers is seen. They are carried to the site in cages covered with blankets and literally fed into the setts just by removing the end of the cage, which is facing the entrance of the sett, so that they can run inside. The decision was made to come out a week later while they were still enclosed in the area around the sett. They wanted to film the landowner putting the feed down for them and then to watch and see if the badgers came out as it started to get dark. Johnny does filming himself but this site was one that belonged to a keen group of people who like to watch badgers and they had built an elevated tree house so they could watch in comfort.

So the film crew went up in the hide and filmed Johnny coming from the Land Rover with his camera and stand, and talking to me and Sarah, who had come to feed them, as we walked towards the enclosure. We were all miked up. Pausing by the side of the area, Johnny asked Sarah what she was going to do and then said to me, 'Well, if we set up here, we may be lucky to see them coming out.'

We both stood and watched as Sarah switched off the electric fence, climbed over and spread the food around. Returning over the electric fence, she switched it back on. Standing all together, Johnny now was whispering. 'So,' he said very quietly, 'how long do you think, before they start to come out?'

'Fairly soon,' said Sarah, and we stood waiting in silence. The midges were starting to bite but we soldiered on. Very quietly, Johnny set up his camera and got it resting on the legs. 'This,' he said whispering, 'is so exciting. We are hoping to see some of those tiny cubs that we watched in Pauline's kitchen.'

Just then a black and white face appeared at the sett entrance. Hesitant, it waited and sniffed the air. 'Yes!' Johnny said in an excited whisper, 'I can see one and I think it's coming towards me.' He checked the view through his camera and moved it forward slightly. 'It's still coming, I can't believe that ... and yes, there is other one!' and he moved the camera and legs forward again.

All of a sudden there was a crack, Johnny was jumping up and down with his arms crossed and hands under his armpits. 'Ooooh, f***!' he said, and he wasn't whispering. The badgers shot back down the sett. Johnny had moved his camera forward and the legs had touched the electric fence. Regaining his composure, a trooper indeed, he carried on. Amazingly, the badgers did come out a bit later so all was not lost. It was practically pitch dark before the film crew came down from the hide very jubilant in the footage they had got.

'Did you see me get that f***ing electric shock?' said Johnny.

'Got the lot,' the cameraman said with his thumbs up. And would you believe it – they did indeed show the whole thing in his programme!

* * *

Wintertime is the best time for me to do talks and I had been invited to give a talk in Essex. Several members of the Badger Group in that area were going to attend. It was in the days of slides. I don't work from notes and tend to use the photos as prompts. Whether I was tired or not, I don't know, but I was busy talking about cormorants and Vanessa, from the audience, called out, 'Is that a white cormorant?' I then realised that I was talking to a slide of a gannet. I apologised and at least the audience laughed.

At break time, Vanessa came over and said, 'I hope you didn't mind me correcting you.'

I laughed. 'I really didn't realise I was saying the wrong bird. I must be getting old.'

'That's alright. It's like you said that hedgehogs have to be at least 500 kilograms to be able to hibernate, but I'm sure they knew you meant grams!'

I put my hand over my mouth, 'Did I really?'

'Yep,' she gloated.

I made sure in the second half that I corrected the weight given for hedgehogs to hibernate before people started to order artic lorries to bring hedgehogs down to us.

* * *

And when I got home, I was sure I heard rattling of saucepans. The glis glis from years ago had died and everything had been quite quiet for years. I knew that there were glis around as we often found a tail, rather like a squirrel's tail and obviously not as tasty as the glis itself, which was the remnant of Gremlin's nightly patrols. I pulled open the drawer where we keep the dog food and bowls and a glis was sitting right in the middle of the drawer blinking with the sudden light. He sat tight, looking around and then up at me.

I quietly closed the drawer.

9

Highs and lows

E ven when we were open to the public and when Nikki was still with us, we had a supporter called Bill Harrison. Bill was a famous healer and had his own home and sanctuary in Wedmore. He often had workshops and this would be for people and for animals too. We sometimes took our resident animals and our pets for healers to lay their hands on.

Now I have to be honest, I don't have a strong belief in these things, hence why Bill would often call me Thomas (doubting Thomas from the scripture). I have an open mind and do believe that there are things in life that cannot be explained away and certainly many people followed Bill and his work. In a way, I think the very fact of having empathy with animals, caring for and helping them is a quality that we don't all have and maybe there is a 'psychic' side to what we do. Certainly I believe that you can't teach empathy and you either have it or you don't.

I can look at a mammal and will be able to tell if it is ill, maybe how much fight that animal has and there are times when I will call it a day when I know that I could do more for an animal, because I know that it has given up. Equally there have been animals that I have gone further with than I would normally do, just because, from their eyes, I can tell that they still have the fight to survive and I will do all that I can. I can't do that with birds so I have always said when doing our Wildlife First Aid courses: do what you know you can do best. There's no shame in not trying to do everything.

Having said that, I once visited the RSPB reserve at Dungeness in Kent with a friend, a keen bird man. At the reserve they have a fantastic viewing area with telescopes so that you can see all manner of waders and sea birds enjoying the habitat that suits them so well. Using the telescope, I scanned the horizon while my friend proudly waited for me to exclaim at the variety of birds foraging and flying in.

Having finished my viewing, I turned and said, 'There's a cormorant over there that's not very well,' pointing in the distance.

Exasperated, he looked down the telescope. 'Where?'

'Over there, just where there's a sand bank – to the left. I can tell from the way that it's standing.'

'I can't believe, out of the thousands of birds that you could have looked at, you go and find one that's,' and he signalled his fingers to denote speech marks, 'not feeling very well!'

'There you go,' I said, 'it's just one of those things.'

Needless to say he has never taken me to another bird reserve.

Bill Harrison often did evenings of clairvoyance in aid of Secret World in Burnham-on-Sea and it was fascinating how he was able to tell people about themselves and sometimes family members. I know many people don't agree with such things but, like religion, if it gives people an inner strength, there can be no harm in it.

Sadly Bill committed suicide. I am sure there were so many people who had been helped by him in so many ways, who would have dearly wished to have supported him at this crossroads but it was not to be. It was because of his love of Secret World that the annual Healing Weekend, held normally at his sanctuary, was hosted by us and it took place on our home ground. All manner of workshops, fortune telling, mystical items, natural potions, jewellery, clothing and crystals filled huge marquees. Butterflies, banners and feather dream catchers fluttered in the wind and the smell of incense drifted over the site. A continual programme of healing, music and entertainment filled the three-day event. The weather was fantastic and many ladies wore floating summer dresses and flower garlands in their hair. There was also a Mr Whippy ice cream van, which necessitated several visits by me to the event.

Simon was patrolling the event on his bike with Rocky the Great Dane in hot pursuit. There were many wary looks from people queued up at the burger van when Rocky decided to join the queue. He is the epitome of the dog in the Scooby Doo cartoon but there was still that natural concern because of his huge size. Simon dearly loved the gentle giant but Rocky still had a real problem with self-harming by chewing his feet. Simon really had to keep an eye on him because, in a matter of minutes, Rocky would make his feet bleed and although poor Simon had tried everything, there seemed to be no pattern as to why he did it. He had taken him to an animal behaviourist, had sought veterinary advice and a dog training programme – all sadly to no avail.

It was probably my second trip up to the event (for an ice cream) when I walked past the tent where they were doing 'Healing for pets'. A friend near the entrance recognised me and called me over. We stood chatting and I took the opportunity to see inside the tent where different photos of animals that had been treated by this guru were on show. There was soothing music being played and soft rugs covered the floor, obviously to make the patients feel at home. A windbreak (like you see on the beach) had been set up to give privacy to the client and their pet. I could see that the lady was busy talking to them and then realised that I recognised the back of the head and shoulders of the client together with the back view of the dog's head – both at the same height. Rocky turned his head and I'm sure if he could have done, he would have winked. I withdrew and went and got my ice cream. Anything is worth a try!

It is a popular event that we host for them every year. They are all such lovely people and many are 'in tune' with the natural world. I was tempted to have my fortune told. Travelling was in my sign, that life would be full of ups and downs in the next few years but it would all come right in the end. I was also told that I had worked hard through my life but had been lucky – a great believer in fate. How true!

* * *

2010 was to start with a trip to Australia. Sheena, a friend of long standing, had been one of the £10 Poms. In the 1960s people were encouraged to emigrate to Australia with tickets only costing £10.

You had to stay for at least a year otherwise when you came home, you had to pay back the remaining price of the ticket. She loved it out there but returned after a couple of years. However – as and when she could afford it – Sheena returned for holidays.

She had always nagged me about going out there and I had always said 'When I'm sixty we'll have to go.' Well, when 2010 arrived it was my 60th year so I had no excuse for not going! Sheena was going with her friend Fiona and Derek was with me, so four excited people met up at Heathrow for the epic trip. I remember sitting having lunch thinking that for three weeks I wasn't going to have to cook a meal.

Luckily, Fiona and Sheena are great organisers so the programme was planned – a visit to Sydney Zoo for me to meet a friend who was doing research on the Australian rat, a visit to Cairns to the tropical rainforest arranged through a BBC filmmaker that I knew whose daughter was one of the guides up there and a couple of days with a couple who had visited England in the last year who did wildlife rescue in Sydney. They had come and stayed with us so that they could see badgers and other British wildlife – we were going to see the work that they did.

It was for just over three weeks and we were going in January before any badger cubs were likely to arrive. The only thing was that it would be in the Australian summer and I'm not a lover of hot weather. We were staying with a friend of Sheena's who had known her from the days when she worked in a hotel in Sydney. Mike was one of the people caught up in the Hungarian uprising and he left Hungary in 1956 and took on Australian nationality. He is a lovely guy who is happy to share his home with all people, young and old, and indeed, when Simon and Nikki went out in 1998, Mike was their first landing point before they started their year-long trip around the country.

Mike met us at the airport on a beautiful sunny day. The long trip had not been a problem for me, having the ability to fall asleep as soon as my body isn't moving. I must admit I was somewhat amused by some of the movements of others on board the plane who were taking to heart the very serious need to move around to avoid blood clots. There was a difference, I felt, between moving around and using the back of the seat to hold on to and go through routines in the aisle that were somewhat similar to a ballerina practising at the bar – but each to their own.

Mike's house was very homely, with a fridge full of lager which we all were very grateful for on many occasions. He was a great cook, too, with lots of stews and ever the host with food always available. Mike had lots of different friends who, like him, were retired and enjoyed nothing more than to visit and put the world to rights and talk politics. It was lovely to sit on the veranda in the evening watching the sun go down, seeing the small lizards dart after the insects, and the noise of crickets unable to combat the banter that was going on in the house.

Mike was a mechanic and had his own garage at one time and his passion was for Mercedes. He had an old model that Fiona was brave enough to drive. A lot of the time we caught the bus into Sydney and Sheena was keen to show us this beautiful city and the best day has to be on Australia Day when all the boats came into Sydney Harbour, an incredible sight, and all manner of street entertainers. Stilt-walkers mingled in the crowds as the sound of the music from several groups of aborigines playing their didgeridoos and drums in traditional costume, competed with other musicians vying for attention.

Sheena had booked surprise tickets for the Sydney Opera House but it was to see the Beach Boys – not an opera. We giggled as the audience filled with people from the silver brigade, knowing full well that we (apart from Fiona) were part of them. Even people with sticks and zimmers took their seats but obviously not everyone was of a great age. Despite the equally elderly age of two of the original group it was a fantastic night, which had even the oldest struggling to their feet to clap in time to the music. Truly, a night to remember.

We enjoyed a beautiful drive to the Blue Mountains, a wonderful balloon flight over Sydney, as well as a trip to Cairns to see the tropical rain forest and the Barrier Reef. I probably didn't get the best out of the Barrier Reef being one of those people who just can't stand getting their face wet and despite encouragement from the team leading the expedition, I failed. We were there at the time of the possible jellyfish season so everyone had to wear a blue wet suit to protect themselves. Already feeling self-conscious, it wasn't helped by the captain of the boat likening us to a group of sperm! The art of wearing flippers and walking backwards into the sea from the beach where we all landed did little to reduce our embarrassment – and we have the photos to prove it.

Martin and Julia, our guides, arranged a night walk so we could see possums, bats and even an echidna, an animal with

. . . the Captain likened us to a group of sperm!

spines like a hedgehog although they are longer and the snout is almost like a beak. We also visited a bat hospital and took incredible walks through the rain forest with colourful birds and huge trees of unbelievable age.

Just Derek and I had a weekend with Diane and her husband that we had met the previous year. Mike belonged to a group called 'The Spooky Men'. It is a group that is very popular in England and they visit and tour every other year. They appear in theatres and music festivals around the country. They had enjoyed staying with us and invited us to spend a couple of days with them while in Australia. Mike was appearing with the group on the Friday night so we were travelling with them to the venue. The group were then going on with their tour and Diane was going to take us to their home in the forest.

Diane collected us from Mike's house. She is a short, stout, no-nonsense person who could, I imagine, handle most situations – especially as she dealt with rescues involving the Australian Brown Snake. This is a snake that is so venomous that you even have to be careful handling the sack that they have been in as the poison is so potent. She opened the boot of the car for us to put our luggage in and moved over the hamper, which contained our lunch for our journey to Canberra. Diane noticed our surprise at the content of the boot but quickly explained that the chainsaw was just in case, when we went to the forest, we were blocked by a fallen tree. The gun was because of the wild boar running around the forest and it was always good to have if you find anything that had been hit by a car and needed 'finishing off'.

On the way, we called in to meet Carol, a friend of Diane's, who also did animal rescue. There were lizards in tanks and colourful birds in cages including baby roos in bags in the kitchen that reminded me so much of Mr Woo. She explained that in Australia so many of the kangaroos get run over on the roads that rescuers always check them to see if there are any babies in their pouches that are still alive. Once checked they mark the body with a large red cross so that other people, driving past, will know that they have already been looked at.

The one animal I really wanted to see were the wombats and Carol had several in her care. They are so like badgers and their pens had to be strong to keep them in, just like our pens. Having strong muscular shoulders, wombats can dig as well as badgers and also, different from badgers, they have large front incisors like rodents so can gnaw their way through material such as roots and bark. Having a very handy husband, Carol had very cleverly built her pens with metal garage doors! Whilst these animals can come out in the evening and at dawn, they are mainly nocturnal and we never did see one in the wild.

I liked the fact that as marsupials they had a pouch, but it faces backwards so that when they are digging, the baby doesn't get a whole lot of earth in its face! Their young are born in the spring after only 20–21 days and are the size of a baked bean. Just the same as the kangaroo babies, they are called Joeys and they climb up the fur into the pouch and attach themselves to the teat. It will be 6–7 months before they are old enough to leave the pouch and wean.

Just like badgers they are very slow-maturing animals but they can live up to 26 years in the wild, which is way more than a badger who on average is only going to survive 3–5 years – with a huge loss in their first year. I guess wombat babies are safe as long as their mothers remain healthy. Wombats dig extensive burrows and chambers but tend to live singularly, which is very different from our gregarious badgers. With the same power as a badger, fences and other obstacles are not much of a problem and being a protected animal can create tricky situations in gardens and under roads. They are found almost everywhere from mountainous areas, in forests and even in heathland.

Luckily they have a very slow rate of digesting their food, taking anything from 8–14 days to complete the process. This helps them to manage in drought seasons when, as herbivores, there is little or no grass or shoots for them to forage on. They have very thick skin and like badgers probably show little sign of wounding when hit on the road but this is because the skin is almost elastic and can take high impact. In size though, they are huge – at least twice the weight of badgers being 20–35 kg and with extremely long claws. They defend their territories and mark with faeces, which are shaped like a cube. How clever is that? Cleaning out would be a lot easier if our badgers did that!

Carol took us to one of the enclosures and let two of the wombats out. These were common wombats, but there are the north hairy-nosed wombats and the southern hairy-nosed wombats (I would have thought they could have given them better names). They were fantastic! They chased around with the allowed new freedom. They are just very tubby, metre-long bears with short stubby legs and hardly any tail. One was a grey colour and the other a sandy brown but they can be dark brown or even black.

Diane explained that they suffer from mange (tiny mites that bore through the skin causing hair loss and eventual loss of energy that results in death) – similar to our foxes. She has invented a way of applying medication by putting a plastic pot on a metal frame sited over the tunnel entrances. The pot can swing on the frame and as the wombat comes out, it tips the bottom of the pot and the liquid is poured over the back of the animal as it exits. This has proved very effective and fewer wombats are being lost because of this awful parasite.

It was the highlight of the weekend, although we really enjoyed the evening with the Spooky Men Chorale with their humorous songs. Diane's woodland home really was deep in the forest and we drove almost an hour and a half into the woods before we came to their home. They really were miles and miles away from the next person and yet with generators and spring water, there was everything you could need. The vegetable garden had to be fenced in against the wildlife but other than that, there were no fences as the land attached to the house was so vast.

How sad that just as we have lamping in our country, where sick people ride out with guns and shoot anything and everything that they see, the same happens over there. The wild boar is the main target – just like the poaching of deer in our country – but nothing is safe. With little possibility of catching them, all people like Diane can do is collect number plates and descriptions, if they can at anytime – and maybe that's another reason for having a gun? Certainly on one of our trips out, a kangaroo had been placed in the middle of the road in a macabre stance, just to show, Diane said, that these evil people had been around. What is the matter with the human race?

* * *

With so many memories in such a short time, it was a holiday I will never forget but I couldn't be happier once my two feet were back on the ground in this country and eventually back in my own kitchen.

It was only a matter of a few weeks later when we received a call from some people who were renovating a house in North Wales. They weren't living in the house but travelled there on the Saturday to check the property as there had been a lot of rain and they were concerned that the house may have flooded. When they arrived all was well with the house but as they walked around they heard some crying coming from a metal drum that was on its side. Peeping inside, they saw some tiny badger cubs and were immediately concerned for their safety as it was February and it was very cold. They decided to leave them for a while hoping that the calling would bring the mother out to collect them and they kept away from the area so that they wouldn't prevent any chance of the mother coming to them.

They returned by the afternoon and were mortified to find they were cold, no longer calling and were almost dead. They got in touch with us and we advised that they picked them up and we would organise a relay to transport them down to us. They rang half an hour later, elated that as the cubs warmed up in the car, they became more active and were calling again. We explained how important it was for them to be kept at body temperature – not too hot – as this can cause dehydration.

I know a vet nurse who lives near Birmingham and I contacted her. Ems is one of those people who would do anything for animals and she was soon on the first leg of the journey, armed with a hot water bottle, carrier and fleece. I had every confidence that she would be able to do what was necessary to help their survival once she had them. At the same time Dave Pulley, one of our Secret World Response Drivers, started his journey towards Birmingham to collect them from Ems when she got home. By the time the cubs arrived in my kitchen, it was nearly midnight.

Dave came in carrying a knitted woollen hat. Three small little mammals were curled up inside. They were so tiny, I thought at first they were baby rabbits (not the first time this mistake has been made!). But no, as I lifted them out, each was a tiny badger cub almost the size of my thumb. Amazingly their umbilical cord was missing, meaning they had to be at least 2–3 days old. We believe the sett must have become flooded and the sow needed to move them into the metal drum for safety but why she would have left such tiny cubs on their own we shall never know. I weighed each tiny cub and placed them into an incubator which was already running. Saffron, a little boy, weighed 76 gms, Nutmeg, a little girl, weighed 72 gms and Lavender, a little girl and the smallest of all three weighed only 58 gms. When you consider that a pack of butter weighs 250 gms, it will give you an idea of how tiny they were.

These tiny cubs needed to be fed every two hours to start with. Placing a teat on the end of a 1 ml syringe and warming some milk for them, I started to feed them. They had been warm for quite some time now and were all very keen to feed. Normally the milk is taken with screwed-up noses as it doesn't taste right, but all these guys were so hungry, they failed to complain. Using a 1 ml syringe means that you have to keep filling it up but it also means that the milk flow is slower and hopefully stops it going into their lungs, which can cause pneumonia. The good thing about their age is that they would have had the first milk from their mother, the colostrum. This contains all the antibodies of their mother and helps them against infection in their early days.

My time was almost consumed with their feeds through the day and night, which tends to mess up my body clock as I grab sleep when I can. It's easier to sleep in the kitchen – in the end I can almost do the feeds in my sleep! But I love doing it and the night times are always the best when all the activity has stopped. The hospital room and Jasmine room where all the small casualties are kept are now in darkness and just the glow of the infrared lights and the whirr of the incubators disturbs the silence. I probably spend too much time as I sit in the kitchen remembering so many badger and otter cubs that have been cared for here – and the sadness of those that haven't made it. I'm wondering if these small cubs will survive and what sort of world we are going to put them out to if we are lucky enough to be successful.

Nutmeg, Saffron and Lavender grew day by day from tiny pink and black forms to shiny black and white tubby cubs. Keeping them infinitely clean, changing bedding every feed and sterilising all equipment, I managed to get them through the very difficult first days, which are crucial to their development and survival. Luckily I didn't have to worry about being absent from the marital bed as Derek had gone off with his cricket team for a tour in India.

This was the time when Derek was only just entering the world of texting and realised how useful it can be when you are in a country with a different time clock. The weather was fantastic but Derek had found it very hard to see people who had so little. A lot of the time they were being hosted by players that had come over to England and played with the East Huntspill team in past years, so they were visiting places that were not necessarily tourist areas.

He had to get up early on one of the days as the team had to travel a fair way to the Taj Mahal and in hot weather travelling is best done in the early morning. The plan was to be up and ready to leave by 5 a.m. Derek was sharing a room with his friend, Matthew, and he set his alarm for 4 a.m. so that he could get up and shower first. The phone beeped and Derek forced himself out of bed although he was still very tired (but you have to remember there would have been the obligatory few drinks before bedtime). He showered and called Matthew, telling him the bathroom was free. Derek dressed as Matthew showered and got ready. It was only as they were just going out of the room that Derek glanced at the clock. It was 2.30 a.m.! I had sent a text that had pinged and Derek had mistaken it for the alarm. As you can imagine Derek was not too popular and was not allowed to have this incident forgotten through the remaining part of the tour.

* * *

'Pauline, Pauline,' shouted Simon. I heard the cry and knew from the tone that something terrible had happened. I rushed into his flat to see my son almost in tears.

'What?' I'd not seen him so upset for years.

'Rocky,' he replied, 'Rocky, he's dead.'

We both went into the lounge and Rocky was laid on the settee looking for all the world as if he was sleeping – but he was dead.

'Oh, Simon,' I said, putting my arms around him, 'I'm so sorry.'

'I went out to the office early, to get some work done before

181

everyone came in – and you know how he isn't always keen on getting up early – and when I called him and he didn't come, I thought he was choosing to sleep a bit longer.'

We had a cup of coffee and talked. He was probably the most difficult dog you could imagine. Having come to stay with us because Simon's brother's family had moved to Saudi, Simon and Rocky were inseparable. Even when Simon was at his desk, if someone came into see him, Rocky would always put himself between the person and Simon – almost like a guard. On the rare occasions that he was left with me because Simon had to go away, the joy when they both met again was equal on both sides. You remember the silly things, the time Rocky ate a coffee and walnut cake whole in two gulps from the cake stall at the open weekend. How Simon had fallen in to a pool on the beach and Rocky had gone in after him although he was terrified of water. How when dogs manage to eat something they shouldn't and then spend the next few days farting – well, a dog that size ...

Then it was time to talk about the logistics. Rocky was an eight-stone dog and Simon started to organise a mini digger to bury Rocky in the front garden. There's one thing about Secret World, when something sad happens, everyone feels the sorrow and sympathises. With a tree to mark his grave, Rocky joined the many other pets that over the years, including my Alsation cross, Murray, and Mr Woo, have been buried close to us in our front garden.

I then went and did a silly thing. Thinking it would help, but doing it far too soon, I went out and bought a black Labrador puppy. I thought it would ease the pain and being a Labrador, when Simon went surfing in his camper caravan, it would love the water. But Simon was quite cross. He was really hurting but there was also a lifting of a huge responsibility, which Rocky had become with the constant watching of him for chewing his feet. There was such a close attachment to Simon that he had to be considered in everything that Simon chose to do. Not everyone wants an eight-stone dog visiting no matter how much of a friend Simon is!

The puppy was very definitely dumped in the kitchen, not that I minded but it was an extra dog I was going to have to explain away when Derek came back from India. By then we still had Max who had come to us as a collie cross who in true collie style would spend most of her day guarding the front gate. We also had Albert, a kind of large Jack Russell (a Parson Jack Russell I believe).

Splish, Splash and Splosh – raining otters

Dormouse on a Rose that Jonathan Ross loved

Jonathan the badger cub

Chocolate brown when first born

Stunning when adult

Turning red at four to five weeks

Maurice 'playing' with Stuart

Maurice the polecat

Trap camera image of sow climbing the gate

Simon with a swan and Dave Pulley, one of our Response Drivers

Simon with Marie Denston 'the dog'

The swan rescue on Boxing Day

A swan each!

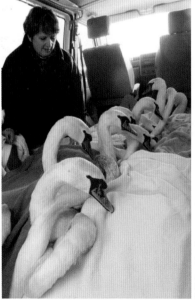

Warm and safe now

Swans under the heat lamps

Time to go home

A bath at last!

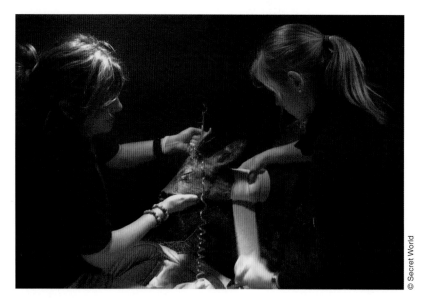

Sara Cowan (vet nurse) and Tash Strelzyn (vet) helping a roe deer

My smallest badger cubs ever –
Saffron 76 gms, Nutmeg 72 gms and Lavender 58 gms

Albert had come and stayed with us several times as my daughter Kerry's marriage had broken up and he was a visitor whenever she had to go away, but he also spent quite a lot of time on his own. We eventually claimed custody and gave Kerry visiting rights, which worked out well! Both dogs were fairly senior and were not impressed with this black ball of energy. Max definitely didn't want to know but Albert in the end put up with having his ear chewed and took on the responsibility of teaching the new puppy the time when people and food were around, such as coffee and tea breaks, and of course lunchtime. He eventually realised that this attractive puppy seemed to catch everyone's attention and it paid off to stick with her. She was named Molly.

I hoped that Derek coming back from a wonderful trip to India was going to feel guilty and allow me the puppy. In fact he did, but I think that was more to do with the enormous amount of time he spent in the toilet for the first few days having returned with Delhi belly, after which he was too weak to complain! Molly was very good at worming her way into affections even though she failed with Simon.

It was a few weeks later that we were joined by Sara Cowen as our veterinary nurse. Sara had come from Wildlife Aid in Surrey where she had starred in a series of programmes called Wildlife S.O.S. so was recognised by many people. Sara had always wanted a dog and so took on Molly who had the best of both worlds. She had Sara's undivided attention at home but could come in at work times and join the other dogs at the centre.

* * *

Work was going well with the new grassed enclosures that we were erecting in the home ground. These were going to be two badger paddocks with a central corridor and then four L-shaped fox pens around each corner so that there could be no nose contact with other wild badgers that live on our land. These pens have wired overhangs to stop animals from climbing out and in and they are totally wired underneath so that no digging out can occur, but there is a depth of earth to allow natural behaviour of digging and foraging by both badgers and foxes.

These enclosures were only made possible by Animal Friends Insurance and Pollyanna Pickering who donated towards this project. As with all orphans, it's so important for them to have large natural enclosures away from the main buildings allowing development and wildness in the final stages of their rehabilitation.

Three of our existing fox pens were to have ponds put in them to become water paddocks for swans, herons, ducks and herring gulls. With the ever-growing number of casualties, these extra facilities were crucial.

Saffron, Nutmeg and Lavender had moved from the incubator in the kitchen and were now in the cubby hole. This gave them more space to play and they were getting stronger and were able to move around the kitchen whilst I cleaned out the cubby hole. They had been joined by a female called Sage who had been found up above ground next to her dead mother. All four were now 500 gms and over and were starting to play and even chew on a custard cream, meaning that they will soon start to wean. They were still on four feeds a day and even as eight-week-old cubs, were still demanding a lot of my time. Paperwork goes by the board, I'm afraid, until there is more time. It was great thinking that they would be able to go into the new pens that were being built. Little did I know that this was never going to happen.

We had a call-out to a greenfinch in someone's garden. Much to the amusement of the rescuer it turned out to be a very tame parakeet. Simon was smitten and had a cage put in his kitchen, offering to care for him while we tried to find out who he belonged to. Again he bonded very well with Simon and would ride around on his shoulder, even happy to be in the office with him. Despite articles in the local paper, his owner was never found.

One day, I went into Simon's kitchen and took no notice of the fact that George, as he was named, had flown on to the floor. Unaware of what was happening, I didn't see that he was striding over to me and on reaching me, attacked my legs. Shaking him off my jeans, it all seemed amusing but when it happened again to Sara in the office, we realised that we had a problem. A further 'attack' occurred with a volunteer and so George was banished and went to live with a friend of mine called Jane who has several parrots and parakeets. It seemed silly that such a small bird could cause so much havoc.

About the same time one of our tiny call ducks was brought in from the poultry pen. He was off his feet and needed treatment. He became very lonely while inside and seemed to perk up when people were around so, until he was able to get up on his feet, Simon was given him as alternative to the dreaded George. There aren't many offices with a duck sitting on the filing cabinet quite happy with all that was going on around him. He was far more popular than the evil parakeet and in time, he got better and returned to his more natural home.

We were now into early summer, and the dry weather had already been with us for weeks. Hosepipe bans were being implemented and there were constant scare stories in the news about the low level of water in our reservoirs. The drought continued and we were hearing stories of badgers coming out during the day, unable to find food and water, and the number of badgers coming in to us was far in excess of what we would normally have. We suddenly had problems with coccidiosis, which was being brought in by the compromised badger cubs that were arriving in very poor condition. It is one of those things that are ever present in animals but when they become stressed through extreme conditions, it can increase to the point of being lethal. We had to shut down the Millie Block and barrier nurse the area. We stopped all badger cubs coming into us from other wildlife rescue centres and had to ask them that when the outbreak was over, that they did a test for coccidiosis prior to sending them to us. Several cubs were found to have high infestation and had to be treated before we could accept them.

To lose any cubs causes heartache and it was only through Sara and the staff being so vigilant with the barrier nursing that we were able to save some of the cubs. Secretly I was so relieved that my four from the cubby hole were all safe and well.

Sadly, because of the outbreak, we didn't use the new enclosures as we didn't want to infect them in any way. But the badgers all had grassed enclosures – they just weren't so huge.

Ems, who had kindly done the first leg of the relay to bring the tiny badger cubs to me earlier in the year, rang with a query over a tiny mammal she was rearing. She emailed me a photo to see if I could recognise if it was a ferret, stoat or weasel. Seeing the tiny dark baby, which was no bigger than my finger, I sadly told her that I thought it was a mink. It still had its eyes closed but was feeding well and she was really upset that she would have to put it to sleep as mink are non-indigenous and classed as a danger to our wildlife. Personally, I believe that their numbers have declined dramatically as we rarely see one ourselves and with the increasing population of otters, a far larger and stronger mammal, I think they are doing a very good job of displacing mink.

The only reason that we have mink in this country is because of ill-conceived ideas of releasing them from fur farms to stop this industry. Right or wrong, it did result in the farming of animals 'solely or primarily' for their fur being banned in 2003. We have had a tame mink in the past and, as they are a solitary animal, I told Ems that if she wanted to tame it, we would be able to use it as a display animal, one occasionally found in Britain.

The mink is denigrated for being the cause of the disappearance of the water vole; I think we have to remember that total clearance of scrub along both sides of the many rhynes and waterways has also had an effect on these mammals. So Maurice the mink continued to thrive.

* * *

The summer days started to shorten and at least long spells of rain helped the gardens and reservoirs that were so dry. It is towards the end of the summer that the Badger Conference is held somewhere in the country depending on which Badger Group is hosting it. Usually we go to universities that accommodate conferences whilst the students are away; we were travelling up to Derbyshire. Sara was coming as she was doing a presentation and so was Andy in connection with his release work. Cori, who was also coming, was someone who helped me with my correspondence. Cori is mature but also slightly eccentric so an entertaining weekend was expected.

We all packed our luggage in the car, along with our display stand and sales goods. Sara, Cori and I sat ready and waiting as Andy went off for something he had forgotten. He returned to the car and got into the driving seat. He was wearing tractor safety ear muffs. Sara poked him in the back.

'What on earth have you got those on for?' she asked.

'If you think I'm going to put up with you lot chatting all the way to Derbyshire, without preventative measures, you can think again!' said Andy – he was joking.

The weekend went well. It's always good to meet up with other people around the country who are doing their best to protect badgers and help with problems that arise. Many groups do rehabilitation so it's good to chat with other like-minded people and get tips about treatment and care. It's always a mix of presentations of many different subjects but I have to admit, I find it hard to sit through talks that involve persecution. We have to accept that sadly badger baiting and digging goes on despite the badger being a protected animal and, since the ever-increasing call for a badger cull because of Bovine TB in cattle, it continues to escalate.

On the way back we stopped at a service station and unfortunately arrived the same time as a couple of coaches. We reached the toilets at the same time as other travellers and there was a queue. Sara and I managed to get to the toilets before Cori so once we washed our hands we waited towards the back for Cori. Now, Cori is very blessed with a large bosom and having washed her hands she side-stepped along the queue, which was still fairly long. With her back to the queue she made her way towards us as there wasn't much room but became very flustered as each hand drier turned on as she passed by – much, as you can imagine, to our amusement!

By this time, Ems' baby was weaned and ready to come to his new home. Ems had become very attached to the little fellow and brought him down to our centre. Coming into the kitchen, Ems was keen to show me her little boy. As soon as she opened the box, I realised that I had made a mistake. Maurice was not Maurice the Mink – Maurice was a polecat. I had never thought that it could have been a polecat, we certainly don't get them in our area but up near Birmingham where the polecat is spreading out from Wales, it was quite possible. I couldn't be absolutely sure as it is quite difficult to tell the difference between a true polecat and a polecat-coloured ferret. It was fabulous to have a polecat to be able to show people, but I felt guilty that because of me, he hadn't been reared for release, which Ems would have done equally as well.

Maurice was happy with his three-storey home and we did actually take him to a talk being held by Johnny Birks who is an authority on polecats. Johnny was amazed to see such a friendly polecat and was sure that he was a true one. Stuart, one of our volunteers who has been with us since 1985, has always loved the ferrets and was more than happy to keep up the human contact with Maurice so he could be shown to people. I do have a fantastic photo of Stuart with Maurice hanging from his ear, but he was only playing – honest!

* * *

Blackberries, leaves starting to turn brown and misty mornings – all signs of the autumn starting to arrive, it's a time I have always loved. It's the time when many of our orphans go to their new homes. The fawns, the fox cubs and the badgers, all on their final

journey towards freedom. My little four who had remained together as a family group went for release on 2nd November. It's
always with a hope they will be safe. We have done as much as we
can with the rearing and care. Andy had found a release site where
they were able to create their new home from a deserted rabbit
burrow. Given a temporary sett made from straw bales, they were
to start digging on the first night. Once designed and complete,
Saffron, Nutmeg, Lavender and Sage moved in to their des res
with the added bonus of straw that they could pull in as extra bedding whenever they needed it. We make sure that the landowner
will continue to feed them through the winter as there is little for
them to find as food and they won't fully know the area and the
food sources until they build up their own knowledge.

They were probably the lucky ones as we were to have one of
the coldest winters on record, which was going to take its toll on
all wildlife. The freezing weather and snow started almost in the
first week of December. Roads became impassable with many
people not daring to go out. Transport was difficult with smaller
roads not salted so people in small villages were unable to get out.
We were very lucky that most of our staff were able to get in and
supporters with 4x4s helped us with rescues. Any animals were
coming in starving and hypothermic. Birds like herons, ducks and
egrets were unable to get food with most waterways turned to ice
and by the time we could catch them, they were beyond help.
Birds of prey were another group of animals severely affected by
the unbelievably cold weather. A white Christmas was guaranteed
with the coldest temperatures ever recorded since met office
records started in 1910.

Amazingly, many of our volunteers still turned in despite the
cold. Brenda is one of our volunteers still prepared to come in
even though she is in her 70s. We usually managed to pick her up
from the village shop, which was near her home. Wrapped up
with a scarf and hat with thermal gloves she waved as the van
came towards her. The van slowed and she climbed in. She was
somewhat surprised that it was someone she didn't recognise but
thought that it must be a new volunteer. Brenda did get concerned
when he took a different route but again thought this was probably due to the difficulty with the snow. Making conversation, she
asked what was the first thing she needed to do when they arrived.
The driver thought that the horses probably needed cleaning first.

'I didn't know we had any horses,' Brenda replied.

At this point the van stopped and Brenda realised that it was a different rescue centre that did domestic animals. It then became apparent that the van driver had stopped because she had waved and had thought that she was a new volunteer for his rescue place. Having finally discovered what had happened, he then went on, leaving Brenda to walk all the way back to the village shop! Luckily she had her phone and was able to ring and get us to collect her. She was somewhat chided for getting into cars with strange men!

There is something special about a white Christmas but for Sara, who was on duty, her Christmas day afternoon and evening was taken up by trying to organise a rescue. A lady who lived down on the moors near the South Drain was worried about a group of swans that were managing to keep a small circle of water free of ice during the day, but at night they were being trapped in the ice and foxes were coming and taking them. By the time she had rung it was too late in the short day to do anything but Sara spent her time getting everything in motion for the following day.

Sara contacted the Burnham-on-Sea Rescue Boat (BARB) and asked them to attend in case anyone fell into the water. She rang all the people she knew with 4x4s who were prepared to give up their Boxing Day to rescue swans and we needed an army of volunteers. By 10 a.m. the rescue was on its way, the 4x4s carried several volunteers and the transporter was taken as well, armed with swan hooks, rope, hot water bottles and blankets. The convoy started and it soon became apparent just how dangerous the road conditions were, particularly as we were going on to the moors where all the fields are surrounded by rhynes, waterways that could not be seen in the snow. The ice on the road was just like glass as we inched our way towards the river. Some vehicles slipped but the drivers were able to control them.

When we got to the house, it was right by a bridge and there was indeed a flock of swans in a small amount of water but the rest of the water was thick ice. The rescue boat was pushed into the circle of water, making most of the swans take to the ice. A few flew away but most were too exhausted to attempt it. Some of the swans had died in the ice, it was a sad sight. Slowly moving on the ice, some of the rescuers lay on their bellies and managed to get a rope around the group of swans and guided them towards the bank. Once they had climbed on to the bank they were guided into a small thicket so that they couldn't fly away.

With everyone surrounding the swans, we all dived for a swan and twenty-one swans were soon being placed in the transporter, covered with blankets and a hot water bottle between each of them. They laid their necks down exhausted and so glad to start feeling warm. It was a fantastic effort from everyone and we all went back to Secret World thinking that it was one of the best Boxing Days we had ever had. Unloading them, they were all placed in our long pen in the Millie Block where deep straw littered the pen and heat lamps slowly warmed the swans up. The whole rescue had taken almost a day as it was now beginning to get dark. Feeling much better, some of the swans started to eat the corn that was put down for them. It was a really good day's work.

In the next few days more swans came in and soon we were up to thirty-four. After four days, the weather started to break and never was a person so pleased to see that than me as this was the day that we had committed to do our annual dip in the sea at Lyme Regis. Driving down with Derek muttering about 'Why do you do such silly things?' – I was pleased to see the branches dripping as the snow melted and blankets of snow cascaded down the roofs of the houses. It'll be fine, I kept telling myself.

Several volunteers brought the birds of prey down and acted as collectors as we had a licence to collect donations from people watching this mad collection of humans in fancy dress. As usual Richard was there to catch the moment of 'running into the sea'. I have to say, it wasn't as bad as I thought it might be but it was the first time that I found it just too cold to swim. Well, we got a cheer from the crowd and perhaps it does show how far we will go to bring in the funds that we need to be able to care for so many animals.

Just a couple of days later, it was felt that the swans had put on enough weight and recovered enough to be released. We arranged to do it on a Saturday so that everyone who had been involved in the rescue could be there to see them returning to the river. We loaded the swans loose in the transporter and van as we just didn't have 34 swan wraps! The swans had been given paddling pools but they hadn't really had water that they could bathe in. Backing the vehicles as near as we could to the river, the doors were opened and a flurry of swans half ran and half flew down to the water. Then a complete whirl of beating wings and dunking heads made the most of deep clean water. Once the excitement was over they glided away.

It was a sight I shall always remember.

10

An emu?

Andy Parr has been our Wildlife Release Manager for many years. Through his own inspiration, he has created ways with trap cameras to monitor our releases. These are cameras that are activated by movement. He has also devised an RFID kit (Radio Frequency Identification) to be able to track animals that we have microchipped over the years. There is a cat flap that will only allow the cat with the correct microchip to enter the house. The aerial is in the frame of the cat flap. By using this frame on its own, Andy had it designed to a size that would fit over a sett entrance, owl box or feeding tube. The information of the microchip number is stored within the aerial memory and when linked to a computer, it will tell you the number but it will also tell you what time the animal went through the reader and whether the animal was going in or going out.

This has been able to be used in many ways. By setting the RFID by a sett where we had released cubs in 2009, we were able to tell that the badgers that were living in the same sett and producing cubs in 2011 and 2012 were indeed the very cubs that we had released. Andy also went back a year later to the sett where Saffron, Nutmeg, Lavender and Sage had been released to use the RFID. He found that they were all still there, and that gives you such a lift – knowing that little ones that we reared, have gone on to survive and lead healthy lives.

The feeding tube is a large ribbed black plastic tube that we often put food into when we have otters, foxes and badgers in pens and also release sites. It allows the food to be put out during the day without other animals such as magpies and rooks, seeing it and eating the food first! The juveniles get used to finding their food inside the feeding tube, and even when released they will still go into the tube to see if a free meal has been provided. With the RFID placed over the front of the tube, we are able to assess if released animals are coming back for it and using trap cameras we can also see their condition.

Andy has also, over the years, assessed certain situations, and with clever monitoring and assessing information from trap cameras and his own observations, he has been able to return orphans to their mothers. This is so much better for them as their natal mother will do a much better job of showing them how to survive.

One late spring, Andy was called out to a stable where two badger cubs had been found. There had been a long spell of heavy rain in the previous week. The owner was not aware of any badger setts near to the stable and was happy for Andy to have a look around when he came to collect the cubs. When he got to the stable, he found that both the cubs were weaned and in good condition. Standing at the door of the stable he looked out across the field next to the stable and could see a small copse that was only a few hundred yards away. He went and had a look and found both adult and badger paw prints in the mud around the water that was quite high in the ditch. He realised that there was a sett there and that it had become flooded. Andy believed that the sow had put the cubs in the stable for safety and that she would return. Coming back to Secret World for equipment and having talked it over with the landowner, Andy then installed one of our badger boxes that our cubs use for chambers, in the stable. He filled it with fresh straw and then placed each of the cubs into the box, first microchipping each one as he placed them inside. He put food down in bowls for the cubs to eat that evening and then shut the stable door. He set the trap camera over the doorway so that he could look at the footage the next day and see whether it had captured the sow coming back for them.

Indeed the next day the cameras showed us 'mum' digging at the stable door but unable to get access to her cubs. Andy's concern was how was he going to allow the sow the opportunity of getting the cubs without leaving the door open which would mean that the cubs could wander off before she came. Talking to him in the kitchen, I suggested, looking at the badger cubby hole, that he placed a board across the gate like we had in front of the cubby hole – high enough to keep the cubs in but low enough for the sow to climb over. This he did, and Andy being Andy, worried that the board was too high, he also installed a step! The trap camera was set again to see what would happen. We had a lovely photo of Mum standing on the step looking over (see photo section) and she did indeed carry both cubs out but sadly this wasn't caught on camera.

Several weeks later Andy returned and found that the sett by the stable had dried out. It was also showing signs of occupancy again. He set the RFID over the sett entrance and also the trap camera and left peanuts outside. The following day – bingo! Both of the cubs' microchip numbers were recorded and the trap camera showed Mum and the two cubs enjoying the peanut supper. This totally recorded the success of cubs returned to their mother but cubs should never be left for a sow to collect unless the situation has been totally assessed. Just because cubs left out have disappeared, does not mean that they are in safe hands. A situation not so monitored, would be classed as an abandonment of a vulnerable animal and therefore illegal. It must be done with great care and skill.

Andy moved down to Somerset from Lancashire and was amazed, once he started working with us, how easily badgers can be handled. Confidence and experience mean that it is an animal that can be handled, assessed and cared for without any need for anaesthetic or restraint – give me a badger over a squirrel any day!

He arranged for several members of the Lancashire Badger Group to come down and camp on a weekend when we were doing a lot of blood testing (this is done under anaesthetic). This was with the badger cubs that were now nearly six months old and two-thirds grown. The badgers were now ready for their third and final test. The members of the group taking part were the ones that got involved with rescue work of badgers in Lancashire but because the population in Lancashire is a lot less than the population of badgers in Somerset, they didn't get called out that often. Andy wanted to show them how easily the cubs could be handled.

They arrived on the Saturday and Andy gave them a tour around our facilities, a talk about his work and they then set up camp. The weather was lovely as it was early summer and Andy was going to take them out for an evening walk showing them badger setts and just how the population is higher in the South West than in any other part of the country. The reason for this is because, in our part of the country, farmland is mainly pasture and this is very good for earthworms which make up the staple diet of badgers. Given the opportunity, on rainy nights when earthworms come to the surface, badgers will hoover up 200 earthworms for a full tummy!

The walk went well until Andy discovered a wasp nest that had been plundered by badgers for its larvae store. Using a stick to point where it was, Andy unfortunately got too close to this nest that had already had a rough time the night before. The remaining wasps therefore were on high alert for any other disturbance. Consequently this demonstration resulted in a quick exit from the area with at least two people getting stung. Chatting to them the next morning, the event was described to me with high merriment as everyone gathered for their course on badger handling in the courtyard. This is the favourite place for coffee and tea break as there are picnic tables that the staff use in lovely weather and it's a sun trap.

Seeing them all having a break at mid-morning, I noticed that Andy had a bandage on his thumb on his right hand. Andy had caught his hand as they had moved the heavy boxes. There was a lot of teasing about the safety of 'handling badgers'. By lunchtime, he also had a bandage on his thumb and finger on the other hand – the first time he had been caught by the quick actions of one of the cubs and just a nick from an animal capable of amputating a finger. Even so, despite the injuries inflicted on his students and himself, the course was declared a great success and they all had learnt a lot about handling badgers, catching them etc. – and the only thing dented was Andy's pride. As you can imagine, a great story often repeated!

Andy has designed collapsible bird aviaries, fox pens, otter and badger pens so that almost everything is soft released. This means that they are taken to the location where they are to be released

194

and allowed to get used to their new surroundings before being let go. The added advantage of the confinement allows them to see where food will be placed for them on a daily basis. Then, even when they are released by opening a flap or removing one of the panels, they can return for food that is still supplied to them. This will continue until they become self-sufficient in finding their own food. This is so vital in the early days. Just setting an animal free and seeing it go, may feel good to the person releasing it but what support does it have in the first few days or weeks of being in the wild?

This is why with adult wildlife casualties, we always return them to where they came from because that way, they will know where they can find food and water, where to hide and even where to hibernate. As much as possible we involve the people that have rescued them and this is something rescuers will never forget – that closeness to a wild animal that we take so much for granted because that's what we experience every day.

* * *

We only survive on donations that are given by supporters, raised by our fundraisers or indeed other people from organisations that do events for us. Sometimes an event can be really successful and other times, the weather, time of event, or for other conflicting reasons, an event can sometimes not be the greatest success. The Burnham-on-Sea Lions were going to hold an event to raise funds jointly for ourselves and a domestic animal charity. All the hard work of organising, getting stall holders, purchasing food for the BBQ and a well-supported cake stall were all the ingredients of a successful day but sadly the weather was not with us and few people arrived.

There had been a dog competition organised for the afternoon but there were so few dogs entered, it looked as if it was going to be a flop. Simon, who was with me and Marie, one of our animal carers (Mad Marie as I call her with her red hair – her dedication to animals is almost beyond belief – and has got me into trouble at different times. Ask her about the bullock!) had both made an excuse of going to get something and off they went. Great, I thought, not only am I spending a day in a dripping tent but I'm also on my own!

They returned just before lunch so I forgave them because at least I could wander over and get a hot dog and a hot cup of coffee

– how can summer days sometimes be so cold? By 2.30 the pathetic Dog Competition was about to start. Simon and Marie had disappeared to look around. The start of the competition was announced over the loudspeakers. God, I thought, this is going to be dire. I really felt for the organisers as the few people in the audience dripped under umbrellas determined to see the day out.

Suddenly there was a cheer and laughter and as I looked across, there was Simon striding towards the line-up with Marie dressed in a dog costume, that I had forgotten we had. They had hatched the plan and gone back for the costume. She was merrily trotting alongside Simon on all fours – well, that's a bit of an exaggeration but she was doing pretty well. Simon seriously lined up with the other contenders and each owner in turn walked their dog up and down for the judge to see. When it came to Simon's turn, the 'dog' was very badly behaved and even went up to the judge and cocked its leg. Surprisingly, they didn't win the prize but it certainly brightened a rather subdued day!

People who do fundraising are really fantastic with the variety of dares or events that they carry out. From Freda, one of our volunteers abseiling down the church tower on her 70th birthday, to bikini-clad car washing by grandchildren of our volunteers, it can be just about anything that someone manages to conjure up. Children who have baked cakes, (sponsored silence – that's a popular one!) to those who have 'Go Green Days' at schools when garments of green have to be worn. They have all helped towards us being able to carry out our work – every single penny counts.

* * *

I talk about highs and lows but one of the hardest times was the year after the rescue of the swans on Boxing Day. We were called out to a group of swans found dead down on the moors. Eight swans had been shot through the head. From the way that they had been shot so accurately, it was obvious someone skilled in shooting had carried out the cruel action. Little did we know it was going to get a lot worse before it got any better. We immediately put the story out to the press to see if we could find out any information about who was doing this. Day by day, the numbers of swans slaughtered increased. Even a television crew who came to cover the story, asked for the location of where these dead swans were being found so that they could film it. When they got there, the crew found a further six dead swans recently killed.

People were incensed by the cruelty and started to contact us offering a reward for any information leading to the prosecution of the guilty person/persons. Amazingly, the reward got to £26,000 and there were several people calling in with names of suspected people but not with enough information for anyone to be prosecuted. Eventually there were so many people down on the moors trying to find who was killing the swans that the killing stopped. But now 46 swans had lost their lives, and we wondered how many of them may have been the ones we had saved just a few months before. On the Somerset moors, swan numbers in the winter can be up to over 100 and they do eat a lot of grass, they also cause disturbance to fishing lakes of which there are several commercial ones around in the area, so one could speculate. Sadly nobody was ever prosecuted.

Why is it that wildlife crime is not recorded? Maybe if this happened, we would know the true cost of cruelty in this country – be it badger digging, baiting, dog- and cock-fighting, hunting, shooting, pole traps that snap the legs of birds of prey, wanton poisoning and mist nets to catch finches that are then sold in cages. I'm afraid I'm not brave enough to face up to such disgusting things like Jean Thorpe does, and by the way, how well deserved the MBE that she has been recently been awarded.

Sir Terry Pratchett was one of those people who offered a donation towards that reward for the killer of the swans and kindly gave it to us for our work when no one was prosecuted. Indeed he doubled the donation when he visited and saw the work that we do. He is a very incredible person who faces full on his own demons and yet still produces the wonderful Disc World books that so many people enjoy. Both he and his family support our work and we are so grateful.

Equally the many celebrities that we have met through filming opportunities have become patrons or given us supportive quotes, which I think reflects the reputation of our care and dedication that our staff and volunteers give so freely to our casualties. They see the love offered to every animal no matter how small. They understand that we endeavour to get animals back to the wild but that we would consider euthanasia as an option for those unable to survive in the wild again. I truly believe that wild-born animals should never be committed to a life in captivity when every season and instinct means that they are unable to live a full life. The only animals that we keep are those that have been imprinted and crave human attention.

Derek, my husband, retired in 2011. Yes, there is a Mr Kidner, although he is far happier down the cricket field than helping wildlife! He is the chairman of the East Huntspill Cricket Club, is a member of Somerset Over 60s, plays for the Forty Club that has matches against schools and students – as well as just having taken an umpire's course so he's as potty on cricket as I am about wildlife. Luckily he is kept busy, especially through the summer season which is my busiest time too. He's looking over my shoulder at the moment and I have been told that I have to add that he also likes wildlife, but just doesn't like clearing up after it or having it bite his feet!

When I had my fortune told, the reader said I was lucky with my husband who would be happy as long as I was happy too. When I think of what he has lost over the years: the tourist attraction where he was the owner, to then going out to find a job so that Simon and I could continue the charity; the handing over of the assets freely to the charity when it could have been sold; the money spent on dividing the farm into sections so that the charity could gradually own the farm; the continuous interruptions by staff, volunteers and film crews coming into the kitchen (which to be honest he did find difficult when he first retired but even then he adjusted). Maybe one day, perhaps when we are older, I will sit him down and tell him how much he means to me. The unfailing support in the background, the 'bringing me back to earth' that I need (and resent – a typical Piscean), the support when things go wrong and as Secret World grows, to help me accept change. Through legacies, the charity has slowly been able to buy parts of the farm and there is just one final part for them to purchase for it to be totally secure. Hopefully, they won't turn us out too quickly once it is all theirs!

* * *

The name Pauline Kidner will always be synonymous with badgers and as an ex-dairy farmer, who had a Bovine TB breakdown in our herd, Derek and I join the many farmers who are against the cull of badgers as a means of reducing this terrible disease in cattle. Science quite clearly tells us that culling badgers doesn't work. It is frightening to see that despite the largest experiment held in the world on Bovine TB, the Randomised Badger Culling Trial was to be rubbished and the Conservatives had culling back on the menu as a lobbying tactic for the election.

We were incredulous, when the Conservatives were not only considering starting culling again but were going to run pilot culls in Somerset and Gloucestershire. This was to see if shooting free-running badgers was a safe, effective and humane way of culling badgers. The trials eventually took place in 2013 and, needless to say, the trials were found to have failed all three principles by the Independent Expert Panel who presided over the cull. Too many badgers took too long to die and several conditions of the licences were broken by shooting operators. With over 1000 badgers killed needlessly just in Somerset and over 600 in Gloucestershire in 2013, they plan to kill more in the future. I must also thank Jeff and Pat Hayden of the Badger Trust who helped so much, sometimes just by being on the end of the phone on those really dark days.

I am disgusted at the scaremongering tactics used to raise fears that domestic animals and humans are at risk from badgers. Why when we see over 150 badgers every year from the South West do we see so few badgers with this disease. With clever wording, they confuse infected with infectious. To be infected by the disease means you have created antibodies and could well be the immune animals that will stop the disease. By these standards, if you had a BCG injection when you were at school, you would also be 'infected' and if you were a badger or cow – you would be killed.

Having attended a meeting where farmers were saying that they had hundreds of badgers dying on their land from Bovine TB, I challenged and offered that the next time they found one, they should contact me. I would pay for that animal to be transported to a lab and give it a postmortem to see if it did indeed have Bovine TB. And remember, it is impossible to tell if a live badger has Bovine TB. Needless to say not one person contacted me.

Wouldn't it be wonderful if in a few years' time, I could write and say that the politicians have come to their senses? That they decided to follow the Welsh programme of vaccinating badgers and higher cattle control strategies. This is reducing the incidence of TB in cattle in Wales but no one in the Cabinet seems to be listening. Even more wonderful if in a few years' time badgers have not lost their legal protection and that even more of our wildlife can be protected by the law. We only survive if wildlife is protected –

our very lives depend on insects for pollination – as I have said before, nothing is too small to be important.

There needs to be more support from the public to halt this cruel farce. I am in awe of those who put their own lives at risk by walking the public footpaths during the cull despite guns being used that if the target was missed, the bullets had the capacity of travelling two to three miles. It was incredible that no one was injured or killed. This is not the answer.

* * *

What we do at Secret World is welfare. We're there to stop suffering and the numbers of animals that we put back make no difference to the populations that they are returning to. That's why I have always believed that our biggest responsibility is to ensure that through education by giving talks to schools and groups, we can make people aware of how fragile our British wildlife is. It's every bit as important as the romantic elephants and tigers and other emotive animals which we should be protecting but not at the expense of our own.

I am of an era when, in my youth, we were all fighting for freedom, the equality of sexes, the opportunity to achieve anything we may want to and against weapons of war. Just what have we achieved? The world still seems a pretty sad place in some countries and our children are denied the very freedom that we had when we were young. A recent survey showed that children spend on average less than nine per cent of their time outside. How many mothers would allow their children to 'disappear' for a couple hours like we did, as long as we were back for lunch or tea? Would your children or grandchildren go to woods and build camps, explore the countryside or even just the local playground? They have lost the ability to use their own imagination and instead seem fascinated by the cyber world. If we don't start realising that by extensive home and car ownership, we are affecting wildlife. Farming has to play its part too in providing habitats for wildlife alongside the produce that they grow. Equally we must realise that farming is being driven to intensification because of the low prices we pay for our milk and our food. How can it be right for a pint of milk to be cheaper than bottles of water?

We are so lucky that our project for a Learning Centre has been successful and a grant has been given from the Heritage Lottery Fund to make it happen. It's not been without a few teething problems, but building work should be completed by the end of 2014. This means that not only do we have a facility to welcome children back to Secret World as we did in our open days, but the grant allows us to make the most of the historic buildings of the farm which is Grade II listed so has protected right to its curtilage. I so hope that our new Learning Centre will unlock our natural world to the children and generations to come.

Hopefully, a new Wildlife Teaching Hospital and Educational Centre will be built in the next few years where vets and vet nurses can be trained in the care of British wildlife, something that is not included in the training to become a vet and even the drugs are not licensed. All the experience gained over the years will go towards ensuring that there will always be best care for wildlife and promotion of the need to protect habitats. Already we do Continuing Personal Development (CPD) courses for vet nurses and we host a group of wildlife centres once a year called A Voice 4 Wildlife. We do that so we can help each other in the care of animals, fundraising ideas, up-to-date information on research and, between us, we have over 100 years of experience!

Perhaps it's good that we are also a little bit mad. We were asked to give a home to a red doe that had been reared as an orphan and then released in a village in Devon. She caused a lot of problems. Not everyone wanted a deer walking into the house and everyone definitely did not want her eating their roses. The village was in crisis, half wanting to get rid of her and half wanting her to stay. Polly, as she was named, was eventually given a home at a centre near us that had a red deer herd but sadly, as an imprinted animal she didn't recognise that she was one of them and refused to join the group.

A few years ago the centre closed and Polly pined for all the fuss that the visitors gave her so Mrs Duckett rang and asked if we would take her at Secret World. We were able to accept her as our Woo Pen was quite large and would be adequate for her to live in. We thought it would be good for the few days that we were open, for visitors to see her and realise just how big red deer are. There is always lots of staff and volunteers around for her to see, so even when we are closed to the public, she gets plenty of attention. We went to see her and to arrange transport. Walking out to see her, Polly saw us coming and ran up to us for company. But she was followed by an emu. They had been living together for the last seven years and the emu was also hoping to pack his bags and

An emu?

. . . and the emu hoped to pack his bags and come too.

come too. Well, it would have been wrong to have split this unusual pair and so, yes, we now have an emu!

* * *

I have only taken you through the years from 1999 to 2011 as to what goes on at Secret World Wildlife Rescue. So there are still many stories for another book maybe! All I know is, accepting that I'm getting older, I won't be able to always do the hours I do (but we're a tough bunch – there are many rehabilitators older than me). Hopefully the younger generation will pick up the gauntlet and carry on all the important work. Secret World Wildlife Rescue has grown and is strong, but it would never have happened if my son, Simon, hadn't dedicated 25 years of his life to it. He first started as the Charity Administrator in 1999 after going to University and becoming qualified in Business Studies and Law. Simon has gone from being the only member of staff employed by the charity to now being the Operations and Project Manager with over 30 full- and part-time staff, two charity shops and rescuing over 5,000 wildlife casualties every year – and soon to oversee the Learning Centre as it grows. He's guided the charity through good and bad times. I would have been lost without him.

It's not a job – you live it. I wouldn't have had my life any other way.

And finally ... with thanks

Success and reputation has only come to Secret World because of the fantastic trustees, staff and volunteers who over the years have dedicated so many hours to make the care of wildlife at this centre possible. And the supporters who have financed all that we have achieved so far.

It would be impossible to mention everyone who deserves to be mentioned but I am so glad that Nikki continues to be one of my other 'daughters'. She is now happily married with two daughters of her own. I even have Debbie as another 'daughter'. You have already heard about how dedicated she is, having been with Secret World on and off for over 20 years. Then there are people like Chris and Maggie, volunteers who live in Southampton, who helped so much when we struggled as an open farm and yet they have still come for the last thirteen years on the Sunday of our open weekends to run a tombola stall and get what Maggie calls her 'top up of Secret World'. She was once a wildlife carer also, but through ill health she had to give it up but still misses it.

Pete and Norma are also volunteers and friends who have been with us since the 1990s, travelling all the way from Wales every time that we have events so that they could help us. Norma is the one who makes all the beautiful cards that are sold on our behalf and also amazing decorations for our annual Auction and Ball. Norma also has reared many, many kittens for her local RSPCA and used to rear fox cubs until she also was unable to do it, again through ill health.

Helen Ditchfield who, besides Stuart, has been our longest-serving volunteer although she started in the 1990s and not the 1980s like Stuart when we still had a tearoom and attractions. She does always say she doesn't know why she stays because I'm always rude to her (but I won't tell you which birthday she told me was looming the other day!).

It helps when one has hopes and dreams, to have a mad friend to keep you company. Jane Fry is mine. Incredibly she suffers from osteoporosis, has a pacemaker in three chambers of her heart, to name just a couple of things wrong with her. So she suffers pain constantly but is mad enough to run a rabbit rescue and a mobile surgery in the Forest of Dean. This is just to help all the forest people, who often don't have transport and, on many occasions, are unable to pay for the treatment her surgery gives even though she keeps her prices as cheap as possible. Yet persevere she does. She is helped by an all too frightening helper called Ann, who keeps Jane in check and who, I might add, Jane would be lost without. Ann, a human Rottweiler, is amazing for her age and come snow, rain or sunshine, she's up at Jane's every day.

Thanks to Liz Mullineaux, our consultant vet, a manual is available through the BSAVA that any vet can have on their shelf, and covers every kind of wildlife found in this country. Their typical injuries, their natural parameters like their blood pressure and if you're lucky enough to get the casualty better, the way to release them. Through Liz's tremendous energy in the care of wildlife, we have a wealth of knowledge. She is a colleague and a friend I value dearly.

My dream has always been to see the charity secure so that if anything happens to me, I would know that the work would continue in my name. A friend, Jeff Cark, died from cancer a year ago and it brings home your own mortality. Jeff was one of those people that belonged to the Badger Trust and also the Surrey Badger Group and nothing was too much trouble. He would just always be there whenever you needed him, there when you were unloading display stuff for a conference, there with a group for our Auction and Ball, there when we needed help on our so busy Badger Bonanza open weekends, always held at Easter. People travel from far and wide so that they can see the orphan badger cubs – the only time we allow it. He was always a phone call away. I never really had the chance to thank him and say how much he had helped. So many of us still miss Jeff. Maybe I should sit down with Derek sooner rather than later and spend more time with the rest of my family too.

I never want the ethics to change and I will fight to ensure that we continue in the belief that every animal is important to us no matter how small or how common. I hope there will always be dedicated people who, like me, believe that 24/7 care is crucial to stopping suffering. People who realise that it can only be done with help from volunteers as we could never afford to employ people to cover all those areas. Everyone needs support and, in life, you collect those people that you would trust with your life.

Secret World has a wonderful atmosphere and we try to make everyone feel that they are part of a family. Just like families, there will be niggles but, just like families, we get over them. We are all working to the same aim.

Special thanks to . . .

Sue Gard and her brother Bob for editing and typesetting the book free of charge to help the charity.

Jason Venus for donating the fabulous cartoons.

Steve Hilling for the design of the cover and plate sections.

Martin Wase for the photograph used for the book cover of the swan and cygnet. (Aptly named A Place of Safety)

Also, a big thank you
to everyone listed below who supported
A Place of Safety

Linda Houston
Tecni Group, Inspired Solutions
Centaur Services Ltd
Lakeside Holiday Park, Burnham on Sea
Chris Cornell
Vera Copp
Marion Escott
Gwen Mugleston
Elaine Lambert
Anna Wallace
Linda Barratt
Greg Rose
Lady Maria Dolan
Iris Parker
Debbie Carter, Neil & Lily
Roger Lucken
Peter & Norma Knight
R A Cottrell
Pat Lincoln
Jenny Schofield
Felicity Drew
Vera & George
Chris & Maggie Fry
Sholing Valleys Study Centre
Deborah Parkin
Janet Feltham
Una & Richard Hadaway
The Reeves Family
Carol Blakeley
Alison & Gray
Debs & Dale Tovey
Sam Buckland, Steve & Ruby

Arik Schulte
Joanne Lumb
Heather Rabbage
Paula Heakin
Julia Dillon
Nicki Salmond
Pauline Churcher
Jessica Norrell-Goldsmith
Stephanie O'Brien
Tracey Pares
Shelley Allen
Jane Stamp
Janet & John Vinnicombe
Sue Wells
Vic and Marie Booth
Gloucestershire Wounded Badger Patrol
Pat Hayden
Lynn Ford
Charlotte Pearce
Terry & Vera Jones
David & Pamela Silcock
Lynn & Trevor West
Barbara Garrett
Jack & Zoe Haines
Shane Hippisley
Steve Warwick
Myra Cox
Lewis Hollister
The Tessier family
Lisa Elder
Mary Elder
Jane Fry
Ann Waite
Tarnya Knight
Jill Wiles

Secret World
Wildlife Rescue

Will you help Secret World continue to grow?

At Secret World, we have a very clear vision: to prevent British wildlife suffering needlessly and inspire in everyone an understanding and love of wildlife and the countryside. We work to deliver this by providing the only 24/7 rescue service in the South West. Caring for sick, injured and orphaned wildlife, rehabilitating the animals that come into our care and returning them to the wild wherever possible. Through Pauline's skills and experience we are developing a centre of excellence where all British wildlife can receive the best care and people will be inspired to learn about the world of wildlife – encouraging everyone to discover what they can do to protect it.

Casualty numbers are increasing

But the better we get, and as our reputation grows, we find that we are receiving more and more animals into our care. And each animal has a cost associated with it, whether that cost is for vet fees, for nursing care, for specialist feeds or for equipment. **In 2013, Secret World cared for over 5,500 animals and birds and at the time of writing this, incoming cases have increased by a third over last year.**

Please help us rescue those that need us

There has to be room for everyone!

Donations are gratefully received
– and if you pay tax, we can claim Gift Aid!

So, can you help us continue our vital work? We don't receive any government support and rely entirely on the generosity of people like you. **If you would like to support our animal care**, our learning programme for schools and young people, or our casualty rooms, the best way is by donating a small sum every month, and to gift aid it so that it is worth even more. You can do this by signing up to a direct debit, or even have this taken from your monthly pay by your employer. **This way, we can plan our finances to ensure we can afford to deliver the best possible care all year round.**

Sponsor our new
Wildlife Learning Centre

Why not hold a coffee morning in aid of us?

Legacies are our lifeline

But we do understand that some people can't afford this, and many people decide that although they can't afford to donate money now, they will leave us a gift in their will. These legacies make a huge contribution to our costs, and we appreciate every penny. **Leaving a legacy often means that we can develop our buildings and care facilities, ensuring our facilities are the best they can be.**

If you would like to find out more about the many, many different ways you can help us, please visit our website at www.secretworld.org, or call us on 01278 783250.

Each casualty receives the best care